AF647042

Tribal Women's Voices in Theological Discourse

Tribal Women's Voices in Theological Discourse

Editors
Lovely Awomi James
Akani Kinimi

Women Study Center
Eastern Theological College, Jorhat
&
Christian World Imprints
Delhi

© Editors

First Published in 2020 by

Women Study Center
Eastern Theological College
Rajabari, **Jorhat-785014**
etcollege@yahoo.co.in
http://etcollege.in
Phone: +91 376 2361219

&

Christian World Imprints
Christian Publishing & Books from India
C-3, Shop No. 14, Ground Floor
Wazirpur Industrial Area, **Delhi-110052**
cwidelhi2017@gmail.com
www.ChristianWorldImprints.com
Phone: +91 11 41526079

ISBN: 978-93-5148-406-6 (HB)
ISBN: 978-93-5148-407-3 (PB)

All rights are reserved. No part of this publication can be reproduced, distributed, performed, publicly displayed, stored in a retrieval system, made into a derivative work, transmitted or utilized in any form or by any means; electronic, mechanical, photocopying, recording or any information storage system, without the prior written permission of the copyright holder(s), as indicated, and the publishers.

Jurisdiction: Any conflict or dispute in relation to this publication shall be adjudged in accordance with the laws of India and the matter shall be subject to the jurisdiction of the Courts, Tribunals or any other Forums of New Delhi, India, only.

Disclaimer: The views, facts, contents, any copyright material used and analysis arrived at in the Articles included/published in this work are solely of the individual Contributors and Editor(s) who assert the right to be identified as Authors; the Publishers - Women Study Center, Eastern Theological College, Jorhat and Christian World Imprints, Delhi - do not take any responsibility for the same in any manner whatsoever.

Printed in India.

Contents

Editorial

Tribal theology in the region today is gaining ascent in its content and perspectives through the unceasing participation and contribution of tribal theologians and scholars – both women and men. We have now to a very great extent courageously transcended the epistemological domination and monopoly of the west and other so-called advanced peoples and cultures over ours. We can now proudly hold that ours is a purely tribal contextual theology – that we are the creators of our own theology. In this theological process, we reflect upon, speak about and share our beliefs, experiences and dreams for our peoples and our future in the light of the teachings of the Word of God, the Bible and our faith in the lord Jesus Christ. This way, our theology becomes original, concrete, meaningful and significant for transforming and practical relevance. As such, this small work is a result of one such effort with the aim of contributing toward tribal theological discourse mainly through the voices of tribal women, though we have two works included here from two of our male tribal biblical scholars but they are exceptionally necessitated as they represent the wholehearted support of those tribal men toward the empowerment and progress of tribal women in theological discourse. We hope the research works from various tribal theologians presented here will bear upon the readers a deep sense of critical theological reflection as well as would enrich our tribal Christian faith-based lives.

The first article, *Tribal Women's Voices in Tribal Theological Discourse: Keynote Address*, by Zhodi Angami, skillfully opens up the discussion for a critical review on most of our hitherto misconception concerning the tribal women of North East India. He argues that "the dominant tribal narratives, controlled and expressed by men, have given us false images of how tribal women are loved, respected and enjoy high status in tribal societies," and that these narratives of men perpetuate and re-inforce the marginalization of tribal women in the region. He then proposes for creation of new narratives (welcoming even counter narratives) in order that both women and men as complete human community could truly work together for a just society and life. He thus sees facilitating tribal women's voices in tribal theological discourse as a dynamic move towards de-centering the dominant narratives and ushering in of a balanced and holistic tribal theology for all.

Jesus Christ in Tribal Context Today: A Theological Exploration, by Lovely Awomi James, sets out to respond to the Christological question, "Who is Jesus Christ for us tribals?" and states that "it all begins and ends with confession of our faith in Jesus Christ and how we live out that faith in concrete context." According to her, tribal Christians at present are in serious need of re-orienting their understanding of their faith in Jesus Christ, making Christ real in their day-to-day experiences. She states that this is so because tribal society is riddled with all kinds of problems and issues such as poverty and the divide between the rich and the poor, corruption and unethical lifestyles, moral degradation, nominalism, depression and loneliness (especially amongst the younger generation), and sickness etc. It is within and for this context that the writer proposes a tribal incarnational method in understanding and interpreting (Incarnational Hermeneutics) Jesus Christ for the tribals today - allowing Christ to be incarnated into our lives and into our situations only can make Christ real to us and she works this out by utilizing tribal thought forms and terminologies for Christ.

A Contextual Reading of Paul's Haustafel Manifesto in Ephesians 5:21-33 with Special Reference to Husband-Wife Relationship: North East India Tribal Perspective, by Razouselie Lasetso, gives a clear exegetical study of the text on Household codes and drew out its theological implications for tribal Christian homes with special attention upon husband-wife relationship and the importance and significance of Christian order and decorum in the family. He specifically takes serious note of the contemporary family environment where there is so much confusion and problems that threaten the stability of spousal as well as family relationships. The article strongly endorses that order, peace and harmony are necessary requisites for any Christian couple/family but that it should all be undergirded and qualified by mutual love and submission.

The Song of Deborah (Judges 5) as a Riposte: A Woman's Perspective, by Akani Kinimi Longvah, critically studies the role of Deborah, a powerful symbol of female potential for leadership, authority and strength for the welfare of the people and community. The writer reflects upon how Deborah acquired all these while being placed within a historical context of rigid patriarchy. The Song of Deborah calls for women across time, cultures and borders to have determination, confidence and courage to break through the stereotypes to make it possible what might seem impossible or impermissible, all with the power and strength from God – our Creator.

Women in Pauline Writings: A Liberative Perspective Towards the Ministerial Role of Women, by Manini Chuseote, analyses the active role of women in Pauline churches as well as in Paul's own ministry. Apostle Paul, while many admit him to be a complicated figure when it comes to his teachings and attitude towards women and their place within the historical-cultural settings of his time, nevertheless clearly portrays women within the egalitarian context of the ministry of the Kingdom of God. The writer notes that Paul addresses his women co-workers on personal and commendable terms as is evidenced by their tangible devotions and contributions toward the Lord's ministry. Her writing therefore posits that the Gospel can be used as a powerful source of reconstruction and transformation in the midst of all the human-made cultural divides that often legitimize the oppression of women (or men) from fully realizing their call and potential for the ministry of the church and society at large.

Woman's Work for Women: The Life and Work of Anna Hasseltine Kay Scott, by Narola Imchen, makes a critical review of the history of Christian mission in North East India from a woman's perspective. She argues that even though in reality women missionaries equally worked and contributed in the history of Christianity right from its inception, it is the male missionaries who get the credit, recognition and acknowledgement in the annals of Christian church history. She admits that this was mainly due to the patriarchal nature of the society in the then period. As such, women who invested all of their lives' energy, time and devotion to the mission of the church alongside their male partners, were ignored, neglected or forgotten and rendered almost invisible. Taking this issue very seriously, Imchen in her research paper takes up a woman missionary by the name Anna Hasseltine Kay Scott, to study her contribution – a woman who first committed herself to serve as a missionary in a far-off land, marries Edward Payson Scott and came to Nowgong, Assam. The passion, determination and the commitment, with which Anna Hasseltine worked even after her husband's early death, speak volumes about the contribution of a woman in the making of history of Christianity in the region in particular and in the world in general.

The Participation of Women in the Society with Special Reference to Chakhesang Community: A Holistic-Missiological Approach, by Mekronyi-ü Thele, employs a holistic view and makes a careful tracing of the participation of Chakhesang women in the society - both traditional and modern context and draws out their significances to empower the Chakhesang women in contemporary Naga Society for a fuller participation in both the church and society. In particular, she provides concrete evidences to support her claim through the lives and contributions of individual and corporate Chakhesang women who played very important roles in building the life of the Chakhesang community through the avenues of home (families), departments, associations and social and religious agencies.

Reading the Nexus between the Domination of Women and the Domination of Nature, by Lovely Awomi James, is a critical research on how women's Eco philosophy unearths the philosophical roots of the deep connection between the domination of women and the domination of nature. It critiques the Christian tradition, western philosophy and patriarchy for their roles in strengthening the clubbing-together of women and nature under the category of the inferior realm of existence while placing and legitimizing men, the Divine and intelligence (male intelligence), at the realm of the superior. The writer then studies how women have taken the courage to not just critique the philosophical, religious and cultural traditions but also to deconstruct them and build upon the significance of women-nature spiritual nexus as an earth-centred or creation-centred spirituality that could contribute toward our search for healing the wounds inflicted upon both women and nature by the dichotomic-male-centred spirituality.

Reclaiming Women's Spirituality, by Esther Jish Rengma, discusses the necessity and significance of reclaiming women's spirituality. She particularly addresses the subject of Christian women and spirituality and argues that the key to reclaim women's spirituality is to first claim our conscious and responsible selfhood, without which it cannot be done. She clearly presents how tribal Christian women's spirituality has always been at the centre of tribal life – be it in the church, family or society – and yet how tribal women have been made the unacknowledged/the invisible toward the visible reflection/ manifestation of tribal Christian life. As such, the significance and necessity of reclaiming women's spirituality and thereby giving it a visible and concrete place in today's context.

Towards a Substantive Role of Women in Naga Society, by S. Akatoli Chishi, takes a positive stance that Naga women can play substantive role in Naga society. This hypothesis is worked out by critically studying the traditional Naga society and its cultural structures where women exercised their freedom and potential only within certain permissible areas and all the while restricted from venturing out of their culturally-conditioned space and roles but now through the introduction of modern education and advent of Christianity, Naga women could cross over those barriers. The writer then proceeds to work on toward empowering Naga women through the principles of self-esteem, awareness, power of choice, rediscovering of women's role in Naga tradition embracing femininity.

Construction of Gender Role in the Society, Vimeno Lasetso, addresses the oft confused concepts of sex and gender and proceeded to differentiate between the two. She discusses how gender as a social construct, is being used by patriarchal culture and its social system to discriminate women to the point of rendering women (the female sex) as the inferior sex. She addresses the serious issue of gender in the society today and draws upon the biblical understanding of gender to draw out theological implications for addressing the issues related to gender in the society today.

Tribal Narrative Communication, by Marlene Marak, beautifully captures the power of tribal narrative communication and takes the readers down the lane of tribal world – the world of stories with storytelling as their main vehicle of communication. It is through this narrative communication of storytelling that tribals communicate, circulate and pass down the knowledge of their origin, identity, culture and their world from generation to generation. The writer also in particular recognizes the significant role of the womenfolk as primary storytellers alongside menfolk in tribal society. To support her view she nostalgically recalls her own grandmother who served as a powerful storyteller when the writer was a young girl. Towards the end, the writer posits forth the possible place of tribal narrative communication particularly storytelling for doing tribal Christian theology and for re-reading the biblical stories of women for meaning and relevance.

Liberative Symbolism of the Spirit/s: A Tribal Feminist Pneumatology, by Eyingbeni Hümtsoe-Nienu, begins by addressing the subject of tribal perspective on the doctrine of the Holy Spirit and she critiques that this subject on the third person of the trinity is "comparatively less discussed" and "much lesser on tribal feminist pneumatology." The writer then goes on to argue that the scantiness of tribal discourses on the Holy Spirit is not due to any lack of resources as such but due to the general neglect of the subject in both Christian theology as well as in feminist theology. The writer then critically draws out the non-discriminatory, liberative and inclusive nature of the work of the spirit(s) in tribal culture whereby both women and men were equally empowered to serve the people and the land, which is also very evident today in the workings of the Holy Spirit in the lives of the women in the church and society. The writer arrived at this conclusion through a liberative approach in interpreting the work of the Holy Spirit whereby the spirits then and the Holy Spirit now become "a symbol of women's liberation from any oppressive and suppressive theology and practice in the church and community."

Tribal Understanding of Priesthood and Its Relevance for Today, by S. Akatoli Chishi, studies the tribal concept and praxis of priesthood in the traditional society and unearths that "the main quality which qualifies" individuals to the office of priesthood or "sets them apart from others was their knowledge of the sacred and the profane." Critically analysing the concept of priesthood in the tribal traditions with comparative reference to the biblical office of priesthood, the writer concludes that it becomes imperative for us to take under our serious consideration the tribal priestly elements if we desire for an integrative form of priesthood in our land. Some of those values and elements she strongly endorses include: the sense of the sacred, corporate existence, sense of justice, commitment to one's cause etc. In her conclusion, she left the question of priesthood of women in an open-ended form, inserting her response with counter questions upon contemporary nature of priesthood and who determines a candidate's eligibility and genuine call to priesthood etc.

Tribal Ecclesiology, by Esther Jish Rengma, begins with the presupposition that "the present structure of the Church is male oriented and so it is difficult to include women's concerns and marginalized people's needs." She argues that the patriarchal culture of the tribals, the inherited patriarchal theology and ministry from the west could all be the causal factors for an ecclesiology that is male-dominated and discriminatory toward women. Having said that she goes on to delineate what constitute the true ecclesia of Christ, building upon the biblical principles for the body of Christ as well as drawing the traditional sources of tribal communitarian culture and traditions for our tribal church today. In her own words, "we need to envision a new paradigm of church for the tribal communities where the church as the body of Christ is fully accomplished. Church should become a common place where people irrespective of gender, economic status, educational background or social standing, feels comfortable and able to freely mingle with people from all the section of the community," as people of God and the church as an earthly agent of God's kingdom.

Reading Rizpah's Lament (2 Sam 21:1-14) vis-à-vis Tribal Women, by Akani Kinimi Longvah, employing feminist critical biblical interpretation attempts to bring the story about the lament of Rizpah and contemporary issues of violence, injustice and the soul-wrenching lament of the families of victims (especially that of women) as conversation partners so as to draw out powerful social-moral and theological implications for us today. The article recalls Rizpah's lament and amazingly long vigil over the corpses of her slain sons so as to protect the bodies from being attacked by vultures and other creatures. She guarded them for so long that eventually led King David to grant them decent burial as well as collected the bones of Saul and Jonathan for the same. This is a very powerful story that can be read in conversation with contemporary stories and events of powerful protests across the globe via non-violent ways and methods against different forms of oppression and assaults. This lament method can give us strength to counter violence and bring transformation in our world as a potential and dynamic source for "resilience of the human spirit that desperately seeks to survive even amid the most terrible of circumstances."

Hearing the Voices of Female Commercial Sex Workers (FCSWs) in Nagaland: Tribal Women's Perspective, by Zuchobeni Ezung, opens up the critical discussion on the contemporary church's role and mission towards the vulnerable, the outcast of the society. The writer presents a case study analysis of the Female Commercial Sex Workers in Dimapur, Nagaland and records some of their stories, stories that unveil the sad plights of their life situations and experiences; she also critically evaluates the role of her tribal church in ministering towards or amidst these vulnerable outcasts of the tribal society. What she unearths is that churches are not doing not even near enough in their social and spiritual service. Thus employing the Solidarity approach of Mercy Amba Oduyoye, she calls for the tribal churches to stand in solidarity with, to become inclusive, to do away with the expectation of perfectness in creation and to become advocates for the voiceless section of the society namely the Female Commercial Sex Workers in our tribal society.

Barrenness in Women: A Retrospect, by Elivi, makes a critical theological study on the issue of barrenness in women and the plight of barren women in particular. She particularly sets her study within the context of NEI tribal culture and society. Barrenness in women has very serious implications upon the lives of barren women in the tribal society. The writer makes a brief yet critical study on the biblical teachings concerning fertility (children) and barrenness and draws out theological insights to help address the plight of barren women in particular and the urgent need of transforming the tribals attitude toward barren women in general.

We (the editors), wish all the readers of tribal theological reflection a meaningful time of reading.

Editors

1

Tribal Women's Voices in Tribal Theological Discourse: Keynote Address

Zhodi Angami

Introduction

Many tribal men, and some women too, suffer from self-delusion. Self-delusion is the act of allowing yourself to believe with absolute certainty, despite verifiable evidence to the contrary, something that is not true. The lie that many believe to be true is that gender discrimination is absent in the tribal societies of North East India, when in fact tribal societies are fiercely patriarchal. In tribal societies, women do not have any decision-making powers in the family, church, and society.

Tribal women are often told that they enjoy a higher status than women in other parts of the country. That is like telling a battered wife that she is lucky her husband has not thrown her out of the house. Many tribal writers keep harping on the view that tribal women have the right to choose their life partner. They ignore the fact that in many cases, girls do not choose their partner because marriages are arranged. Girls, who have been socialized to be polite, obedient, submissive and virtuous, cannot think of refusing marriage proposals brought to them by their elders.

Tribal customary laws, which are not written or coded, is followed in the Indian tribal societies.[1] These customary laws deny women their rights to equality, justice and political representation. In accordance with tribal law, women in tribal societies do not have the right to inherit ancestral land. Women do inherit clan land among the matrilineal societies of the Khasis, the Jiantias, and the Garos of Meghalaya, yet even there the decisions concerning land are made by men.[2] To assume that women in matrilineal societies are empowered would be wrong because matrilineal does not equal matriarchal. Matrilineal societies are patriarchal andthe administrative and political powers are monopolized by men.

In 2017, women of Nagaland, under the leadership of Naga Mother's Association, sought to contest in the urban local bodies' election as the then government of Nagaland upheld the 2006 Nagaland Municipal (First Amendment) Act which granted 33 per cent reservation of seat to Naga women in local bodies.The move to reserve 33 per cent of seats for women in local political bodies is an application of Article 243T of the Constitution of India, 1949. However, the bid of women to participate in governance was met with violent protests, arson and boycotts by powerful tribal bodies dominated by men such as the Naga Hoho (a body of all the eighteen tribes of Nagaland), Eastern Naga People's Organization (a body of six Naga tribes), Naga Council, Ao Senden (a body of the Ao tribe), Lotha Hoho (a body of the Lotha tribe), Sumi Hoho (a body of the Sumi tribe), Angami Public Organization (a body of the Angami tribe) and others.The protestors claimed that the reservation was against Article 371A of the Indian Constitution which gives special provisionsto respect and protect the customary laws and practices of Nagaland.[3] Following directions from their tribe's organizations,

---

[1] K. S. Singh, ed., *Tribal Ethnography, Customary Law and Change* (New Delhi: Concept, 1993); Walter Fernandes, Melville Pereira, Vizalenu Khatso, *Tribal Customary Laws in Northeast India: Gender and Class Implications*, Legal Awareness Series, 4 (Guwahati: North Eastern Social Research Centre, 2008); Melvil Pereira, et al., eds., *Gender Implications of Tribal Customary Law: The Case of North-East India* (Guwahati: North Eastern Social Research Centre, 2017).

[2] Pranab Kumar Das Gupta, *Life and Culture of Matrilineal Tribe of Meghalaya*, 2nd ed. (New Delhi: Inter-India Publications, 1989); A. K. Nongkynrih, *Khasi Society of Meghalaya: A Sociological Understanding* (New Delhi: Indus Publishing Company, 2002); Julius Marak, *Garo Customary Laws and Practices: A Sociological Study* (New Delhi: Akansha Publishing House, 2000).

[3] For critical analyses of the issue, see Dolly Kikon, "What Kind of Nagaland are We Moving Towards? A Naga Feminist Reflects on the Row Over Women's Quota," in *Scroll*, 02 March 2017, https://scroll.in/bulletins/236/mercedes-benz-owners-can-now-hold-the-key-to-their-dream-car-quite-literally (accessed on 15 August 2019); idem, "Nagaland and the Fight for a Women's Quota," in *open Democracy*, 17 March 2017, https://www.opendemocracy.net/en/5050/nagaland-fight-for-women-quota/ (accessed on 15 August 2019); Lianboi Vaiphei,

the Chakhesang Mothers Association (a body of the women of the Chakhesang tribe), the Angamimiapfü Mechü Krotho (a body of the women of the Angami tribe) and Sumi Totimi Hoho (a body of women of the Sumi tribe) dissociated from their parent body, the Naga Mother's Association. Some of the tribal groups also excommunicated women candidates of their tribe for choosing to contest in the polls while others threatened to excommunicate and ostracize them if they take part in the elections. Consequently, 140 candidates withdrew their nominations.[4] Since its inception in 1963, there has not been a single woman legislator in the State Assembly, which has sixty seats. Rano M. Shaiza is the only Naga woman to represent Nagaland in politics. She is thefirst and only woman Member of Parliament from Nagaland. She was elected to the Lok Sabha after defeating the sitting Chief Minister, Hokishe Sema, in 1977.

The reason why I'm pointing out some of these issues is to highlight the fact that the dominant tribal narratives, controlled and expressed by men, have given us false images of how tribal women are loved, respected and enjoy high status in tribal societies. These dominant narratives perpetuate and contribute to the marginalization of women. Society, church and theology will be best served if we create new narratives, or even counter narratives, that will dismantle our perceived reality, debunk myths about equality and unmask the ugliness of gender discrimination in tribal cultures. This will be possible only when we change the lens through which we view our culture, practice and history. Decentring the dominant narrative by adding women's narrative, or seeing from women's perspective, is one way of achieving that. Decentring will enable us to reverse inequality by placing in the centre those who are suffering from injustice.

I see the task of facilitating tribal women's voices in tribal theological discourse as a move to decentre the dominant narrative. Undoubtedly, tribal women's voices can be a valuable contribution to tribal theological discourse. It is significant, in my opinion, that I'm a man talking about women's voices. The issue is not about women struggling for space in the theological field, it should be about women and men working together for a more just society. I believe that theology developed by men alone will be skewed, limited and not truly beneficial for all.

"Equality and Tradition Clash as Naga Women in India's Northeast Fight for Political Representation,“ in *The Conversation*, 3 March 2017, http://theconversation.com/equality-and-tradition-clash-as-naga-women-in-indias-northeast-fight-for-political-representation-73804 (accessed on 15 August 2019).

[4] A follow up is found here: Makepeace Sitlhou, "Threatened, Excommunicated and Banished: Where Do Women Candidates in Nagaland Stand Today?" in *Scroll*, 23 December 2017, https://scroll.in/magazine/859390/threatened-excommunicated-and-banished-where-do-women-candidates-in-nagaland-stand-today (accessed on 15 August 2019).

Are There Women's Voices in Tribal Theological Discourse?

This question is not difficult to answer. Tribal theological discourse itself occupies only a tiny niche in theological discourse and it is barely acknowledged in the field of theology. Additionally, there are only a few major works on tribal theology. A glance at those works gives the answer: Women's voice is missing in tribal theological discourse. I'm not saying that women have not engaged in theological discourse at all. There are a few books and a good number of articles published in books and journals. However, those works have not been considered as central in tribal theology or as representing tribal theological thought. Furthermore, not all works done by tribal women can qualify as tribal women's voice in theological discourse.

Tribal women's voice is not women doing theology. Tribal women have done theology that employs the same methods and principles developed in Western patriarchal settings, accepting the masculinist models of theology. Tribal women's voice is not simply those that talk about women. Tribal women have talked about women and women's issues without questioning the patriarchal gender paradigm and gender stereotyping. Tribal women's voice is not even primarily about supporting an egalitarian gender perspective; it is possible to posit egalitarian views employing contextual approaches (such as feminist theory). Tribal women's voice is all about women doing theology with their own categories, methods, approaches, languages and values. Finding tribal women's voices in tribal theological discourse is a step in that direction. Our ultimate aim is to make the presence of women an integral part of tribal theology.

Tribal Women as Theologians

Women have been critics of the theology determined, defined and dominated by men. Tribal women have spoken often of the egalitarianism in biblical texts. They have drawn their inspiration from the creation account in Genesis 1:27 where both female and male are created in God's image. They have reread the stories of women in the Old Testament. There is the story of the midwives, Shiphrah and Puah, who defied the Pharaoh (Exod 1:15-21) and thereby became participants of God's redemptive work. Miriam, Hannah, Esther, Ruth, Rahab, Jael, Tamar, Jephthah's daughter and other women have been read in various ways through women's perspective.Women scholars have referred to the female disciples of Jesus. Luke tells us that there were many women who were followers of Jesus and who provided for Jesus and the twelve disciples out of their resources. In fact, Luke names some of them along with the Twelve: Mary Magdalene, Joanna, the wife of Herod's steward Chuza, and Susanna (Luke 8:1-3). Mark also informs us that the women at the cross were the ones who used too follow him and provided for him in Galilee: Mary Magdalene, Mary the mother of James the younger and Joses, and Salome (Mark 15:40-41). Mark adds that many other women had followed Jesus to Jerusalem. Likewise, Matthew tells us that there were many women followers at the cross and among them were Mary Magdalene, Mary the mother of James and Joseph, and the mother of the sons of Zebedee (Matt 27:55-56). In the gospels, following Jesus means being his disciple. Thus, the gospels testify that a large group of women were disciples of Jesus who followed him, supported him, and served him throughout his ministry. Women have also argued that women were Apostle to the Apostles. In all the gospels women are the first to visit the tomb of Jesus on Sunday morning, the first to see the resurrected Messiah, and the ones who received the commission to carry the good news of the resurrection to the male disciples (Mark 16:1-7; Matt 28:1-8; Luke 24:1-10; John 20:1-2). Women have harped on the eschatological vision of a new inclusive humanity envisaged in Gal 3:28.

However, simply pointing out the role played by women in the history of Israel, in the life of Jesus, and in the ministry of the early church and relating them to the situation of women in the church and society today does not constitute the voice of tribal women. Tribal women's voice must arise from the world of women and not from the world made by men. What I mean is that tribal women will have to speak in the language of women, using their own social and cultural symbols. If women learn, speak, write, teach, and preach the same way men engage in those activities, there will be no new perspective in our theological enterprise and no opportunity for real transformation in church and society. This is the reason we are now attempting to look at some of the basic Christian concepts, models and symbols such as christology, pneumatology, ecclesiology, ethics, history, communication, scriptures, and priesthood to interpret or restructure them as women. It signals the transition of women from critic to theologian.

Women's Voice in Tribal Theology

At the risk of oversimplifying complex issues or distorting the matters under consideration, allow me to comment briefly on some of the areas of tribal theology that women can articulate—not as feminist or women's perspective to be attached to tribal theology as a subsidiary wing but as an articulation of tribal theology.

Tribal Ecclesiology and History

First, let me say something about tribal ecclesiology and history. I think tribal ecclesiology will benefit greatly from combining history and theology. It is in history that we will discover women have been central in the ministries of the church. Women were not only central figures in the ministry of Jesus but they played significant roles in the early church. In 1971, grave portraits of two female bishops, Cerula and Bitalia, were discovered in the catacomb of San Gennaro, beneath the city of Naples. The portraits of Cerula and Bitalia might have survived the attempts to destroy evidence of ordained women bishops because they were underground. The frescos have been dated to the late 400s or early 500s. Cerula is painted with her hands raised, with the Greek characters *alpha omega* and the *chirho* painted over her head. On either side of her head, there are two books emitting tongues of fire, with the names of the four evangelists written on them. Bitalia is painted in the same posture as Cerula, with the open books and *chirho*.[5] It is only in the ordination of bishops, and none other, that the open gospel books were, and still are, placed over their head. The tongues of fire on the books represented the inspiration of the Holy Spirit in the preaching of the bishops. In the early church there were women bishops, presbyters and patrons. There were women writing Christian documents, preaching, prophesying, evangelizing, discipling believers, baptizing, presiding over the Lord's Supper, and performing various ecclesiastical roles at least until the sixth century. There are many such visual evidence that women served as bishops, priests, deacons and other liturgical orders.

What went wrong? How did the church become an institution led only by males? Why did women stop to function as church leaders and ordained ministers? Was it because of the influence of Greco-Roman culture? Was it Emperor Constantine who airbrushed women out from the history of Christianity? Certainly Constantine's conversion to Christianity served a political purpose. His empire was caught up in civil wars and embracing a single faith was meant to unite the warring factions. But, Constantine needed a militant kind of Christianity, without women, which would be acceptable to his soldiers and which they could more easily compel others to accept. These views are open to debate. What we do know is that the movement to eject women from ministry began in the writings of some early theologians in the third century and received ecclesiastical approval in the Council of Nicea in 325 CE which banned women from the clergy. The Council of Laodicea (between 343-381 CE), forbade women from entering the altar area and from presiding over churches. In the Fourth Synod of Carthage in 398 CE, it was decreed that women, however learned and holy they may be, should neither teach men in an assembly nor baptize.Yet in the fifth century it was still a common practice to ordain women as deacons. The Council of Chalcedon in 451 CE attempted to put an end to this practice and ruled that women under the age of forty should not be ordained as deacons.

---

[5] Ally Kateusz, *Mary and Early Christian Women: Hidden Leadership* (Cham, Switzerland: Palgrave Macmillan, 2019), 156-61.

Those ordained as deacons become eligible for ordination as priests later on. The Eastern Church continued to ordain women until the ninth century. In the Catholic church, it was during the 12th and 13th centuries that women were removed from ordained ministry. Not only that, but attempts were also made to destroy evidence of ordained women in the past.[6] Despite repeated legislations by the church against the participation of women in ministry, there has been women (and men) who defied those unjust legislations and continued to answer their call from God to serve in the ministries of the church. Sadly, the majority followed the authoritarian pronouncements of the church.—for them, the authority of the church superseded the authority of Scripture and the authority of Jesus Christ.

Tribal ecclesiology may learn from the history of Christianity, from the mistakes of the past. History shows that the church has been embroiled in sin. It denigrated women, removed women from priesthood, silenced them, hated them, hunted and burned them at the stake as witches, and regarded them as the source of sin. The depth of sin within the Christian psyche is seen in the fact that many people still do not find anything wrong to consider women as inferior to men, unfit to represent the male Saviour. Throughout history, the church has subjugated women and it has been the loss of the church that it chose to besexist, misogynistic, and discriminatory.

The history of Christianity in North East India is not as bad as the history of the dismal failure of Christianity in India nor as terrible as the history of atrocities by the church in the East and West. But, it is not a pleasant story either. Christianity came to North East India from the West and the Christians of the region inherited its hierarchical ecclesiological structures, authoritarian practices and the misogynistic theologies. This is why we need to formulate a tribal ecclesiology that recognizes men and women, and children and grownups as embodying the body of Christ together.

Tribal Christology

Next, let us consider tribal Christology. Some work has been done in this area by various scholars. Takatemjen portrayed Jesus as *Lijaba*, based on the Ao Naga folklore of *Lijaba* and the two sisters.[7] Hemkhochon Chongloi articulated Kuki Christology based on the institution of *Indoi*.[8] Bendangla Longkumer formulated an Ao Naga women's Christology in which Jesus is

---

[6] Gary Macy, *The Hidden History of Women's Ordination: Female Clergy in the Medieval West* (Oxford: Oxford University Press, 2012); Gary Macy, William T. Ditewig, Phyllis Zagano, *Women Deacons: Past, Present and Future* (New York: Paulist Press, 2012).

[7] Taketemjen, *Studies on Theology and Naga Culture* (Delhi: ISPCK/CTC, Aolijen, 1998), 55-68.

[8] Hemkhochon Chongloi, I*ndoi: A Study of Primal Kuki Religious Symbolism in the Hermeneutical Framework of Mircea Eliade* (Delhi: ISPCK, 2008), 284-87.

seen as *Arasentur* (an Ao Naga women shaman), emphasizing the healing ministry of healing.[9] L. H. Lalpekhlua, in his PhD thesis constructed a Christology for Mizo people in which the Mizo conceptual framework of *pasaltha* is related to the person and work of Jesus Christ and Jesus' self-giving life and ministry, incarnation, suffering, and death on the cross are seen as manifesting the Mizo principle of *tlawmngaihna.*[10] Yangkahao Vashum expounded a tribal Christology of Jesus Christ as ancestor and elder brother.[11] These few examples serve to show that there is a lively discussion of tribal Christology in North East India. I will not enter into a conversation with the works mentioned above. Instead, I wish to offer some general insights into the issue. Drawing parallels between tribal culture and the life and work of Jesus Christ helps us to understand Christ from our own perspective—to meet him in our own culture. However, there are limitations to this method. For instance, we often find theologians making comparisons without considering the biblical text, which is the primary source of theology. Very often, we come across theological discourse that read the context into the text rather than reading the text to a given context. Another drawback is that christological constructions that do not embody the full soteriological dimension of the work of Jesus Christ will not be helpful nor desirable. Thankfully, there are signs that tribal christological discourse is moving beyond comparative studies and has started to grapple with ontological questions.

A tribal women's approach to Christology could attempt to answer a few questions. Why is Jesus important? Is the maleness of Jesus significant for salvation? How does the humanity and divinity of Jesus impact the status and role of women in church and society? Is the crucified Christ or the resurrected Christ more relevant for tribals? What is the place of the female gender in tribal understanding of the humanity?

Tribal Narrative Theology

Finally, let us turn to tribal narrative theology. Tribals are storytelling people. Our oral stories include stories about the family and clan, origin of the tribe or humanity, folklore, female and male heroes, supernatural legends about gods,

---

[9] Bendanglemla Longkumer, "Weaving Christology from Tribal Women Perspective: An Ao Naga Reading," *Journal of Tribal Studies* 15/2 (July-December, 2010), 29-45.

[10] L. H. Lalpekhlua, "A Study of Christology from a Tribal Perspective: With Special Reference to Mizoram, Northeast India," (PhD Thesis, University of Auckland, 2005), published as *Tribal Christology: A Tribal Perspective* (Delhi: ISPCK, 2007).

[11] Yangkahao Vashum, "Jesus Christ as the Ancestor and Elder Brother: Constructing a Relevant Indigenous/Tribal Christology of North East India," *Journal of Tribal Studies* 13/2 (July-December, 2008): 21-36. See also idem., *Christology in Context: A Tribal Indigenous Appraisal of North East India*, Christian Heritage Rediscovered 49 (Delhi: Christian World Imprints, 2017).

spirits, and humans, and the like. This tendency for storytelling should not be left out in reconceiving tribal theology, tribal ecclesiology, and tribal Christian worship. In tribal societies, women played an important role as storytellers. They were largely responsible for remembering the story of the ancestors of the tribe and preserving those stories by weaving their symbols into the tapestry of shawls and *mekhelas*. They also told personal stories of love and loss and stories of hopes and aspirations through the medium of songs and dances. Why should this be left out in tribal Christian life? In many churches, men have become the sole storytellers of our faith and practice, legitimizing women's subordinate position in church, family and society. Our Christianity will be richer, fuller and truer if women are not silenced but given space to tell Christ's story. We have to bear in mind that storytelling does not take place in a vacuum and that storytellers do not simply repeat a fixed story. No. The storyteller brings her own story with her, blends it with the story of Jesus and becomes one with the story of Christ. In that way, her story becomes Christ's story. Tribal Christology is Jesus Christ performing his story in our stories. Tribal history is not only his-story but her-story. Tribal ecclesiology is women and men becoming Church, becoming a part of the story of Jesus Christ.

Conclusion

This symposium will be significant as we will hear some of the voices of women. In the coming days, we will hear more and more voices from various fields, including those areas we could not cover in this symposium, such as tribal women's voices in biblical studies, pastoral care, counselling, worship and preaching, and the like. One of the advantages of tribal women is that more and more women are getting trained in theological colleges and joining church ministry upon graduation. Even more significantly, a growing number of women are getting higher degrees in theological education and quite a few have become theological educators, capable of passing down inclusive theological perspectives, biblical interpretation, and ministerial development to the next generation. Women have struggled long and hard. Yet many churches are hostile to women's leadership and participation in decision-making bodies. It is in that context that I wish to remind my sisters that you don't have to knock down the church doors that are closed, and you don't have to demand equality from those who don't understand Jesus and the Way of his realm. It is Christ who calls women to follow him and minister to those in need. The church is not church without women. So, those churches which do not accept women are not truly church. Forgive those sinners. Our Lord Jesus himself did not follow the norms of his society nor the rules of his culture. You, and I, can do the same. We can be mavericks, blazing a path all our own, and show our brothers from the other side what it means to follow Christ.

2

Jesus Christ in Tribal Context Today: A Theological Exploration

Dr Lovely Awomi James

Introduction

Tribal theology is progressing at a respectable pace today, thanks to the tireless, continuous efforts of the tribal theologians and scholars. Since the early 1990s tribal theology in the North East region has been making its existence felt through the work of the pioneering tribal scholars and till date we see the chain of tribal theological discourses being nurtured and maintained. In all of its reflections and formulations, the crux of the discourse is, "what does our faith in the lord and saviour Jesus Christ mean to us?" Or, "who is Jesus Christ to us?" It all begins and ends with our confession of our faith in Jesus Christ and how we live out that faith in concrete context. As such, the question or the subject of Christology is central to our tribal theological discourse. The hypothesis of this paper is this: Tribal Christians at present are in serious need of re-orienting their understanding of their faith in Jesus Christ. This is because tribal society is riddled with all kinds of problems and issues and in this situation one is compelled to ponder over the question of the authenticity and efficacy of their Christian faith. Some of the serious problems are poverty and the divide between the rich and the poor, corruptionand unethical lifestyles, moral degradation, nominalism, depression and loneliness (especially amongst the younger generation), and sickness etc. The writer strongly believes that there is a serious need to make a critical reflection on our understanding of Jesus Christ, the centre of our faith and see how we interpret and present him as the God-Incarnate in our situations to comfort, guide, heal, restore and transform our lives. This paper therefore attempts to critically explore the tribal Christological formulations and understand how they meaningfully and concretely relate with the lives and experiences of the tribals in today's context.

Before we proceed, however, the present writer would like to throw a serious caution before the audience and the readers: when tribal men speak and write theology, they are automatically taken as tribal theologians whereas, when tribal women speak and write theology, they are sidelined or compartmentalized as women's perspective or at worst *feminist* (with negative connotation) perspective; in other words, tribal male theologians and scholars equal to the voice of the whole tribal community/tribal world but tribal female theologians and scholars equal to the voice of tribal women (gender-identifying) and mistaken as mainly "for" or "in-relation-to" tribal women over against men. This is one serious injustice and oppressive practice within tribal theological discourse. Therefore, the present writer would like to spell out very clearly that this paper is not to be taken as a tribal woman's perspective in a limited sense but as a paper on tribal Christology written by a full-fledged tribal theologian first and then only if necessary by a tribal woman theologian. Moreover, the writer will be utilizing few indigenous concepts from within her own Sumi Naga tradition whenever necessary.

1. Definition and Meaning of Christology

Christology is a branch in theology that deals with the person, nature and works of Jesus Christ – the second person of the Holy Trinity – the God-Incarnate. Jesus Christ is the central figure whom the Old Testament foreshadows and the New Testament witnesses and proclaims as prophecy become real. The importance of Christology for Christianity cannot be contested because without Jesus Christ, Christianity would never emerge. And thus down through the history of the Christian church, numerous efforts were put in to understand, define and interpret the person and work of our Lord Jesus Christ. All of these efforts were driven by people's desire to make Jesus Christ meaningful and relevant to the life and faith of the people, without distorting the truth as revealed in the Bible. The central objective of the present paper on tribal Christology is not on the traditional doctrinal aspect of Christ's person, nature and work as such but specifically on the meaning and relevance of Jesus Christ in the contemporary tribal Christian life and situation.

2. Methodology for the Present Study

In Matthew 16:13-16, Jesus puts forward two heavily-loaded questions before His disciples: "Who do men say that the Son of man is?" and, "But who do you say that I am?" The first refers to opinions, views, attitudes and assumptions of the general others while the second is a direct question addressed to His closest friend(s) and disciple(s). Christological reflections and formulations can take either of the two approaches – the former is objective in approach which has its own advantages yet cannot be considered valid or authentic in the real sense of the term. It lies in the category of the general, impersonal reflections and responses. It cannot have concrete relevance and meaning. On the other hand, the second question is direct, personal and therefore subjective in approach. There is no place for assumptions, views or opinions derived out of what others say/think or out of the general ideas prevalent but it completely requires a response derived out of personal, contextual and concrete experience and knowledge. As such, any Christological reflection that takes the first approach can have very little relevance or authenticity. It is only when our Christological understanding follows the second approach will we be able to truly bring about serious reflection and formulation that will have a concretely relevant and meaningful impact upon our tribal Christian life and faith. Therefore, we need to begin our Christological exploration by asking the question, "Who do we (tribals) say that Jesus Christ is today?"

Next, in our Christological study, we also need to be reminded at all times that the context of the people with whom and for whom we are theologizing should be considered first before we proceed to interpret Jesus Christ for our people. This is to avoid repeating the same old mistake of the early missionaries who attempted to transplant onto our land the message of the gospel developed in the west for the western people and context. Example, "Jesus is the Answer!" reads a banner and someone confused asked, "But what is the Question?" What the writer is trying to say here is that, in order to respond to the question of who Jesus is for us today, it is a must that we first and foremost understand our living context, our experiences, needs, struggles, issues and problems, joy, aspirations and our culture as a whole. In simple terms it means allowing Christ to incarnate into our lives and into our very own concrete historical context. This will then guide us to deeper understanding of our faith in Jesus Christ and responding to his love, grace and salvation within our given situations.

Therefore, our methodology for the present study on tribal Christology follows tribal-incarnational method wherein Christ is understood as present and dwelling amongst us tribals, and therefore it requires that we understand and interpret Christ in our local cultural categories truly suited to our historical, existential situations. Christ should be seen as intimately involved and connected to us, rejoicing, mending, suffering, healing and transforming lives of the tribals. This incarnational method/approach is firmly rooted in the scripture as given in John 1:14;[1] John 6:38;[2] Luke 19:10;[3] John 10:10;[4] John 3:16-17.[5] By tribal-incarnational method we mean that we allow Christ Jesus to be personally incarnated (read *truly become real, situated*) in our living context so that as tribal Christians we do not identify ourselves merely as God's people or as followers of Christ by mouth or by name alone without any concrete meaning and relevance but as genuine Christians whereby our faith profession and our total way of life are guided, empowered and transformed by the person, teachings and promises of our lord Jesus Christ. The incarnation clearly shows us that God is present in a particular culture, speaks within that culture so that people can understand and respond to Him. In other words, the incarnation "tells us that God is intent on communicating about himself."[6] The incarnation gives us strong biblical basis and model of theological engagement – that God comes into our world out of His love in order to heal, transform and save us and our world. Tribal incarnational method requires that we contextualize the gospel in ways that respect and honor tribal culture and our existential situations and at the same time allow the power of the gospel to be truly incarnated within us so that it empowers, transforms and guide us toward the realization of God's reign amongst us. As such, our tribal incarnational hermeneutical approach proceeds with the question, "who do we say Jesus Christ is, for us tribals living today in the context of the 21st century?"

Having discussed briefly on the methodology of the present study, the writer would like to caution that this paper is not to be taken as an exhaustive/ complete Christological formulation being presented for us to ponder over and question about but rather it is to be taken as a working paper brought forth for us to critically engage in a discourse with a view to filter our thoughts and reflections and set forth how we can understand, interpret and present who Jesus Christ is for us tribals in today's context. In short, it will be is more like a team deliberation on tribal Christology that requires our combined efforts so

---

[1] "And the Word became flesh and lived among us, and we have seen his glory, the glory as of a father's only son, full of grace and truth."

[2] "For I have come down from heaven, not to do my own will, but the will of him who sent me."

[3] "For the Son of Man came to seek out and to save the lost."

[4] "…I came that they may have life and have it abundantly."

[5] "For God so loved the world that he gave his only Son, so that everyone who believes in him may not perish but may have eternal life. Indeed, God did not send the Son into the world to condemn the world, but in order that the world might be saved through him."

[6] Cf. Olugbenga Olagunju, "Incarnational Christology in Johannine Gospel: Implications for African Christianity," in *https://www.biblicaltheology.com/Research/Olagunju003pdf*, 23. (Accessed 22.10.2018).

that we have a more inclusive, comprehensive and wholesome reflection on tribal Christology.

3. Development of Tribal Christology thus Far

Without going into detail, let us quickly and briefly recall some of the significant Christological reflections and interpretations developed by our tribal theologians thus far.

Renthy Keitzar, engaging the indigenization/inculturation method he endorses the importance of communicating the gospel (Jesus Christ) in tribal cultural thought forms. In his own words, Keitzar states that in formulating (tribal) Christian theology we contextualize the gospel message and "taking stock of all we have in the past, we interpret these things in terms of our socio-cultural traditions and contemporary realities."[7]

K. Thanzauva employs communitarian approach and engages the synthetic-praxis method/model whereby there is given a space for a synthesis of gospel and tribal culture and out of that synthesis tribal Christians are guided toward active praxis – living transforming Christian lives, leading the society towards the realization of the Kingdom of God.[8] In this approach, Jesus Christ is presented as the liberator of the tribals from sin, struggles and pains through God's act of *Tlawmngaihna* (tribal altruism – self-abnegation, self-sacrificing)[9] and as such Christ is God's *Tlawmngaihna* incarnate and personified.

A. Wati Longchar employs Space/Earth/Creation-centred approach and critiques the traditional western theological method and the missionary theology that is completely anthropocentric (human-centred). He argues that the early western missionaries and evangelists neglected the holistic salvation and emphasized only upon the salvation of the souls such that tribal Christians began to neglect the physical, material and cosmic aspect of faith life. According to him, Christ was presented only as the saviour of human souls and therefore this limited the whole of the gospel message and its relevance for the tribals whose existence and whose identity were very closely connected with and to the land, space and creation.[10] Hence, this necessitates re-interpretation of God as Lijaba – the Earth-entering, Earth-dwelling, immanent God and saviour for the tribals.

---

[7] Cf. Renthy Keitzar, "A Study of the North-East India Tribal Christian Theology," in Renthy Keitzar, ed., *Good News for North East India: A Theological Reader* (Guwahati: CLC, 1995), 40.

[8] Cf. K. Thanzauva, *Theology of Community: Tribal Theology in the Making* (Aizawl: MTC, 1997), 84. (Hereafter cited as Thanzauva, *Theology of Community*).

[9] Cf. Thanzauva, *Theology of Community*, 129-133.

[10] Cf. A. Wati Longchar, *The Tribal Religious Traditions in North East India: An Introduction* (Jorhat: ETC, 2000), 147.

Yangkahao Vashum employs contextual hermeneutics in his Christological formulations. He utilizes tribal symbols and images of Christ to make Jesus Christ meaningful and relevant in the context of the tribals. The biblical image of Jesus as the Lamb of God (John 1:29[11]), is reinterpreted and re-presented in tribal language and category by using the image of *Rooster* (sacred sacrificial animal in tribal culture). Offering unblemished rooster for sacrifice on behalf of individuals or community[12] with the objective of taking away suffering, sickness and troubles, was one of the central components in tribal religious tradition. Furthermore, he uses *Jesus Christ as Ancestor*, *Jesus Christ as Elder Brother* etc.[13] As Ancestor, Jesus fulfils the role of perfect mediation between the spiritual world and the material/physical world[14] and as Elder Brother par excellence, he fulfils the role of the firstborn son (Luke 2:7; Matthew 1:25),[15] serving as the role model[16] in responsible living and service of others.

L. H. Lalpekhlua employing Contextual Christology for Mizo context interprets Jesus Christ as *Pasaltha* (ideal/good/brave man) and incorporates the Mizo ethics of *Tlawmngaihna* in his Christological formulation. Jesus Christ in Mizo context thus is the upright, ideal, brave and good God-man who embodies and exhibits all the elements of *Tlawmngaihna* that he selflessly and bravely went to the cross, overcoming all evil powers and finally conquering sin and death for our salvation.[17] As such, Jesus Christ is the *Pasaltha Tlawmngai* for the Mizo tribal Christians.

4. Who is Jesus Christ for the Tribals Today? A Theological Exploration

This section is solely concentrated upon some of the possible tribal Christological categories using tribal cultural images, symbols and metaphors for meaningfully understanding and relating Christ's salvific person and his teachings amongst the tribals today. The writer would like to caution the readers that no image, symbol or metaphor that we use for Christ is absolute,

---

[11] "...Here is the Lamb of God who takes away the sins of the world."

[12] Cf. Yangkahao Vashum, *Christology in Context: A Tribal-Indigenous Appraisal of North East India* (New Delhi: CWI, 2017), 136. (Hereafter cited as Vashum, *Contextual Christology*).

[13] Cf. Yangkahao Vashum, "Jesus Christ as the Ancestor and Elder Brother: Constructing a Relevant Indigenous/Tribal Christology of North East India," *Journal of Tribal Studies*, 13/2 (July-December, 2008): 21-36. (Hereafter cited as Vashum, *Jesus Christ as Ancestor and Elder Brother*).

[14] Cf. Vashum, *Jesus Christ as Ancestor and Elder Brother*, 31.

[15] Cf. Vashum, *Jesus Christ as Ancestor and Elder Brother*, 30-31.

[16] Cf. Vashum, *Contextual Christology*, 140-141.

[17] Cf. L.H. Lalpekhlua, *Contextual Christology: A Tribal Perspective* (New Delhi: ISPCK, 2007), 204ff.

normative or complete for the very fact that Christ as God-Incarnate transcends all our finite languages, thoughts, knowledge and our world. No image that we employ is perfect for we can only image or conceptualize the infinite and the divine in limited, finite human categories. Augustine, the great Bishop of Hippo (354-430 A.D.), rightly commented that even the person who says the most about God is but "dumb" and yet, our only alternatives are to speak in halting, inadequate words or to remain silent.[18] Most importantly, the present Christological categories/images are solely selected according to the urgent needs and challenges of the contemporary tribal socio-religious, political, cultural and economic situations.

4.1. Jesus Christ as *Timijhulholokau Lhou-u*: The Human Face of God (Immanuel - God with Us) in Concrete Historical Context

Christology must begin with God and incarnation – God-Incarnate. The story or the event of Christian faith begins and ends with God in Christ and the salvation that he brought for us and for the whole creation. We cannot compromise on that no matter how we try to twist and turn or try to outsmart each other's theological formulation with our abstract, philosophical and high intellectual reflections. The Bible is our basis and the Bible reveals that truth concerning God's initiation for our salvation. Jesus Christ is God in human form, the human face of God. God enters time and space through the Incarnate Word – the Logos – our Lord Jesus Christ. The central message of Christian faith is this: that God came down and became one of us and dwelled amongst us for a purpose, in and through the person of Jesus Christ. The Sumi Naga tribal term *Xakulu-u Lhou* is the translation of *Saviour God* or the *Creator/ God who saves*. As God (*Alhou-u*) Jesus saves (*Xalu*) for, no mere human can save), and as human, he embodies and experienced our nature and existence – our limitations (except sin) and our struggles and saves the total human from the depravity of sin and death. As Divine-human or as God-in-human-form (*Timijhulholokau Lhou-u*), he bridges the gap between God and the world becoming the mediator and thus reconciles us and the world to God.

4.2. Jesus Christ as the Path and Guide to True Religiosity/Spirituality

In the Context of Religious Nominalism and Fundamentalism, who is Jesus Christ to us? Without discrediting the existence of the minority faithful and upright tribal Christians, tribal Christians can either be just plain nominal or fundamental/rigid Christians as is apparent in today's context. Many tribal Christians are Christians in name only. They wear their Christian identity as an outward badge for purpose of registry rather than for any real Christian

[18] Cited in Sallie McFague, *Metaphorical Theology: Models of God in Religious Language* (Philadelphia: Fortress press, 1982), 1.

living. Tribal society is crowded with more of professing Christians than with practicing Christians. Jesus in his own religious context: In the context of false, empty, showy religiosity - ***John 14:6*** *I am the way, the truth and the life. No one comes to the father except through me.* Refer also Matthew 23:5ff.[19] Mark 7:6;[20] Matthew 6:1[21] etc. Who do we say Jesus is in such a context of shallow religiosity and spirituality of the tribal Christians? Can he be imaged as the tribal priest? The shaman, religious/spiritual guide? Through whom people are taught and guided toward upright way of life – in perfect and peaceful tune with God and with the world of creation.

4.3. Jesus Christ is the Moral Teacher/Elder (*Akukhu-aye Shikukau-u/Kichimikivimi*)[22]

Tribal society today is gradually sinking into moral degradation. The question is, who is to be blamed? Or, what are the factors responsible for it? While there may be different and several opinions to answer these questions, the present writer strongly believes that one of the main reasons is a theological one – that people are not genuinely/deeply rooted in their faith life. Nominal Christian life and corruptive lifestyles are becoming the order of the day whereby people are easily affected and influenced by the secular, global culture – young and old alike. One example is, a decade or two back, tribals were busy copying the western white culture and lifestyle but today in North East India, especially among the younger generation and the womenfolk, Korean culture/lifestyle is becoming popular for imitation/adoption. In addition, individualism and materialism are taking over the tribals Christians in which even the church is not spared or exempted. Tribal culture is slowly disappearing and its moral, ethical values are neglected as primitive, shameful and irrelevant – developing our own local imperialistic attitude and outlook whereas the real irrelevant foreign culture(s) is/are adopted as relevant and worthy by the tribals. Traditional values of altruism, selflessness, service for others, social graces and etiquettes and respect of elders etc., are all being replaced by self-centredness, mannerlessness and disrespectfulness in the society. In this context, can we develop a Christological image/metaphor of Jesus as the Excellent Moral-ethical Teacher or Elder? Jesus as *Akukhu-aye Shikukau/Kichimikivimi* can offer the tribal Christians scope to teach them of the gospel principles of love,

---

[19] "They do all their deeds to be seen by others…"

[20] "He said to them, Isaiah prophesied rightly about you hypocrites, as it is written: 'This people honor me with their lips, but their hearts are far from me.'"

[21] "Beware of practicing your piety before others to be seen by them; for then you have no reward from your Father in heaven."

[22] A Sumi Naga term referring to an excellent moral-ethical teacher or an elder who justly executes his/her duty of being a role model for guiding others toward just, moral and ethical life.

purity, justice, originality, selflessness and Christian sharing and unity which are also very much entrenched in traditional culture of the tribals.

4.4. Jesus Christ: The Sustainable Farmer/Cultivator (*Alokutsu-lukichiu*) – The Sustainable Economist

Tribal Christians can be economically divided into three main divisions – the very rich, the moderate and the very poor. Without neglecting the middle/moderate class of tribals, the writer would like to draw our attention to the extreme opposite groups with special emphasis upon the very poor of the rural villages and towns. The former class is constituted by the educated, well-employed, and ill-gotten wealthy individuals and families, who form the affluent group while the latter is constituted by the uneducated, unemployed, just, simple and struggling population. We cannot even imagine the possibility of measuring the huge gap of disparity between these two social divide groups. In tribal context, a wise farmer/cultivator assesses all aspects of agricultural life when it comes to maintaining sustainable livelihood. He/she assesses the ecological conditions – the seasons, atmosphere, the air, the rain, the sun and the soil before one sets out to sow/plant/harvest etc., food crops. For such a farmer/cultivator, there is no question of lacking, hunger or greed. Everything one does depend upon the favourability of the ecological environment and resources and upon and within one's own inherited or acquired territory of the field/plot of the land. As such, there is very little or no space at all for anyone to accumulate unethical measure of wealth and resources.

Can we image Jesus Christ as a sustainable farmer or economist for the tribals to direct us about hard work, just and sustainable earning? Jesus as presented in the gospels taught adequate lessons on believers' attitude toward and management of wealth and resources. During his own days, he encountered people who were steep into economic poverty and economic sin. Read Mark 12:31; Luke 12:15; Luke 6:38; John 10:10; Matthew 6:25-34 and Acts 2:42-47 etc. Jesus' economic messages were centred on the principles of sharing among the believers, of blessing others with our wealth, of fair trade, and of ridding oneself of the sin or greed and economic corruption.

4.5. Jesus Christ: The Divine Healer (*Shikipivi-lhou-u, Tu-umi*)

Today in tribal society many individuals and families are seen wrestling with the problems related to diseases and illnesses. Problems related to health are taking over the lives of the tribals at a very fast pace. Almost every individual/family affected. Many have lost their loved ones and many continue to foresee such possibilities. Physical sickness is seriously destroying many tribal Christian homes, rendering them physically, mentally, emotionally, materially and spiritually drained and without hope. We can also consider the ever-increasing cost of health care today – with only the unjustly rich people able to afford. The gospel presents Jesus as the Healer, the Restorer of people's health and life. Healing was an essential part of Jesus' ministry. The gospels clearly testify that it was his divine compassion for the sick, poor and suffering that always drew Jesus toward his healing ministry. Countless of people – young and old were healed. The blind, the lame, the deaf, the mute, the demon-possessed, the leprous, the bleeding and even the dead were brought to him for healing (Matthew 1816; 12:15; 14:14; 14:36; 15:30; Mark 6:56; 6:5; 7:37; Luke 4:40; 5:17; 9:11 etc.). To present Jesus as the healer we have sufficient tribal images/symbols of *shaman* (indigenous physician/healer), *Tu-umi*, *Arasentsur*, *Shikipivi-lhou-u*. In the tribal tradition, it is the shaman, the traditional healer, who ascertains the cause of sickness and works out the remedies for healing and restoration of health[23] and life. Therefore Jesus as the healer - traditional healing image can restore the tribals to their faith in God, who is the healer of all their ailments.

4.6. Jesus Christ: The True Friend and Confidant (*Akusau-kuchou/ Akusau-kiviu*)[24]

This image of Jesus Christ as the *True Friend* and *Confidant* is mainly developed out of tribal women's personal and internal relationship with God.[25] Tribal Christians as individuals and as communities are invaded by the pressures of today's world in many different forms and manners. Whether old or young, many go through untold measures of stress, depression and loneliness in life. We become victims of these problems due to various factors – work-related, relationship problems, studies, career, family, societal, pressures of sky-high expectations, health issues etc. One of the serious problems that we face in our tribal society is the rise of suicides rate especially amongst the younger generation. Within such a context, how best can we image Jesus Christ than as the *Akusau-kuchou* or *Akusau-kiviu* – the True Friend and Confidant? How many of us, of our family members, of spouses, of friends are friendless? How many are slowly dying inside of loneliness, without hope, without answers, with unspoken fears, struggles and with dark secrets? Can we offer a fitting image/presence of God to such suffering people amidst us? Yes, we can. Jesus as the *Akusau-kuchou/ Akusau-kiviu* – the *True Friend and Confidant*.

---

[23] Cf. Bendanglemla Longkumer, *Christ, The Healer: Exploring Indigenous People's Spirituality* (ND: CWI, 2018), 122-124.

[24] A Sumi Naga term for True/Genuine/Best friend.

[25] Cf. Lovely Awomi James, "Re-Imaging God from Tribal Women's Perspective," in Marlene Ch. Marak, ed., *Inspiring Change: Tribal Women and Men Reading and Doing Theology* (Jorhat: WSC-ETC, 2015), 60-74.

Conclusion

Employing tribal-incarnational methodology, the present paper made a humble attempt to understand and interpret the relevance of Jesus Christ into the real life situations of the tribals in North East India. Tribal-incarnational methodology in doing tribal Christology enables us to understand and meet Jesus Christ, the significance of his person, his teachings and his work from within our own tribal culture and using our own tribal categories, images and language. The paper highlighted the necessity for tribal Christological formulations and argues for a contextual, incarnational re-presentation of Christ for meaning and relevance for the tribal Christians today as they struggle with various existential problems and issues.

3

A Contextual Reading of Paul's *Haustafel* Manifesto in Ephesians 5:21-33 with Special Reference to Husband-Wife Relationship: North East India Tribal Perspective

Razouselie Lasetso

Introduction

Paul's most extensive treatment on *haustafel* (household code) in relation to gender roles is found in Ephesians 5:21-33.[1] This passage is the centre storm on current debate concerning structure of authority in the marriage relationship.[2] It had its beginning with the emergence of women's movement, particularly feminist biblical hermeneutics, which drastically provoked people's understanding of marriage and gender roles within it. In this connection, there are at least three divergent views found today. First, the group that strongly believes in the chain of authority – with God, Christ, husbands, wives, children, slaves in the descending order. In this they prefer to hold on to the traditional understanding of "rule and authority over" of husbands over their wives. The second view, particularly held by the feminist camp, calls for egalitarian model of family in which no one seems in charge but where

[1] Other texts on household codes are Col 3:18-4:1; Titus 2:1-15; 1 Pet 2:18-3:7.

[2] David M. Park, "The Structure of Authority in Marriage: An Examination of *Hupotasso* and *Kephale* in Ephesians 5:21-33," *Evangelical Quarterly* 59/2 (1987), 117.

everyone is free to do what he or she thinks. They advocate for removal of all gender-based distinction including husband-wife distinction. They want everything to be egalitarian.[3] They believe that since in Christ we are all new creation the old social paradigm of hierarchies has no place in Christian life (2 Cor 5:17; Gal 3:28).[4] They view such biblical passages which enjoin her submission as applying only to that culture and therefore not applicable to modern marriages.[5] The third view is the one which is sandwiched in-between these two contrasting views characterized by confusion and obscurity.[6]

These views are not foreign to the tribal world of North East India. Rather, they are also prevalent in the understanding of gender roles in the tribal family. This presents us the setting for a contextual reading of the text from the tribal perspective to draw its significance for today. But, before we take up the passage for study a brief note on the husband-wife relation among the tribals of North East India befits the discussion here.

1. Context of the Husband-Wife Relationship among the Tribals of North East India

The structure of the tribal people of North East India is patriarchal and as such male domination of both the family and the society is prevalent in the region. The family setup is generally patriarchal, patrilocal and patrilineal among most of the tribal communities of North East India, with the exception of the Garos, the Khasis and a portion of the Lalungs which is matrilineal and matrilocal. But, even these cultures practice patriarchy not matriarchy. Therefore, in the tribal culture, generally speaking, it is the male who rules the household as women are considered the weaker gender. Therefore, patriarchy is pervasive in the region, where women have little or no say at all in the affairs of the community and the family. The structure of authority in the tribal household is therefore customarily patricentric where the male head controls every decision, all property, members of the family and the wife.[7] And even to this day tribal families generally adhere to the traditional model of family relationship.[8]

---

[3] Steven J. Cole, "What Do You Mean, 'Submit'? (Ephesians 5:21-24),"https://bible.org/seriespage/lesson-3-what-fo-you-mean-submit-ephesians-521-24 (29/8/2017).

[4] Marg Mowczko, "Paul's Main Point in Ephesians 5:22-33," margmowczho.com/pauls-main-point-in-eph-5_22-33 (3/9/2017).

[5] Cole, "What Do You Mean, 'Submit'? (Ephesians 5:21-24)."

[6] Park, "The Structure of Authority in Marriage," 117.

[7] Limatula Longkumer, *Women in Theological Education: Pedagogical Issues* (Bangalore: BTESSC, 2012), 151.

[8] NarolaImchen, "A Search for Liberative Elements for Women Within the Patriarchal Culture of NEI," in *Doing Tribal Christian Theology with Tribal Resources: Cultural Resources from North East India*, edited by Razouselie Lasetso & Eyingbeni Hümtsoe (Jorhat, Assam: ETC Programme Coordination, 2009), 210.

Women's status in the tribal society is therefore not very encouraging. They are made voiceless by the long standing traditions of male domination and in silence they bear the brunt of male chauvinism.

In the realms of the household, wives are expected to be submissive and are considered as created mainly for household chores, procreation and nurturing their husbands' progenies. In marriage, as Lovely Awomi James laments, "After marriage, by virtue of her inferiority as a female . . . she has to relegate herself, her independence, her energy and her time to shoulder the responsibility as a wife to her husband, . . ."[9] Often it is lamented that wives are reduced to the status of a slave in the tribal world.[10] In the name of patriarchy, tradition, and biblical sanction (misinterpretation of Scriptures) men continue to violate women through violence and abuse. In North East India, Assam and Tripura account for the highest incidences of domestic violence. Domestic violence is very much prevalent in the region and despite its severity most have sadly accepted it as personal and domestic affair that need not be intervened by external force.[11] As a report on violence against women in North East India states; "Due to strong patriarchal structure of society, women have been relegated to a subordinate position. Consequently, many forms of domestic violence have received public sanction and are as such not considered to be within the ambit of DV."[12] This is seen in the fact that many tribal women consider it sinful to reprimand their husbands for any violence. Rather, they even consider it "a 'husband's privilege' to strike the wife."[13]

Husbands' ill-treatment of wives among the tribals in North East India is manifested in the form of violence which includes physical, verbal, psychological, and spiritual abuses. With regard to domestic violence in regard to physical abuse R. L. Hnuni observes that it is an,

> . . . expression of the husband's claim of superiority over the wife. This practice is common among the uneducated and the educated alike, and in rural as well as urban areas. In former days in Mizo society, before and

---

[9] Lovely Awomi James, *Tribal Theology: Reviewing the Naga Traditional Worldview*, Christian Heritage Rediscovered – 48 (New Delhi: Christian World Imprints, 2017), 111.

[10] Lungsangliu, "Role and Status of Rongmei Naga Women in the Traditional and Present Society," in *Women Then and Now: Sharing Untold Insights on Women of North East India*, edited by Narola Imchen & Eyingbei Hümtsoe (Jorhat, Assam: WSC-ETC, 2011), 4.

[11] Eyingbeni Hümtsoe-Nienu, "Theological Response to Domestic Violence," in *Voices Against Domestic Violence: Biblical, Theological and Sociocultural Appraisal of the Experiences of the Oppressed Tribal, Children, Men and Women*, edited by A. Tali Ao (New Delhi: CTC & CWI, 2016), 109.

[12] "Violence Against Women in North East India – NCW," *http://ncw.nic.in/pdfreports/Violence%20against%20women%20North%20East%20India%20-%20An%20Inquiry.pdf* (11/9/2017).

[13] "Violence Against Women in North East India – NCW."

> after Christianity when a husband got angry he would first go and drink and get drunk so that he could beat his wife as he would not like to do so with a clear conscience. Today even without getting drunk a husband would beat his wife when he gets angry. Throughout the ages women have been suffering at the hands of their husbands. While some women would run home to their parents, the others would endure it silently with a painful heart.[14]

This is unfortunate because such incidences prevail even in the Christian families. Another form of the domestic violence is driving the wife away from home. In such a situation women find themselves in helpless situation with nowhere to go, and often families are reluctant to take them back. Social stigma for such women driven away from home is very high.[15] Such violence and cruelties committed against women/wives by their own husband is condemnable. But, sadly this has been taken in most quarters as part of family life where the church and society do not address the issue relevantly. In the words of Eyingbeni Hümtsoe-Nienu,

> The fact that Christianity is the religion of most of the tribal communities in the Northeast India region has not positively transformed the general quality of human relations. The ancient distinction founded on gender, class, age, tribe, etc., continue to affect the way we relate to one another.[16]

Even today, as in the old, in many homes of the tribal world of North East India, wives are physically, mentally, spiritually and verbally abused as part of the family ritual. Wives are often objects of abuse in many tribal homes even to this day. The lack of balance in relationship and the absence of love within the families in the husband-wife relation are due to the strongly entrenched patriarchal mind-set of the tribal people. This is an area of concern in this age where Church buildings stand tall in the region. With this we now turn to our text in hand.

2. The Text (Ephesians 5:21-33)

Ephesians 5:21-33 is crucial to the understanding of the mutual obligations of husbands and wives in Christian marriage. Some consider the passage as a text of terror.[17] Many consider the hierarchical structure of the passage as oppressive.[18] Some treat it as an apologetic statement to the Roman

---

[14] R.L. Hnuni, *Vision for Women in India: Perspectives from the Bible, Church and Society* (Bangalore: Asian Trading Corporation, 2009), 80.

[15] "Violence Against Women in North East India – NCW."

[16] Hümtsoe-Nienu, "Theological Response to Domestic Violence," 109.

[17] Frank Logue, "A Text of Terror: Ephesians 5:21-33," *http://kingofpeace.org/sermons2002-2003/sermon-082403.htm(9/9/2017).*

[18] Park, "The Structure of Authority in Marriage," 123.

government.[19] Some people, because of such text, call Paul the chief chauvinist in the Bible,[20] while some exegetes are hermeneutically controlled by egalitarian texts such as Genesis 1:26-30 and Galatians 3:28 to interpret the controverted texts like Ephesians 5:21-33; 1 Corinthians 11:3-16; Col 3:18-4:1;and 1 Tim 2:11-15. In this regard Stephen Clark observes, "Foundational to their hermeneutic is the conviction that subordination is inconsistent with the equality specified in these texts and therefore, the controverted texts cannot express a universally applicable subordination."[21] But, such an approach where a straightforward passage of Scripture that deals with gender roles within marriage like Ephesians 5:21-33 the legitimacy of the so-called control factor in the egalitarian hermeneutics is questionable.[22]

Rather, a proper exegetical method needs to be employed to derive the crux of such passage. An exegetical and philological reading of some the debated terms in this paper therefore becomes crucial in understanding the full import of Paul's perception on the Christian *haustafel* as embedded in Ephesians 5:21-33. The text talks of "submission" (*hupotassō*) and "respect" (*phobeō*) as the wife's response, and "head" (*kephalē*) and "love" (*agapē*) as response of the husband in the marriage relationship. Therefore, these words need special attention in dealing with Paul's *haustafel.*

But, before proceeding further, a note on the placement of verse 21 in the text must be made. The placement of this verse in the various translations is interesting to note. Some put it as conclusion to the previous passage (vv.15-20), some put it independently between verse 20 and verse 22, some insert it as the introduction to the *Haustafel* (vv. 21-33). Some commentators opine that the editor seems to have created verse 21 as an introductory note to the *haustafel.*[23] And as Muddiman observes, "the doxological phrase at the end of verse 20 makes a satisfactory closure and would surely force the reader to draw breath for a new paragraph. And in terms of content, 5.21 changes the subject and forms an introduction to the section that follows."[24] Therefore, it is better to take verse 21 as part of the whole *haustafel* passage. This would also explain the supply of "submit" in verse 22 which is actually derived from verse

[19] Craig S. Keener, *Paul, Women and Wives: Marriage and Women's Ministry in the Letters of Paul* (Peabody, MA: Hendrickson Publishers, 2004).

[20] Robin Scorggs defends against such allegations as baseless rather he sees Paul as the "only consistent spokesman for the liberation and equality of women in the New Testament," Cited by Alan F. Johnson, "A Review of the Scholarly Debate on the Meaning of 'Head' (kefalh) in Paul's Writings," *Ashland Theological Journal* (2009), 37 (35-57).

[21] Clark, "Exegesis 20: Headship in Ephesians," *Foundations* 35 (Autumn 1995), 19.

[22] Clark, "Exegesis 20: Headship in Ephesians," 19.

[23] John Muddiman, *A Commentary on the Epistle to the Ephesians* (London & New York: Continuum, 2001), 257.

[24] Muddiman, *A Commentary on the Epistle to the Ephesians*, 256.

21. Therefore, taking verses 21-33 as a unit we will look into those pertinent words like "submit," "head," "love" and "respect," in the text to draw the meaning Paul possibly might have implied.

3. Context of Paul's *Haustafel* Manifesto in Reference to Husband-Wife Relationship

In order to understand the purpose why Paul wrote this code the way it is written, we need to first understand what marriage and family were like in the cultures which surrounded the New Testament world. To this aspect we now turn our attention.

3.1. Greek Family

To the ancient Greeks the household was a vital social institution through which order was maintained in the society. Therefore Greek teachers offered their advice to the *paterfamilias* (father/male head) on household management. These discourses given by the teachers came to be known as "household codes" (*haustafel*). One of the most extensive and referenced discourse is that of Aristotle's instruction in the fourth Century B.C. This includes how the *paterfamilias* should manage and control his wife, children and slaves. It must be noted here that, Aristotle is acknowledged as the one who introduced the three pairs of relationship into the household codes with the father as the authority.[25] In regard to the Greek family, Craig S. Keener states that, "the man in charge of the household was often even compared to a king, since the family was viewed as a microcosm of society."[26]

Monogamy was the predominant practice among the Greeks, however, marriage was contracted mainly for the convenience of the men. Men marry primarily for legitimate heirs to his properties through his wife. The wife was literally kept in seclusion at home. She was not allowed to take part in public life. She was not allowed to walk in the streets alone.[27] She was not allowed to join the men of the household, not even for meals. Her role was one of servitude and chastity, whereas the husband could go anywhere and find any woman for partnership.[28] Women were usually married young, as young as 13-15. Men can nearly be in their forties. The logic behind such gap in age is that man can more easily teach and control her the way he wished his household to be managed.

---

[25] Keener, *Paul, Women and* Wives, 146.

[26] Keener, *Paul, Women and Wives*, 146.

[27] William Barclay, *The Letters to the Galatians and Ephesians*, NDSB (Bangalore: Theological Publications in India, 2013), 196.

[28] William Barclay, *The Letters to the Philippians, Colossians and Thessalonians*, NDSB (Bangalore: Theological Publications in India, 2013), 187.

The wife's subservience in the Greek family is also seen in that fact that, "eroticism being part of the Greek life, a husband did not need a wife for companionship, love, or sexual fulfilment. It was not considered immoral for husbands to have affairs. However, there were serious penalties for an adulterous wife. The wife's legal position to her husband was much like a child or a slave."[29]And in Greece there was no proper legal provision for divorce and as such divorce was comparatively easy. Both the husband and wife could initiate divorce but the wife needs to seek divorce through the *archon*, while the husband need not go through such process. Thus wives were easily discarded on personal whims. The wife's only security was her dowry since on divorce it must be returned. Therefore in Greek culture there was little commonality between the husband and the wife.[30] In regard to the Greek family William Barclay observes, "Home and family were near to being extinct, and faithfulness was completely non-existent."[31] Husband-wife relation was therefore greatly impaired in the Greek world.

3.2. Roman Family

The Roman wives had more freedom than their counter parts. They could own property and also could obtain a divorce. But, nevertheless the power over the family was clearly the husband's or father's privilege.[32] The Roman *patria potestas* (father's power) gave the Roman *paterfamilias* (father, grandfather or great-grandfather) absolute control and authority over the family.[33] The *paterfamilias* was accountable for the behaviour of the family, including wife. In such a setting a wife was required complete submission to their husbands.[34] Thus serving wives who managed their household well and are obedient were extolled.[35] In Paul's days Roman family was in shambles and it has even been said that "women were married to be divorced and divorced to be married."[36] In other words divorce was rampant. To this, "the biblical scholar Jerome declares it to be true that in Rome there was a woman who was married to her twenty-third husband and she herself was his twenty-first wife."[37] The whole

[29] Joanne Krupp, "What About Submission and Headship?" (28/8/2017).

[30] Krupp, "What About Submission and Headship?"

[31] Barclay, *The Letters to the Galatians and Ephesians*, 196-197.

[32] Krupp, "What About Submission and Headship?"

[33] Catherine C. Kroeger, "Head," *Dictionary of Paul and His Letters*, edited by Gerald F. Hawthorne, Ralph P. Martin, Daniel G. Reid (Downers Grove, Ill: Intervarsity Press, 1993), 376.

[34] Keener, *Paul, Women and Wives*, 165.

[35] Keener, *Paul, Women and Wives*, 165.

[36] Citing Philosopher Seneca. Barclay, *The Letters to the Galatians and Ephesians*, 197.

[37] Barclay, *The Letters to the Galatians and Ephesians*, 197.

atmosphere surrounding the Roman family was adulterous and the marriage bond was crumbling down.[38]

3.3. Jewish Family

Marriage was, at least in theory, a highly esteemed institution among the Jewish people. And the Rabbis encouraged that everyone must be married. In Jewish marriage male domination was pervasive as in the Greco-Roman society. Wives generally fulfil their marital roles in submission to the wishes of their husbands.[39] This is not a surprise when we see the fact that Jewish women were considered merely as a thing or possession of her husband. Philo, the Hellenistic Jewish philosopher, writes in relation to the stability of the Jewish home, "Wives must be in servitude to their husbands, a servitude not imposed by violent ill-treatment but promoting obedience in all things."[40] Similarly, Josephus, the Romano-Jewish scholar, historian, and hagiographer wrote, "The woman, says the law, is in all things inferior to the man. Let her accordingly be submissive, not for her humiliation, but that she may be directed, for the authority has been given by God to the man (*Ag. Ap.* II.199)."[41] In a marriage relationship the wife's primary duties were household management and servile approach towards the husband. She was required to obey her husband as a master, which was considered a religious duty.[42]

She was voiceless and without any legal rights. The only ground in which the wife can initiate divorce was when her husband contracted leprosy, gave up his faith or is involved in sexually assaulting a virgin. Contrary to her lack of legal rights for divorce men can initiate divorce rather easily. The divorce law as enshrined in Deuteronomy 24:1 was interpreted by two schools of thought on the phrase "something indecent." The conservative school of Shammai interpret the phrase as referring only to adultery. But, the school of Hillel advocated for a liberal interpretation which could include spoiling the husband's dinner, walking in public with head uncovered, and speaking ill of her husband's parents in the hearing of her husband, argumentative, troublesome or quarrelsome. She could be divorced even if the husband found

---

[38] Barclay, *The Letters to the Galatians and Ephesians*, 198.

[39] Park, "The Structure of Authority in Marriage," 121.

[40] Quoted by David L. Balch, *Let Wives Be Submissive: The Domestic Code in 1 Peter*, SBLMS 26 (Chico, CA: Scholars Press, 1981), 54. Cited by Timothy G. Gombis, "A Radically New Humanity: The Function of the *Haustafel* in Ephesians," *Journal of Evangelical Theological Society* 48/2 (June 2005), 317. See also Craig S. Keener, *Paul, Women and Wives*, 165.

[41] Quoted by Balch, *Let Wives Be Submissive*, 54. Cited by Gombis, "A Radically New Humanity," 318. See also Keener, *Paul, Women and* Wives, 165.

[42] J. Jeremias, *Jerusalem in the Times of Jesus*, trans. F.H. Cave and C.H. Cave (Philadelphia, 1969), 369. Cited by Park, "The Structure of Authority in Marriage," 121-122.

a more attractive woman than her.[43] It is evident that the interpretation held by the school of Hillel was the popular one. In the context of divorce according to the Mosaic law "all a man had to do was to hand that bill in the presence of two witnesses and the divorce was complete. The only other condition was that the woman's dowry must be returned."[44] The position of wives was so uncertain that many Jewish girls were refusing to get married at the time of Christ's coming.[45] And by Paul's time divorce had somewhat become easy.[46]

The husband as "head" in the sense of absolute power and ruling authority and submission of wife in the sense of servitude in the ancient culture was standard practice. Submitting to one's husband in servile response was the definition of a good wife in the ancient society.[47] Because of the general imbalance in the marriage relationship in the surrounding cultures in which wives were hardly considered as partners in marriage and in which "the husband became the unquestioned dictator"[48] Paul[49] needed to instruct the Ephesian believers how husbands and wives need to relate to one another in marriage as partners.[50] This occasioned him to write his *haustafel* as a Christian witness in a decaying world. Therefore, reading Paul's *haustafel* in this context is crucial to the understanding behind Paul's purpose for writing such a code.

4. Exegetical and Philological Study of Terms

Under this section an examination of the four crucial words in Ephesians 5:21-33 is attempted. Properly put into perspective they may hold the key to the correct interpretation of the Pauline *haustafel*. The words dealt under this section are *hupotassō* (submit), *kephalē* (head), *agapē* (love), and *phobeō* (fear/respect), which are the determinative words in Paul's *haustafel* in relation to the first pair – husband-wife.

4.1. Submit (*Hupotassō*)

The verb *hupotassō* in verse 21 is a participle used in place of an imperative which is Paul's call for mutual submission among believers. What did this call imply for the three pairs of relationship which Paul enshrined in his overall *haustafeln* (Eph 5:21-6:9)? A study of the following verses is significant to

[43] Barclay, *The Letters to the Galatians and Ephesians*, 194-195.

[44] Barclay, *The Letters to the Galatians and Ephesians*, 195.

[45] Ibid.

[46] Ibid., 194.

[47] Keener, *Paul, Women and Wives*, 166.

[48] Barclay, *The Letters to the Galatians and Ephesians*, 189.

[49] Pauline instruction on the household code is challenged as not original. However, we shall not delve into this matter due to want of space. Yet, it must be noted that the significance of the author to infuse Christian values into the household code is not diminished in any way.

[50] Krupp, "What About Submission and Headship?"

answer such questions. With the general tone set at verse 21, Paul directs his attention to wives first to define what he meant by the call for mutual submission. The verb *hupotassō* in verse 22 is not found in the older manuscripts, it is inferred from verse 21. The verb is a compound word in Greek which is made up of the preposition *hupo* meaning "under" and the verb *tassō* meaning "to arrange." It is "a Greek military term meaning 'to arrange [troop divisions] in a military fashion under the command of a leader'. In non-military use, it was 'a voluntary attitude of giving in, cooperating, assuming responsibility, and carrying a burden.'"[51] Therefore as a word *hupotassō* means "to subject or subordinate" oneself, something or someone to someone else. In classical times, "submission" involved compliance to the wishes and desires of the authority in question.[52] However, in Paul's usage it does not imply an absolute obedience.[53] Verse 24 defines the meaning more clearly when it used the same word to describe the submission of the Church to Christ. Therefore, wives are exhorted to submit to their husbands as the church submits to Christ. And as Stephen Clark observes, "the submission of the Church is a loving submission, not a servile affair."[54]

There are at least three interpretation of the verb *hupotassō* worth our attention:[55]

1. The so-called evangelical feminism holds on to the mutual submission interpretation in terms of equality. They take Ephesians 5:21 as the guiding principle of mutual submission that eliminates any hierarchical variances based on gender in the home and even in the church. They also appeal to Galatians 3:28 as the basis for doing away with all gender based hierarchical roles in the family and the church.
2. The second view does not take "mutual submission" in verse 21 as referring to everyone in the church. Rather, it is opined that it refers to wives, children and slaves submitting to the husbands, parents, and masters respectively, which is explicitly described in the following verses. Their main argument is that the semantic meaning of *hupotassō* never means "mutual" in its sense. It always exclusively meant someone subjecting to the one in authority.
3. The third view holds that there is a sense of mutual submission in Christian relationships. This view does not do away with the

[51] "Hupotasso," *http://www.biblestudytools.com/lexicons/greek/kjv/hupotasso.html* (9/9/2017).

[52] Park, "The Structure of Authority in Marriage," 118.

[53] Krupp, "What About Submission and Headship?"

[54] Clark, "Exegesis 20: Headship in Ephesians," 17.

[55] Cole, "What Do You Mean, 'Submit'?"

> understanding of hierarchical roles but stresses on maintaining relationships by laying aside our rights and serving one another in love and respect. It argues that even those in the position of authority should submit to those under their authority by serving in love rather than by being self-assertive. They take the example of how Jesus laid aside his rights and washed the feet of his disciples even though they were under his authority.

Of these interpretations the last one merits our attention because Paul in no way abolishes gender-based roles.[56] And moreover this has never been as issue in the history of the church until the raise of feminist movement.[57] Therefore, caution need to be employed in uncritically attacking the gender-based roles in the family.

In the *oikonomia* tradition of ancient times wives were never directly addressed. Rather, the *paterfamilias* are usually the focus of the instructions of the sages on how to manage and control the household including their wives. But contrary to current practice, in Ephesians 5 "Paul addresses the wives directly, exhorting them to participate fully and willingly in the New Humanity."[58] It must be noted that God had ordained and instituted authorities for the proper functioning of his creation. There are at least seven explicit areas in which God has ordained authority: Submission to God (James 4:7); Submission to the governmental authority (Rom 13:1-7; 1 Pet 2:13-14); Submission to Church leaders (Heb 13:17; 1 Pet 5:5; 1 Cor 16:15-16); Submission of wives to husbands, of children to their parents and slaves/servants to master (Eph 5:22-6:9); Mutual submission in the body of Christ (Eph 5:21).To challenge any of these areas as out-dated or invalid in modern context is to challenge all the institutions God ordained for the smooth functioning of His creation. Submission in no way negates the nature of God. The supreme example of submission is given in the act of Jesus washing his disciples feet (Jn 13:13-15). His submission did not make him any smaller he was still the Lord and Teacher.

Elsewhere also, in contrast to what seemed a one-sided demand for submission in the *haustafel*, "Paul himself acknowledged that certain degree of mutual submission was appropriate between husband and wife (1 Cor. 7.4)."[59] Someone succinctly observed that wives' submission is defined only as respect (5:33)[60] and not in terms of servitude. This interpretation suits what follows in the instruction to husbands.

---

[56] Cole, "What Do You Mean, 'Submit'?"

[57] Cole, "What Do You Mean, 'Submit'?"

[58] Gombis, "A Radically New Humanity," 325-326.

[59] Muddiman, *A Commentary on The Epistle to the Ephesians,* 257.

[60] Keener, *Paul, Women and Wives*, 171.

To say that the Scriptures would command indefinite submission to abusive and tyrant husbands contradict the very essence of God. Paul never tells husbands like the sages of the surrounding cultures to manage and control their household, particularly their wives. Above all it never teaches the husband to get their wives to submit to them.[61] "Submission" to Paul is not a mindless obedience but rather it is the attitude of mutual acceptance that yields to the desire of the other. It is best defined by *phobos* (fear/respect) in verse 33, as we shall see later on. Submission to the husband is enjoined as the wives' response in the Christian *haustafel*, albeit not in the way surrounding cultures expect the wives' unlimited submission to the *paterfamilias*. Rather, submission now bears a Christian basis: *as it is in the Lord*.[62] In the words of Manfred T. Brauch, " . . . a radically new self-submission of wife to husband is now given."[63] That is, as the Church submits to Christ so wives are to submit to their husbands (Eph 5:24).

4.2. Head (*Kephalē*)

Perhaps one of the most misleading and debated word in the New Testament that came with the raise of feminist movement is the Greek noun *kephalē* (head). From the middle of the twentieth century heated arguments have ensued not over the word itself but over the figurative sense of the term.[64] Literally it means the physical head, "the head of a person or an animal." But, the word *kephalē* in the controverted texts such as Ephesians 5:21-33 and 1 Corinthians 11:3-16, do not bear a literal meaning rather it is used figuratively. And the interpretation of this figurative meaning has been elusive among scholars. In the tribal world, as in many cultures, when we use the word "head" it automatically implies "ruler," "leader," "chief," "boss," "director" and so on. Thus, it connotes the sense of one having "power" or "authority over" someone.

We need to ask then what the word *kephalē* meant in the ancient culture and how Paul understood it and used it in his writings, particularly in his *haustafel* instruction. This is a significant term that needs a careful philological study to decode the meaning Paul might have intended in his usage. It is interesting to note that English versions like NKJV, RSV, NIV, TNIV, NEB, ESV, and NASB cautiously render the literal meaning "head" for *kephalē*. Some versions like GNT, GNB, and TEV however translates the

---

[61] Cole, "What Do You Mean, 'Submit'?"

[62] Delling, "upotassw," in *Theological Dictionary of the New Testament* (Grand Rapids, MI: Wm. B. Eerdmans Publishing Company, 2000, c1964), CD-ROM.

[63] Manfred T. Brauch, *Hard Sayings of Paul* (Downers Grove, ILL: InterVarsity Press, 1989), 216.

[64] Johnson, "A Review of the Scholarly Debate on the Meaning of 'Head,'" 35.

word *kephalē* figuratively as "authority over," "supreme over." The Living Bible's translation is more interpretive; "a husband is in charge of his wife in the same way Christ is in charge of his body the Church" (Eph 5:23).[65]

Scholarly debate on the meaning of *kephalē* started with the work of Stephen Bedale which came out in a short article in 1954.[66] Following this work at least three prominent views have been suggested: That *kephalē* means "source," "origin," "temporal priority," is held by scholars like Stephen Bedale,[67] Mickelsens,[68] Catherine C. Kroeger,[69] and Manfred T. Brauch.[70] That it means "authority over" is held by J. A. Fitzmyer,[71] Wayne Grudem,[72] and Craig S. Keener.[73] Third, that the word means "preeminent," "foremost," "representative," is held by scholars like Andrew C. Perriman.[74] Thus, one can see the divergence in the understanding of *kephalē* which leads to problems of interpretation of Paul's *haustafel* in Ephesian 5:21-33. Of the three views held the last one does not have proper attestations by the Greek manuscripts therefore we shall not dwell much on this view.[75]

It is interesting to note that scholars like the Mickelsens who hold on to the view that "head" is to be understood as "origin" or "source" do so by basing on Liddell-Scott Lexicon which is considered a standard lexicon for all Greek literature from about 700 B.C. to about A.D. 600. But, Grudem critiques that this lexicon is one of the basic tools for studying Plato or Aristotle and that it is not a standard lexicon for the study of the New Testament Greek. Grudem rather opines that Bauer-Arndt-Gingrich-Danker (BAGD) is the most standard

---

[65] Brauch, *Hard Sayings of Paul*, 135.

[66] Stephen Bedale, "The Meaning of *kephalē* in the Pauline Epistles," *Journal of Theological Studies* 50 (1954), 211-216.

[67] Bedale, "The Meaning of *kephalē* in the Pauline Epistles," 211-216.

[68] Berkeley Mickelsen and Alvera Mickelsen, "Does Male Dominance Tarnish Our Translation?" *Christianity Today*, 5 (Oct 1979), 20-23.

[69] Catherine C. Kroeger, "Head," in *Dictionary of Paul and His Letters*, edited by G.F. Hawthorne, R.P. Martin, and D.G. Reid (Downers Grove and Leicester: InterVarsity, 1993), 375-377.

[70] Brauch, *Hard Sayings of Paul*, 134-140.

[71] Joseph A Fitzmyer, "Another Look at *kephalē*in 1 Corinthians 11:3," *New Testament Studies* 35 (1989), 503-511.

[72] Wayne Grudem, "Does kefalh ('Head') Mean 'Source' or 'Authority' or 'Authority Over' in Greek Literature? A Survey of 2,336 Examples," *Trinity Journal* 6 (1985): 38-59. See also his, "The Meaning of kefalh ('Head'): An Evaluation of New Evidence, Real and Alleged," *Journal of the Evangelical Theological Society* 44. 1 (March 2001), 25-66.

[73] Keener, *Paul, Women and Wives,* 19-69.

[74] Andrew C. Perriman, "The Head of a Woman: The Meaning of *kephalē* in 1 Cor. 11:3," *Journal of Theological Studies* 45 (1994), 602-622.

[75] Grudem, "The Meaning of kefalh ('Head')," 63.

for the study of the New Testament Greek. In fact the BAGD defines *kephalē* as, "In the case of living people, to denote superior rank."[76] Further, he rightly notes that, "all standard lexicons and dictionaries for the New Testament Greek do list the meaning "authority over" for kefalh, 'head.'"[77]

Greek classicists like Homer, Plutarch, Hellenist Jewish philosopher Philo, and Romano-Jewish scholar, historian and hagiographer Josephus also used *kephalē* in the sense of "leaders."[78] This evidence is interesting to note in the context of some scholars who held that *kephalē* primarily means "source," have done so wrongly. For example, the work of Catherine C. Kroeger who citing John Chrysostom states that ". . . only a heretic would understand Paul's use of 'head' to mean 'chief' or 'authority over.'"[79] Her research method and statements have been vehemently criticised by Wayne Grudem in his substantial work which came out in 2001.[80] Kroeger' sclaims from patristic material like John Chrysostom are proven false and Grudem further points that even patristic material (e.g., Lampe's *Patristic Greek Lexicon*) she used also support "leader, authority over" as the meaning of *kephalē*.[81] This is one of the examples we see *eisegesis* at work in the interpretation of some crucial and yet clear texts.

But as Stephen Clark observes, even if "source" is taken as the meaning for *kephalē* it does not make any sharp difference because "if one confined the semantic equivalent of *kephale* to 'source', one would have to say that the referent in the verse carries authority/subordination connotations because it functions as the basis of the wife's subordination."[82] However, as Wayne Grudem points out, the increasing consensus derived from the major lexicons on "authority over" as the figurative meaning of *kephalē* is well established today and this must guide our writings.[83]

Therefore, weighing on scholarly research it becomes clear that *kephalē* in the context of Paul's *haustafel* bears the meaning of "one entrusted with superior rank, authority or power."[84] But, this is not to be construed with the "absolute authority" of the *paterfamilias* in the ancient *oikonomia*. How then did *kephalē*as "authority over" entail in Paul's *Haustafel* Manifesto? To understand this we now turn to the next determinative word, which is *Agapē*.

[76] Quoted by Grudem, "Does kefalh ('Head') Mean 'Source' or 'Authority,'" 47.

[77] Grudem, "Does kefalh ('Head') Mean 'Source' or 'Authority,'" 47.

[78] Park, "The Structure of Authority in Marriage," 119.

[79] Quoted by Grudem, "The Meaning of kefalh ('Head')," 25.

[80] Grudem, "The Meaning of kefalh ('Head')," 25-66.

[81] Grudem, "The Meaning of kefalh ('Head')," 6. See the article on the full scholarly critique on Catherine C. Kroeger.

[82] Clark, "Exegesis 20: Headship in Ephesians," 15-20.

[83] Grudem, "The Meaning of kefalh ('Head')," 65.

[84] Park, "The Structure of Authority in Marriage," 118-119.

4.3. Love (*Agapē*)

In Ephesians 5:25-33 Paul draws attention to the husband's responsibility in the *haustafel*. Just as he brought to bearing *hupotassō* and *kephalē* in the exhortation to wives in 22-24; he now turns to the husband's role in the *haustafel*, particularly his responsibility towards his wife. He stresses on *agape* (love); emphasized thrice in verses 25, 28, and 33. This word is either taken for granted or ignored in the discussion on Paul's *Haustafel*. The whole discussion on the understanding of Paul's *haustafel* is always clouded by *hupotassō* and *kephalē* which are suspiciously viewed as patriarchal constructs and therefore seen by the egalitarian camp as derogatory.

The failure to pay attention to Paul's emphatic stress on *agapē* misleads the reading of the *Haustafel*. There is no negativity in *hupotassō* and *kephalē* when seen in its proper perspective as in the Pauline *Haustafel* which talks of relationship between parties. In the ancient *oikonomia* "the household codes normally instructed the head of the household how to 'rule' or 'govern' his wife, rather than how to love her."[85] But, in Paul there is a revolutionary approach where husbands are commanded to love their wives in the *haustafel*.

In Paul's *haustafel* instruction he devotes more space to address the role of the husband towards his wife. He emphasizes on *agapē* (love) as the response of the husband towards the wife. The Greek word *agape* that he employs in this relationship is significant. Of the four words for "love" found in Greek language[86] he specifically saw in *agapē*a word that would perfectly define a husband's response to the wife. *Agapē* is the highest form of love in Greek. It is sacrificial love that goes to the length of enduring discomfort, suffering and even death for the benefit of others without expecting anything in return. This word is best exemplified in the sacrificial act of Jesus when he gave his life for the church (Eph 5:25-27). As Paul J. Kobelski states, "Christ's love for his body, the church, is the model for the husband's love of his wife."[87] Thus, as Elisabeth Schüssler Fiorenza notes, "patriarchal domination is thus radically questioned with reference to the paradigmatic love relationship of Christ to the Church."[88] Such love and nothing less is commanded to be the response of the husband to his wife who submits to him in respect of him. Here we find Paul

---

[85] Keener, *Paul, Women and Wives,* 167.

[86] *Agapē* (Divine love, highest or noblest form of love), *phileō* (friendship or brotherly love), *eros* (referring to sexual love, not used in the New Testament), and *storge* (meaning natural affection as love within family members, but always used in the New Testament with the prefix "a" which negates love and therefore means without this kind of love (Rom 1:3; 12:10; 2 Tim 3:3).

[87] Paul J. Kobelski, "The Letter to the Ephesians," in *The New Jerome Biblical Commentary* (Bangalore: Theological Publications in India, 1994), 890.

[88] Elisabeth Schüssler Fiorenza, *In Memory of Her: A Feminist Theological Reconstruction of Christian Origins*, Tenth Anniversary Edition (New York: Crossroad, 1994), 269-270.

giving a new content to the word *kephalē*. To be the "head" of the wife in the New Humanity involves not the traditional authoritarian rule but sacrifice and self-giving *agapē* – love.[89]

Paul further stresses the need for the husbands to love their wives as they love themselves. Here the concept of the mysterious union of the marriage relationship is called forth (Eph 5:31 cf. Gen 2:24). In the mysterious relationship loving wife is loving the self, for the two are no longer two but one flesh (cf. Mk 10:8). At verse 33 Paul once again reiterates this command to love wives before he closed his instruction to the husbands. Paul's command to husbands to love their wives was a revolutionary command in the context of the *oikonomia* of the existing contemporary cultures.

4.4. Respect (*Phobeō*)

As a last note Paul once again reverts to the wife's role in the *haustafel*. She is to "*Phobeō*" (lit. "fear") her husband. The possible meaning of this word in Greek are many; fear, afraid, dread, terrified, reverence, venerate, respect etc. What Paul meant is of concern here. Most of the Bible translations have used "respect" or "reverence" as the meaning for *Phobeō*. But some people object saying that "fear" should be the proper translation for the term and not respect.[90] But, in the context in which it is placed it calls for "respect" and not "fear" in the sense of being deeply afraid. Rather then fear, in the new *haustafel* that Paul lays down wives are to expect love and nurture from their husbands who are even expected to give their lives for them as Christ did for his Church (Eph 5:25, 28-29). Such a person then need not be feared but respected. This is the reason why Paul once again exhorts the wives to respect their husbands at verse 33. "Respect" then is the clearest definition of "submission" on the part of the wife.

5. A Comparative Analysis

In the context of the surrounding cultures which in general practiced divergent views of the husband-wife relationship in the *oikonomia* Paul's projection of the new *haustafel* is significant. Generally in the ancient *oikonomia* wives were literally kept under subordination. Therefore, "submission" in those cultures was superimposed rather than being a voluntary act. An appraisal of the ancient *oikonomia* and Paul's *haustafel* reveals that,

1. In the Christian *haustafel* instructions are directed both to the wife and the husband as equally important members of the *haustafel*. In the ancient cultures wives were not directly addressed.

---

[89] Kevin Giles, unpublished lecture notes. Cited by Alan F. Johnson, "A Review of the Scholarly Debate of the Meaning of 'Head' (kefalh)," 53-54.

[90] "Ephesians 5:33: Is It About 'Deep Respect'?" http://perimeno.ca/Ephesians.htm (12/9/2017).

2. The submission that is commanded of the wives is in respect or reverence of the husband who is commanded to fulfil his marital role in *agapē* towards his wife. The concept of submission in the new *haustafel* has no connection with tyrannical rule of the husband like in the ancient *oikonomia*.
3. The command given to the husbands is a revolutionary approach, for he placed the command in contrast to the prevailing social mores of the New Testament times. Paul's call for "love" as the husband's response in the marital relationship is deepened by his use of the Greek word *agapē* which is the highest form of love. Wives are not to be treated inferior, abused or controlled as in the ancient *oikonomia*. Rather, they are to be loved and nurtured as Christ did for his Church (Eph 5:25, 28-29). In this, Christ's love for the Church becomes the model for the husband to love his wife.
4. Husbands according to the creation order have been given the *kephalē* role in the *haustafel* to love, nurture, and if need be sacrifice their lives for their wives. This is in contradiction to the Jewish teaching that if found in danger the husband's life must be saved first. Paul then equates *kephalē* to *agapē* and Christ's sacrificial death. This redefined *kephalē* not as one person's dominion over another but christologically as service, sacrifice, and love.[91] Husbands are to play the role of the "head" in the *haustafel* by "expressing their authority and power through selfless acts of love."[92]

In the New Humanity as the community was slowly forming herself to take a new shape, members of the new found communities needed a direction in regard to the Christian *haustafel*. In the midst of the confusion about the *oikonomia* in the ancient cultures Paul also saw the need to give a clear direction the new community must adhere to in relation to household management. This is where Paul in Ephesians 5:21-33 lays down the most extensive *haustafel* instructions. Thus, a comparative analysis of the instructions given in Paul's *haustafel* with the surrounding cultures of the Greco-Roman world of the New Testament times reveals Paul's revolutionary stance in regard to the new *haustafel*.

6. Implications of Reading Ephesians 5:21-33 in the Tribal Context

In the cultures of the tribals of North East India Paul's instruction to the wives to "submit" to their husbands, along with the picture of husbands as "head" have been literally interpreted and taken as proof text. The verses in

---

[91] Park, "The Structure of Authority in Marriage," 122.

[92] Ibid.

the passage that explain and clarify the concept of submission and headship are always ignored. This has to do with the patriarchal structure and mind set of the tribal people in which traditionally women have always been considered inferior. Many tribal people rather take scriptural texts such as Paul's *haustafel* in Ephesians 5:21-33 to reiterate their traditional practice of keeping wives subordinated. Thus, physical abuses like wife beating, mental/psychological abuse, spiritual abuse, verbal abuse and all other forms of abuse levelled against wives in the tribal societies are a manifestation of male chauvinism. Tribal people have not been able to come out of this deeply rooted traditional understanding even today. Therefore, there is the need to break free from traditional bondage which often inadvertently keeps people subjugated in their own practices. Tribal peoples' practice of dominating and overpowering wives as inferior and ill-treating them is a serious scriptural omission.

Whereas the headship as implied by its relation with love in Paul's *haustafel* is to govern the Christian family, the headship that is practiced among the tribal people of North East India amounts to oppression for many unfortunate wives, who are forced to submit to the cruelties of their own husbands. Paul's call for mutual love which lives out in respect and love for one another in the Christian family is the model built on the love of Christ. Tribal husbands' attitude towards their wives are still not different from the cultures of the ancient times like the Greeks, Romans, and Jews who keep their women subjugated to satisfy their male ego.

This male machismo attitude and ill-treatment of wives as inferior is one of the reason for many people, particularly many women, to doubt their own Scripture. Tribal Christian scholars should be critical with the proper interpretation of words like "head" and "submission." These terms should not be discussed independently and devoid of "love" as the husband's response. Patriarchal constructs which are harmful to any section of people must be addressed but at the same time one must be guided by proper exegetical principles to understand Scripture so that we will not twist the Scripture in *eisegesis*. A careful and holistic reading of scriptural texts such as Ephesians 5:21-33 need to take root in the tribal families, communities and churches so that both men and women can work towards emancipation by the scriptural principles of mutual love and respect as seen in Paul's *Haustafel* Manifesto.

Conclusion

Paul's *Haustafel* Manifesto in Ephesians 5:21-33 seen in its right perspective bears no derogatory notion against women as it was in the surrounding cultures of the New Testament times. Rather, it bears the power to break the patriarchal domination by men over women in all cultures. This is seen in the fact that in contrast to the surrounding cultures' practice of the *oikonomia* where the institution of marriage was disintegrating Paul sets his *haustafel* as the new way for the people of God. It is a radical call to mutual submission characterized by love and respect. The tribals of North East India need to seriously contemplate on how tradition and the unwritten ancient mores of the tribals pose a serious threat to the health and continuity of the Christian family today. While holding on to the cultural mores of the times the power dominion of the male head is cancelled in the call to love wives in the way Jesus loved his Church and sacrificed his life for her. The *Haustafel* Manifesto that Paul crafted is the model that tribal families (husband–wife) must endeavour to live, where mutual love and respect govern the marriage relationship, instead of struggling for dominion and power that leads to abuses and violence against women/wives. The deeply entrenched patriarchy which draws on dominion and subjugation of wives in marital relationship is unscriptural and out-dated according to Paul's *Haustafel* Manifesto. Rather, mutual submission in love and respect for one another is the new *haustafel* for the people of God.

4

The Song of Deborah (Judges 5) as a Riposte: A Woman's Perspective

Akani Kinimi

Introduction

The book of Judges records stories of the great men and women of valour who were given the title 'judges'. Judges Chapters 4 and 5 tell the story of Deborah, one that is so powerful and unique particularly given the time and era of history for women. We see through her story that she had gained great prominence, distinction, and importance on her own merits of character. And as such, the Song of Deborah has received much attention throughout the history of biblical studies and much has been written about it, and we find different interpretations about the Song. This work aims to explore some of the aspects and nuances of the Song of Deborah that serve as a riposte from a woman's perspective. Deborah's and Jael's role was not a typical role for a woman in a strongly patriarchal society, yet they clearly did not draw back, or were concerned about what others might think. Countering all stereotypes Deborah and Jael had to rise to the occasion to show strength and vigour.

The Historical Setting

The Song of Deborah is widely viewed as among the most ancient of all the biblical material; by its own terms,[1] it describes a period early in the history of the Israelite occupation of the Promised Land, "in those days, when there was no king in Israel..." (Judg. 19:1). The common life of the tribes was organised under a loose confederacy under the guidance of 'judges', inspired leaders who would rise up to rescue the Israelites when they faced aggression from other peoples. In other words, the role of judges in the Old Testament was that of a leader of the Hebrew people, in lieu of a king, as they did not yet have kings. Deborah, a woman, was one of these judges, which was not common.[2]

Several scholars have analysed the text as history, and reached varying conclusions about the historical reliability of the text and the probable geopolitical background. A.D.H. Mayes[3] sees the text as a fairly accurate account of a battle sometime in the course of the second half of the 11th century BCE, and as representing a 'stage in the course of transition by which the Israelite tribes progressed from acting as independent units to employing their combined strength in time of battle'. Niels Peter Lemche, argues that ancient Israel was governed by the rules and values of patron-client politics. Loyalty and deference were the glue holding the structure together. Patrons offered protection for people seeking justice and security, while clients gave tribute and obedient support to the rulers. Even relationships enforced by threat and military power were cloaked in the language of family, friendship, and devotion.[4]

Some Interpretations of the Song of Deborah

The richness of the Song is apparent from the wide variety of research which it has prompted. Some of the earliest interpretations of the song of Deborah are by Origen, Ambrose, and others followed them. Origen[5] is the earliest Christian writer to address Judges; he gave a set of nine homilies on the book. Origen's interpretation is primarily allegorical: Sisera represents the animalistic person, one who is completely unspiritual; Deborah, "Bee," represents the word of

[1] J. Alberto Soggin, *Judges: A Commentary* (Philadelphia: Westminster Press, 1981), 80.

[2] Geoffrey P. Miller, "A Riposte Form in the Song of Deborah," *Gender and Law in the Hebrew Bible and the Ancient Near East*, edited by Victor H. Matthews, Bernard M. Levinson and Tikva Frymer-Kensky (England: Sheffield Academic Press,1998), 113.

[3] A.D.H. Mayes, "The Historical Context of the Battle Against Sisera," *VT* 19 (1969), 353-360.

[4] Niels Peter Lemche, "Kings and Clients: On Loyalty between the Ruler and the Ruled in Ancient Israel," *Semeia* 66 (1994), 119-132.

[5] Origen, *Origen: Homilies on Judges*, translated by Elizabeth Ann Dively Lauro (Washington DC: Catholic University of America Press, 2010), 4.

God, in as much as she is a prophet and that the words of God are "sweeter than honey" (Ps 19:10); Barak, whose name Origen translates "flash," represents the unenlightened Israel, who had a glimpse of God but have subsequently forgotten it; thus, according to Origen, Israel, like Barak, will be led to victory by another, namely, the Christian Church; Jael, Origen identifies as the Church, the one who secured the victory by destroying the unenlightened philosophy of the world (Sisera).

Ambrose[6] holds up Deborah as an exemplary widow and analyses the situation in much the same allegorical way as Origen, treating the victory achieved by Jael as a prefiguring of the Gentile Christian Church's adoption into the children of God. Ambrose reflects the ancient tradition that Deborah is a widow and Barak is her son, although these are stated neither in the Hebrew nor in the Greek text. It is because of this that Ambrose uses these figures as a model for the care of widows and the duty of children to parents. Theodoret of Cyrus[7] treats Judges briefly in his *Questions on the Octateuch* and has brought out some significant remarks on the meaning of the Song of Deborah. He uses it to demonstrate the basic equality of men and women in service to God, so that although the Church might observe one practice, that is, segregation of women, God can and does still use women beyond the Church's specific order.

Norman Gottwald[8] views the poem as recording the victory of "Israel's egalitarian peasant army" against the "imperial ventures" of the Canaanite city states. Robert Alter[9] provides a sensitive analysis of the complex and subtle gender reversals found in the Deborah story. In Alter's account, the 'firmly insistent' Deborah assumes a leadership position throughout in her relations with Barak, the 'very hesitant male field commander'. According to David J. Zucker and Moshe Reiss, the Song is a poetic depiction of a 12th century BCE battle and its aftermath. The conflict is between the forces of Israel and those of a Canaanite commander. They comment that the traditional sexual roles are overturned and subverted in this Song of Deborah.[10]

Feminist interpretations of the Song became prominent since the subject of this passage is one of the few strong, prominent, and leading women of

---

[6] Philip Schaff and Henry Wace, ed., *St. Ambrose: Selected Works and Letters* (NPNF 2nd Series X; New York: The Christian Literature Co., 1896).

[7] Theodoret, *Questions on the Octateuch*, translated by Robert C. Hill (Washington D.C.: Catholic University of America Press, 2007), 327–31.

[8] See, Norman K. Gottwald, *The Hebrew Bible: A Socio-Literary Introduction* (Philadelphia: Fortress Press, 1985); Norman Gottwald, *The Tribes of Yahweh: A Sociology of the Religion of Liberated Israel, 1250-1050 B.C.E.* (Maryknoll, New York: Orbis Books 1979), 503-507.

[9] Robert Alter, *The World of Biblical Literature* (New York: Basic Books, 1992), 42.

[10] David J. Zucker and Moshe Reiss, "Subverting Sexuality: Manly Women; Womanly Men in Judges 4–5," *Biblical Theology Bulletin* 45/ 1 (2015), 32.

Israel. As prophetess and judge, Deborah became a potent symbol of female authority and speech, an obvious exemplar for women aspiring to claim a public voice in the modern and contemporary world. Deborah's poem in Judges 5 is considered as a vestige of an elusive and irretrievable women's history, a heritage which must have been fuller and richer than the extant historical sources have preserved.[11] Clara Neyman comments that "by arousing woman to the dignity of her position we shall again have women like Deborah, honored openly and publicly for political wisdom, to whom men will come in time of need."[12]

The Song of Deborah (Judg. 5:1-31)

Judges Chapter 5 is known as the "Song of Deborah" in which Deborah and Barak sing a song of blessings to God for His deliverance and how God brings His leaders through to victory. It records a stunning victory won by a coalition of Israelite tribes under Deborah and Barak over a powerful army led by the Canaanite Sisera (Judg. 5:1-31). The Song proclaims the military skill and divine favour enjoyed by the Israelite forces. Deborah opens her song with a stirring depiction of a majestic entry of God into the world: "Lord, when you went out from Seir, when you marched from the region of Edom, the earth trembled, and the heavens poured, the clouds indeed poured water. The mountains quaked before the Lord, the One of Sinai, before the Lord, the God of Israel" (Judg. 5:4-5 NRSV). The poem continues by portraying the wretched days before the Israelites' triumph. In those days, the prophetess laments, "caravans ceased and travelers kept to the byways"[13] (Judg. 5:6). Four verses later, Deborah urges her people to speak God's praise after their success and refers to them as "you who sit on rich carpets and you who walk by the way" (Judg. 5:10). She calls the men to attention as she reminds them of the cry of the women. Men are called to take the responsibility to provide direction and protection to the women and children.

The Canaanites appeared in battle with a vastly superior chariot force, of which we may infer they were enormously proud. The Canaanites, moreover, appear to take pride in their organised, sophisticated, and segmented society: it is said, the 'kings' of Canaan who come to do battle (Judg. 5:19). All this pride is turned back on the Canaanites in the form of a taunt, contrasting the Canaanites' boastful claims to power and valour with their humiliating defeat

---

[11] Joy A. Schroeder, "Deborah's Daughters," *Women in the Bible*, edited by Robert B. Kruschwitz (Waco, TX: The Center for Christian Ethics Baylor University, 2013), 44.

[12] Clara Neyman, "Judges 5," *The Woman's Bible,* Part II, edited by Elizabeth Cady Stanton (New York: European Publishing Company, 1898; reprinted Boston, MA: Northeastern University Press, 1993), 18.

[13] This shows that Israel was afraid of the enemy and walked on back-roads, but also walked on crooked roads because there was no one to show them the way.

at the hands of amateur Israelite warriors. Judges 5:24-27 describe Jael as the blessed women who struck and crushed Sisera. Verses 26 and 27 are vital, for these poetic lines indicate an occurring dramatic shift. Unexpectedly, verse 26 shifts from the maternal comfort of verses 24 and 25 to Jael's vicious attack of Sisera.[14] In verse 28, a different shift in perspective occurs, with the Song focusing attention on Sisera's mother. The image of Sisera's mother worriedly awaiting her son's return in verse 28 seems to be Deborah's way of sympathising with the enemy women. Considering Deborah's own role as a wife and a woman in a patriarchal society, she understands the nervous anticipation of a war's conclusion: Sisera's mother not only fears for a loved one's life amidst the violence of warfare, she also fears the personal experience of rape and torture enacted upon enemy women.[15]

Towards the end of the Song, the prophetess calls out against the injustice where men have failed to protect the women. The prophetess exposes the perversion where the men of Israel had forsaken the ways of God and began to worship foreign gods, like as Sisera, where they accept the belief that various powers control the forces of nature. Judges 5:30 says, "Are they not finding and dividing the spoil? A girl or two for every man; spoil of dyed stuffs for Sisera, spoil of dyed stuffs embroidered, two pieces of dyed work embroidered for my neck as spoil?" (NRSV). Deborah's song ends with an end-time proclamation: "So perish all your enemies, O Lord! But, may your friends be like the sun as it rises in its might" (Judg. 5:31 NRSV).

The Song as a Riposte

The Song of Deborah can be read as a riposte form influenced by norms and nuances of the society. A riposte is a form of retaliation against an insult circulated in the culture by a rival group. Characteristic of the riposte is the fact that the insult could not simply be denied or ignored, because its substance had achieved widespread credibility in the broader culture. The riposte deals with this problem by accepting part of a stereotype as true, but reversing the honour-value of the attribution and returning the insult, with interest, to the group from which it originated.[16]

Riposte to Stereotypes

The Song of Deborah responds to a negative stereotype about the people of the hill country of Canaan, i.e. the Israelites, which may have enjoyed popularity

---

[14] Tamara Dixon, "Most Blessed of Women: An Exegetical Study of Women's Roles under Patriarchy in Judges 5: 24-31," *The Review: A Journal of Undergraduate Student Research* 8 (Fall 2006), 8.

[15] Tamara Dixon, "Most Blessed of Women: An Exegetical Study of Women's Roles under Patriarchy in Judges 5: 24-31," 10.

[16] Geoffrey P. Miller, "A Riposte Form in the Song of Deborah," 113.

among their city-dwelling neighbours, i.e., the Canaanites. The hill people were stereotyped as those who lacked social graces and refinement, and that their women behaved like men.[17] This was a common cultural stereotype in the social conditions of Iron Age I culture. The Israelites were people of the hills, who lived in a rural setting of small hamlets and farms; the Canaanites were people of the plains whose social life was organised around cities. The people of the hills were not wealthy, and there is no evidence of urban elite. Conditions of life were difficult, and it is probable that women as well as men had to engage in arduous physical labour. Urbanites of the Canaanite cities may have looked down on and mocked the Israelites for their strange and rude ways. The contrast between city and country appears to be nearly a human universal: country folk, especially people of the hills, are often seen from the urban standpoint as lacking in education, refinement, and social graces, and as economically, politically, and socially inferior compared with the high society of the cities.[18]

The Song of Deborah addresses the essential attributes of the stereotype, and reverses the Canaanites- Israelites' honour value by demonstrating that it is good to have nature on your side, and that any group should be glad to be led by women when the result is a victory as spectacular as the one secured by Deborah and her general. The Song depicts how the sophisticated Canaanite forces were swept away by the forces of nature that are allied with the Israelites, and the Canaanite commander was crushed by a woman.

Reversal of Honour

Honour appears to be an important element in many societies, especially societies that function outside the organising power of an established state. The existence of shame and honour as elements of social control in the Hebrew Bible is indisputable. Ancient Israelite society was deeply concerned about honour, not only the honour of the individual, but also that of the family, clan, and tribe. One's honour was a valuable asset. Victor H. Matthews affirms that the biblical text is a product of a 'tradition-oriented' society, which places a great deal of value on honourable behaviour.[19] Groups would attempt to establish honour for themselves with stories or attributes that reflected on them in a good light, while at the same time attempting to diminish the honour of competing groups with shaming stories or attributes. The book of Judges

[17] Country women were often stereotyped as plain and vigorous, lacking in the beauty and refinement of city women.

[18] Geoffrey P. Miller, "A Riposte Form in the Song of Deborah," 114.

[19] Victor H. Matthews, "Honor and Shame in Gender-Related Legal Situations in the Hebrew Bible," *Gender and Law in the Hebrew Bible and the Ancient Near East*, edited by Victor H. Matthews, Bernard M. Levinson and Tikva Frymer-Kensky (England: Sheffield Academic Press,1998), 97.

presents the social setting of the tribal confederacy as one strongly influenced by norms of honour. Hence, the Song of Deborah is fundamentally structured according to the norms of honour prevalent during those days; however, it contains within it a distinctive riposte.

The Song of Deborah reverses the honour-value of the stereotype of Israelite women, demonstrating that a fierce Israelite woman is to be valued, not mocked. It is only because of Deborah's willingness to assume a male role that the Israelites were freed from the Canaanite threat. Her activity, courage, and authority contrast with the passivity, timidity, and subordination displayed by the royal women of the Canaanite city, just as her milieu in open country contrasts with the housebound environment of Sisera's mother. Sisera's mother lusts after 'dyed stuff' (Judg. 5:30); Deborah seeks honour and victory. The contrast between Deborah and Sisera's mother is reinforced through the subsidiary female characters, the Canaanite princess and the Kenite Jael. The princess lived in a palace and Jael in a tent, but Jael's familiarity with tents and tent-pegs turns out to be more useful than Canaanite feminine arts.[20]

Further, the Song of Deborah is, in form, a riposte uttered by a member of the victorious group after a military victory. It presents the responding group's superior skill in battle and the favour it enjoys in the eyes of a mighty God. Thus, the riposte is a claim of honour for the neglected group. The Song of Deborah bears a remarkable resemblance to the other great biblical Song, the song of Moses and Miriam after the miracle of the Red Sea in Exodus 15.1-21. Both texts celebrate a victory over superior military force; in both the overwhelming power of the chariots is defeated by a flood of water; and both are sung, in part, by a woman.

Qualities of women

The Song of Deborah upholds Israelite women's note worthy qualities. For starters, Deborah herself, a woman, became judge over Israel. It would appear unusual for a woman to exercise authority in her own capacity and not as stand-in or regent for some male figure. Deborah's role becomes even more unusual when we consider that the judges were not selected by dynastic succession. The most common ways in which women rose to power in the ancient world were by their own merit. Deborah was a leader whom the people called on to rouse herself and 'lead out the host': "Awake, awake, Deborah! Awake, awake, utter a song!" (Judg. 5:12). And Deborah indeed displayed qualities that were considered masculine: bold, courageous and determined, and she assumed a man's position, and exercised personal authority that did not depend on men.

Jael also had qualities that did not fit an ideal of protected femininity. She was alone in a tent in open country when Sisera appeared. She was not

[20] Geoffrey P. Miller, "A Riposte Form in the Song of Deborah," 125.

afraid to entertain a strange man, probably in battle dress and dishevelled from his flight. She had no difficulty in taking matters into her own hand and when she drove the tent-peg into Sisera's skull.[21] Canaanite women, in contrast, are depicted as timid and retiring, closeted behind walls and dreaming of the house servants and the booty of dyed cloth their menfolk will bring home from the battle (Judg.5:30). Jael's act asserts that the hospitality of the country folk is not the same as foolishness. Sisera implicitly invokes the country norm of hospitality when he appears at Jael's tent and asks for water. The exhausted Sisera, apparently lulled by Jael's ministrations, is no match for the fate that awaits him at her hands.[22] We may infer that Sisera's confidence in Jael is due, at least in part, to the false stereotype to which he and other city folk subscribe as to the excesses of country hospitality.

Concluding Remarks

Judges Chapters 4 and 5 tell the story of Deborah, one that is so powerful and unique particularly given the time and era of history for women. We see through her story that she had gained great prominence, distinction, and importance on her own merits of character. Deborah was a woman whose confidence was rooted in a close personal relationship with God and in her awareness that God had chosen to use her to guide His people. Deborah was a woman of influence and which opened the way for other women to flourish into their own call and destiny.

Each woman in the Song of Deborah displays an innate possession of individual power, fortitude, and strength uncharacteristic of opposing portrayals of women. Yet, the inner possession of resolve never fully manifested outward, for the women ultimately face victimisation. Tamara Dixon asserts that even the women who conquer and seize victory from the hands of men, Deborah and Jael, are confined to and dangerously condone the limitations of patriarchy (Judg. 4-5).[23] Thereby, reading the Song of Deborah as a riposte from a woman's perspective breaks new ground by bringing out the insights and message embedded in the lines of the Song in the context of socio-political stereotypes. The systematic use of a riposte form offers a lucid and compelling explanation of the role and depiction of the human characters in Judges 4 and 5. God gives equal and unconditional love to all as He searches out the matter of the heart, whether male or female.

---

[21] Judy Taubes Sterman, "Themes in the Deborah Narrative (Judges 4-5)"*Jewish Bible Quarterly* 39/1 (2011), 20.

[22] Geoffrey P. Miller, "A Riposte Form in the Song of Deborah," 124.

[23] Tamara Dixon, "Most Blessed of Women: An Exegetical Study of Women's Roles under Patriarchy in Judges 5: 24-31," 1.

Deborah and Jael are presented as strong, female figures who take control of circumstances instead of submissively waiting to be taken control of. Deborah deplorably utilised her power as a military leader to ridicule the violence impending against other women. Despite being caught between the decisions of men, Jael appears to be the strong; she bravely and decisively takes action. The general expected roles of women are-mother, wife, and daughter and in addition, several unexpected roles. In the expected roles the women presented in the book of Judges are involved in explorations of the ways in which women participate in the structure of society; in the unexpected roles female figures are part of a consideration of how the role of women itself may be defined. Deborah and Jael are portrayed as strong and resolute characters with determination and purpose. There is a nuance of common sexual stereotyping; however, it is turned around in this Song. Here, the potential victims end up as victors.

The reality of many women's lives in the Old Testament times, and even in the contemporary world is 'silence and being silenced'. For those women who experience both the silence of women and their silencing, and the stereotype in which they are held, the Song of Deborah in Judges 5 is a divine booster to break through the stereotypes. It is a call to them to rise to the occasion to raise their voice, and they are to be determined and purposeful in their acts.

5

Women in Pauline Writings: A Liberative Perspective Towards the Ministerial Role of Women

Manini Chuseote

Introduction

The issue of leadership crisis in the ordained ministry is a common concern. The established hierarchical ecclesial structure no longer witness egalitarian ministry that was once active in Jesus' movement and Paul's ministry. Rather, the active participation of women in Pauline churches is found to have become problematic and questioned by the dominant structure. The study draws the understanding of the social behavior of Christian community from the Pauline writings particularly from the Pastorals towards the liberative role of women. The Pastorals exhibit the social problem in regard to women's public participation in the early Christianity. Genuine letters of Paul give evidence of women's active participation in his ministry but the same is not found in the post-Pauline churches. For the liberative role of women in the church and society the feminists critically outweigh the social position of women and the context in which the text is formed and the shift in reasoning that took place. Thus, the study brings forth the position of Paul in the Pastorals and the ecclesial identity of women in Pauline writings from the liberative perspective of women that challenges to identify new directions for mutual empowerment and inclusive community in the household of God.

1. Paul and Women

Paul led a ministry where women had equal mission and function with men. The Rabbinic teachings restrict other men to call a married woman by name except by her husband alone. But, Paul is found to cross such boundaries by mentioning names in his writings (Acts 16) or even calling them by name as recognizing their identity.[1] The Christian teaching that subjugate women's demeanor takes its standpoint on Pauline writings. But, it is when the church was attacked that Paul ordered a subordinate status as a defensive mechanism and so his concern for subordinating women is partly exegetical, cultural and practical.[2] Paul was open to women leadership role. The common terms in Pauline writings such as "co-worker", "brother/sister", "minister/helper", and "apostle" indicate the kind of leadership role women had been engaging in his ministry and served on equal basis. Euodia and Syntyche worked alongside Paul with mutual empowerment (Phil 4:2f.). Priscilla, a prominent co-worker of Paul along with her husband Aquila, worked independently without Paul's authority.[3] Phoebe is another important figure who receives the titles *diakonia* and *prostatis*[4] thus, she held the role of leadership and teaching in the community of Cenchreae. Paul's undisputed letters present prominent and leading women figures as preachers, teachers and leaders of the early Christian community who had the same mission function with the male co-workers. Thus, it shows an egalitarian ministry in the early Christian missionary movement.[5]

---

[1] V. Devashayam, "Paul and Partnership of Women and Men," in *A Reader in Feminist Theology*, edited by Prasanna Kumari (Madras: Gurukul Publication, 1993), 32–40.

[2] Peter Richardson, *Paul's Ethic of Freedom* (Philadelphia: Westminster Press, 1979), 169.

[3] In greeting the couple (Rom 16:3f) Paul addresses Prisca first, signifying her leadership (2 Tim 4:19). Junia and her husband Andronicus are called apostles (Rom 16:7). Elizabeth Schussler Fiorenza, "Word, Spirit and Power: Women in Early Christian Communities," in *Women of Spirit: Female Leadership in the Jewish and Christian Traditions*, edited by Rosemary Ruether and Eleanor McLaughlin (New York: Simon and Schuster, 1979), 29–70. Paul addressing Prisca first suggests of her significant leadership in early Christianity since in antiquity the one with better status and higher social class is named first. Joanna Dewey, "2 Timothy," in *The Women's Bible Commentary*, edited by Carol A. Newsom and Sharon H. Ringe (London: SPCK, 1992), 450–451.

[4] The term *diakonia* appear to be not only itinerant missionaries but leaders in local congregations. It serves in a recognized official capacity as teachers and preachers in the Christian community. The term *prostatis* (helper/patroness), which also means leading officer or governor, is referred to a person with authority (1 Thess 5:12) and the functions of church offices such as bishop, deacon or elder (1 Tim 3:4f.; 5:17). Fiorenza, "Word, Spirit and Power," 35–36.

[5] Fiorenza, "Word, Spirit and Power," 36.

2. Feminist Hermeneutical Reading on the Position of Paul in the Pastorals

The term *feminism* is identified in many expressions yet many have prejudice against the term because of its ideological bias and heresy in particular. Elizabeth Fiorenza defined the term feminism as "the radical notion that women are people."[6] This definition affirms that women are also full citizens and asserts justice without any discrimination against them in every aspect of life. It challenges to bring change in the structure of the society and advocate equality.[7] Paul is the most discussed biblical author while addressing women related issues and he is often misquoted. Paul's teachings and instructions in regard to the public participation of women is determined by the cultural situation.[8] The Pastorals having been written in a late first or early second century in the name of Paul, carries the teaching of Paul to certain aspect but with different notion.[9] The source of the Pastorals which is assumed to have been Hellenistic or Hellenistic Jewish became part of the Christian tradition in the post-apostolic period through the Pauline school of thought. This created a literary form with the object to articulate the theology of women's position in the church and society[10] as the public participation of women in Paul's time became problematic in the new church order in the post-apostolic period. The authentic letters of Paul show egalitarian viewpoint towards women's involvement in the church but the patriarchal outlook of the later Paulinist materials restricts the role of women to silence and submission in the post-apostolic church.[11] On this basis Deborah Krause,[12] Peter Richardson[13] and William O. Walker[14] argue that the Pastorals project Paul but his genuine approach and practice in relation to leadership role of women is absent in the letters which gave a wrong image of Paul in regard to women issue. Timothy and Titus as being the recipients of the Pastorals are instructed to set a tradition by substituting Paul in his churches particularly in Asia Minor in both preaching

---

[6] Elisabeth Schüssler Fiorenza, *Sharing Her Word: Feminist Biblical Interpretation in Context* (Dublin: Colour Book Ltd., 1998), 3.

[7] Fiorenza, *Sharing Her Word*, 4.

[8] Devasahayam, "Paul and Partnership of Women and Men," 32–33.

[9] Perhaps during his absence, Paul writes to the churches and so it is assumed that in this way the letter might have substituted Paul's presence but could not represent wholly Paul. Deborah Krause, *1 Timothy* (London: T&T Clark International, 2004), 1–2.

[10] William O. Walker, "The "Theology of Woman's Place" and the "Paulist" Tradition," *Semeia* 28 (1983), 101–112.

[11] Walker, "Theology of Woman's Place," 111–112.

[12] Krause, *1 Timothy*, 2.

[13] Richardson, Paul's Ethic of Freedom, 170.

[14] Walker, "The "Theology of Woman's Place," 112.

and teaching.[15] Hence, women in the given context of the Pastorals are rarely in any position of structural power and influence.[16]

The authentic letters of Paul portray Paul's attitudes towards the emancipation in relation to gender, class and race than his later letters. Paul strived for equality for the sake of the church.[17] Christians have encountered a legitimate kind of freedom in applying Scripture intelligently and appropriately for a new social outlook which is called a "hermeneutical freedom."[18] Many critics considered Paul as male chauvinist and therefore, it is difficult for the reader to grasp Paul's position with regards to women. The active participation of women in Paul's ministry determines Paul's acceptance of the roles of women in church worship. His instruction towards women on certain behavior and conduct may be because of the problem arising in the churches through that assertion of freedom. The change on the position of women in the family and society from household to obtaining high social position may be further enhanced by maintaining the egalitarian concept of Paul towards gender (Gal 3:28). Thus, the hermeneutical freedom which emphasizes on Paul's view of freedom challenges and encourages women empowerment.[19] Therefore, it can be assumed that Paul is not responsible for the teachings that restrict women's public participation in the Pastorals but the author who is against the leadership position of women in the new church order.

3. Women Leadership in Early Christianity

The prominent figures in the early Christianity were predominantly male leaders. It shows power relations between the genders.[20] Women in the early Christianity are often assumed as marginal figures. Scholars conclude that the early church structure reflects the social structures and values of existing patriarchal Jewish or Greco-Roman society. Fiorenza argues that this reconstruction of early church history is androcentric and functions as contemporary social and theological methodology that determines the self-understanding which justifies the present ecclesial structures of male power.[21] She further remarks that the early Christian community had the theological

---

[15] This tradition shows the importance of ministry to Paul. Hence, the instruction regarding proper conduct in the church to Timothy and Titus links with the stewardship of Paul's words and ministry. The Pastorals present post-Pauline church. Krause, *1 Timothy*, 4–5.

[16] Myra Blyth and Wendy S. Robins, *No Boundaries to compassion? An Exploration of Women, Gender and Diakonia* (Geneva: WCC,1998), 65.

[17] Richardson, *Paul's Ethic of Freedom*, 164–166.

[18] Richardson, *Paul's Ethic of Freedom*, 168.

[19] Richardson, *Paul's Ethic of Freedom*, 169.

[20] Elsa Tamez, "Women's Leadership in the New Testament," in *Concilium* 4 (2012), 77–85.

[21] Fiorenza, "Word, Spirit and Power," 30.

understanding of egalitarian discipleship (Gal 3:27ff.) but they picked up the institutional forms of the close patriarchal cultural system in the later period that resulted in a patriarchal pattern of leadership and exclude women from leadership position.[22]

In sub-apostolic period two New Testament texts appeared: the Gospel of John, where the leadership position of women is identified as leaders, teachers and evangelists and the Pastorals in which women are prohibited from the role of teaching.[23] It was an ideal practice among the lower members of the household in the Roman society to submit to the head of the household. In such context women who fail to submit to male-head are doubted.[24] As a result, the establishment of 'household codes' perhaps was a patriarchal reaction to this women's leadership role within the house churches.[25] These rules of conduct enforced women a passive life to observe the social-patriarchal order in the worship just as at home.[26] Yet, women did not stop from public participation although their leadership was more visible in the heretical movements.[27] The second century writing *The Acts of Paul and Thecla* gives evidence of women's leadership role. The public participation of Thecla retains the authority of early Christian women missionaries.[28]

The Pastorals also presents the significant role of women in propagating Christianity besides their struggles for liberation (2 Tim 1:5).[29] Women continue

---

[22] Fiorenza, "Word, Spirit and Power," 30–32.

[23] Tamez, "Women's Leadership in the New Testament," 82.

[24] In this period the domestic codes of Roman society were employed in the ecclesial structure of the Christian communities. In letters like Ephesians, Colossians and 1 Peter, the husbands reciprocate to the wives' submission with love, but such reciprocity is absent in the Pastorals. In 1 Timothy women are instructed to keep silence (2:11 – 12), children are to obey (3:4), and slaves are to serve and respect their masters (6:1 – 2). Such relationship is to maintain in the church and the leadership role in God's household depends upon it (1 Tim 2:14; 3:4 – 5). Tamez, "Women's Leadership in the New Testament," 82–83.

[25] The early Christian women played important role as leaders in the house church (Acts 12:12; 17:4, 12; Rom 16:3 – 5; 1 Cor 1:11; 16:19) and the gathering was called the "house of God". The whole activity in the house church and the assembly of the Christian community determined the form of church life. Fiorenza, "Word, Spirit and Power," 32–33.

[26] Fiorenza, "Word, Spirit and Power," 37.

[27] Tamez, "Women's Leadership in the New Testament," 83.

[28] Paul charged the apostle Thecla to go and teach the word of God. Fiorenza, "Word, Spirit and Power," 37–39. The un-canonical book *Acts of Paul and Thecla* presents how Thecla escaped from the household and join ministry with Paul. Her refusal of marriage and escape from household for the purpose of public teaching provides images of women leadership in the early Christian text. Rosemary Radford Ruether, *Introducing Redemption in Christian Feminism* (Sheffield: Academic Press, 1998), 26.

[29] Joanna Dewey, "2 Timothy," in *The Women's Bible Commentary* (ed. Carol A. Newsom and Sharon H. Ringe; London: SPCK, 1992), 450.

to remain active in the church even at the later part of the second century as prophets and teachers apart from the office of widows and deaconess but their active participation was rejected all the more by the patriarchal church.[30] According to the historians, the early Christian writers excluded some of the materials in the process of rewriting the early Christian traditions but were selective and that perhaps most of the egalitarian traditions of primitive Christianity are lost. On this basis Fiorenza remarks that the references to women's leadership role in the patriarchal record are found in traces like the tip of an iceberg indicating precious information that has vanished from historical consciousness.[31]

4. Contextual Outlook on Women's Liberation in the Pauline Writings

Women in the Gospels played decisive role as faithful disciples of Christ. In the Apostolic Church Order certain arguments among the disciples' dialogue are found in regard to whether, women can celebrate the Eucharist.[32] This shows the existing burning issue of women's leadership position within the Christian community from the early centuries.[33] In the first century C.E., the hate-filled propaganda against women's liberation prevailed in all aspects of imperial Rome's dominant culture in Judaism and Christianity. Within the patriarchal cultural systems in the history of liberation, voices of women and men for liberation are found in traces in the New Testament texts.[34]

The Pastorals appear as one of the literary documents that contain women's liberating struggles particularly 1 Timothy[35] and the major concerns are on the ecclesial position of women, their apparel and social demeanor of women and their role at home particularly to their husbands.[36] 1Tim 2:11ff gives a social picture of the time where women did not remain silent against

[30] Women actually dared to perform certain roles like teaching, debate, exorcise, baptize. Fiorenza, "Word, Spirit and Power," 51.

[31] Fiorenza, "Word, Spirit and Power," 57.

[32] Andrew and Peter raised the concern of women's ministry in relation to Eucharist. Fiorenza, "Word, Spirit and Power," 56.

[33] The advocates of women's leadership often refer to the passage Gal 3:28 and Rom 16 in support to show that Christian truth is based also on the apostolic authority of women and not only of men. On the other hand, the texts such as 1 Cor 14:33b–36 and 1 Tim 2:9–15 are referred to by the Patriarchal opposition in support to subordinate role of women in church and society. Fiorenza, "Word, Spirit and Power," 56.

[34] 1 Timothy stands one of those texts that gives traces of a history of women's liberation although, Schottroff remarks, "albeit most unwittingly and entirely contrary to its declared intentions." Luise Schottroff, *Lydia's Impatient Sisters: A Feminist Social History of Early Christianity* (London: SCM Press, 1995), 77.

[35] Schottroff, *Lydia's Impatient Sisters*, 73.

[36] Walker, "Theology of Woman's Place," 105.

the oppression of women but assert for their right to learn and to teach besides their domestic role. They sought for freedom not with the role imposed by the patriarchal order (Tit 2:3–5) but they relegated their domestic function with public participation and adopted independent ecclesial position. Therefore, Luise Schottroff asserts, "first Timothy was to bring an end this history of women's liberation, to discredit it and render it invisible."[37] The freedom in the early church, as a body, solely depends on the gifts of the Spirit and today many are looking for that same freedom[38] for egalitarian community.

The identity of women in the Indian patriarchal context is connected with the male members of their families and their social behavior is controlled by the patriarchal cultural and traditional values.[39] Although, the position of women today is uplifted and have more freedom, the traditional notion of women as weak creature, unclean and temptress still continue to influence in relegating the role and leadership of women in church and society.[40] The church's context is not far from such traditional factor that has greatly impacted the society particularly towards the identity and role of women for Christianity has its origin in the patriarchal culture.[41] However, the new humanity in Christ gives a new social identity to every member of the community as participants in New Creation for mutual empowerment and to liberate one another.

5. Ecclesial Models for Liberative Ministrial Role of Women

The model of ecclesial leadership that developed on the basis of patriarchal cultural system of the Greco–Roman society in the late first century enhanced a hierarchical relation within the early Christian community unlike Jesus' time. This image of leadership creates gender polarization in the church particularly in leadership role.[42] Thus, Rosemary Ruether argues the question of ecclesial leadership role of women is undoubtedly a question of the human rights of women for the full humanity in the church.[43] Sociologists, in approving the analysis of power and authority as dominance, affirm that in social relations authority takes the place of domination and that the patterns of elitism and oppression are due to social, political, and economic

---

[37] Schottroff, *Lydia's Impatient Sisters*, 73.

[38] Richardson, *Paul's Ethic of Freedom*, 170.

[39] Nirmala Vasanthakumar, "Role and Identity of Women in the Church," in *Women in Church and Society* (comps. Zubeno Kithan; West Bengal: SCEPTRE, 2014), 374–383.

[40] Vasanthakumar, "Role and Identity of Women in the Church," 376–377.

[41] Vasanthakumar, "Role and Identity of Women in the Church," 377–378.

[42] Rosemary Radford Ruether, *New Woman New Earth: Sexist Ideologies & Human Liberation* (New York: Seabury Press, 1975), 75.

[43] Ruether, *New Woman New Earth*, 78.

inequality.[44] Therefore, for liberative role of women it is vital to restructure the ecclesial models.

5.1. Authority as Legitimate Power

Power may be understood as a means of achieving one's desired ends and social power as the ability of a person or group that reacts to other's behavior.[45] This aspect of power is apparent in the Pastorals. In the early Christianity the leadership role of women is marked by charisma rather than by office. It reflects the sociological fact of the time where women had no right to claim authority of office. It was in this context that women find space and exercise authority based on 'gifts of the Spirit'. Furthermore, one who follows Christ and suffers for Christ willingly is considered as a disciple whose authority appears as that of the Episcopal leadership. However, the prophetic role of women as preaching or blessing the Lord's Supper is later considered as false practice by the institutionalized mainstream church[46] and further determined the authority of women from her social position.[47] Paul's notion on equality in Christ in the Deutero-Pauline letters is expressed in the form of subjection to the hierarchical orders of the patriarchal family.[48] The calling to serve is not to be passive with the dominant cultural system in the church or society nor to subjugate the opposite sex but it is to exercise authority and legitimate power in a new way for the cause of liberation of all and mutual empowerment.[49] A just society demands the service of both women and men in which power is shared equally.

5.2. Ministry as Mutual Empowerment

Women's leadership role in the church is less visible and strongly controlled by the Church hierarchy and so women often questioned "Where do women fit as members of the body of Christ? Given the reality of unequal treatment, how

[44] Letty M. Russell, *Household of Freedom: Authority in Feminist Theology* (Philadelphia: The Westminster Press, 1987), 21.

[45] Russell, *Household of Freedom*, 21.

[46] Rosemary Ruether and Eleanor McLaughlin, "Women's Leadership in the Jewish and Christian Traditions: Continuity and Change," in *Women of Spirit: Female Leadership in the Jewish and Christian Traditions* (ed. Rosemary Ruether and Eleanor McLaughlin; New York: Simon and Schuster, 1979), 19–20.

[47] Although women maintain a subordinate status in all classes, a woman who is from the leadership class exercises authority. It is the wealthy women being active in public roles in the fourth-century Christian asceticism. Ruether and McLaughlin, "Women's Leadership in the Jewish and Christian Traditions," 22.

[48] Ruether, *Introducing Redemption in Christian Feminism*, 26.

[49] For Ruether, διάκονος is referred to kenotic concept of 'self-emptying of power as domination'. Ruether, *Sexism and God-Talk*, 206–207.

do we correct the gender imbalance?"[50] In the contemporary church structure, women's ministry makes visible the charisma in unique and different roles that function for the sake of empowering the whole community.[51] So, the church is responsible to provide ministerial space for individual member to use his/her unique gift/s with confidence to liberate one another.[52] Hence, Ruether argues that mutual empowerment with women will lead to priesthood of all believers in giving a new identity as equal partners in Christ.[53] Leadership functions as a call from within and not to deprive others' rights by certain imposition.[54] Hence, only in the egalitarian communities will there be mutual empowerment in the church.

5.3. Ministry as Equal Partnership

Men and women, as created in the image of God, are partners in life. Jesus accepted and valued all who come to him. Ministry of equal partnership calls for equal sharing and not competitiveness. The prejudices, myths and negative outlook towards women which the Rabbinic Tradition and the Church Fathers have held for long will have to be broken down in order to achieve equal partnership at all levels.[55] Paul, being not only a theological radical but also a social conservative (Gal 3:28; Col 3: 18–4:1), observes the hierarchicalism between slaves and masters, women and men basing on the order of creation.[56] Women's inferiority and negative stereotypes of femininity are often seen in the letters of Paul and church Fathers. However, in Pauline writings, women's active participation in the house-church is found as 'partners in ministry'. But, the degree of administration in the constitution of the church subjugated and oppressed the status of women. Anne Arabome argues that even within the religious community that professes Christ as Liberator, women continue to be treated as inferior beings.[57] Jesus' relationship to authority is marked with

---

[50] Anne Arabome SSS, "Gender and Ecclesiology: Authorities, Structures, Ministry," *Concilium* 4 (2012), 110–117.

[51] Rosemary Radford Ruether, *Sexism and God-Talk: Toward a Feminist Theology* (Boston: Beacon Press, 1993), 207.

[52] Ruether, *Sexism and God-Talk*, 208.

[53] Thomas H. Groome, "From Chauvinism and Clericalism to Priesthood: The Long March," in *The Emerging Christian Woman: Church and Society Perspective*, edited by Stella Faria, Anna Vareed Alexander and Jessie B. Tellis-Nayak (Pune: Satprakashan Sanchar Kendra, 1984), 90–104.

[54] Ruether, *Sexism and God-Talk*, 210.

[55] Gerwin van Leeuwen, "Women in Ministries," in *The Emerging Christian Woman: Church and Society Perspective*, edited by Stella Faria, Anna Vareed Alexander and Jessie B. Tellis-Nayak (Pune: Satprakashan Sanchar Kendra, 1984), 109.

[56] Ruether, *New Woman New Earth*, 67–68.

[57] Arabome SSS, "Gender and Ecclesiology," 111.

love and invitation. His service to others confirms his type of authority which challenged the social structure of the time.[58] It is through service that advocates partnership within the humanity.[59] Therefore, in the church which is identified as the household of God, the role of women must be equally identified as that of the male members.

Conclusion

Power can marginalize people or create an inclusive community. The patriarchal cultural system in the ecclesial structure in the early century relegated the social behavior of women. The Pastorals reflect such reality of women's struggle for liberation from the structured body that limits their role to domestic sphere. The text in the Pastorals that restricts leadership role of women has its own context which cannot be universal to every woman. The deconstruction of biased ministry is seen in Paul's radical stand for freedom when he challenged the existing social and cultural system of the time that there is no longer male or female but all are one in Christ (Gal 3:28). This oneness can be experienced only in the family or household where each one functions as equal partners responsible for mutual growth. Therefore, it is the inclusive community and mutual participation in the ministry that would allow the household of God to experience the new humanity and oneness in Christ.

[58] Arabome SSS, "Gender and Ecclesiology," 113.

[59] Letty M. Russell, *The Future of Partnership* (Philadelphia: Westminster Press, 1979), 73.

6

Woman's Work for Women: The Life and Work of Anna Hasseltine Kay Scott

Narola Imchen

Introduction

Here I want to make a historical review of our Mission History in North East India (NEI) from a woman's perspective. As we know, both men and women participated equally in the history of Christianity right from the beginning, yet due to the existing Patriarchal culture, often the role of women has been ignored or side-lined. When we look at the history of Christianity in NEI, it was the American Baptist Missionaries who made the greatest impact in witnessing Christ in the region. In this noble work of witnessing Christ, both men and women missionaries participated and contributed equally. NEI like any other Patriarchal society is no exception when we look at the Church Histories and Church Records, mostly the work of men are recorded. But, when we go through the journals and reports of the missionaries and books written by missionaries, we find ample evidence of how the women also worked side by side along with the men. Hence, an attempt is made here to look at women in mission from a historical perspective. I want to focus particularly, on the life story of an American Baptist woman missionary, Anna Hasseltine Kay Scott, whose work is very inspiring and encouraging.

But before we come to her story, we shall briefly look at the context from which the women missionaries came.

Women Missionaries: Background Context

At the beginning of the twentieth century, Helen Montgomery wrote,

> For the women of our modern churches it is hard to realize that there ever was a time when there were none of the active and ubiquitous (ever-present, everywhere, omnipresent) women's missionary societies that seem so much a part of the structure of church life.[1]

As we go through the reports and writings of the women missionaries, we find that women had to struggle to take their place alongside men in missionary work. The organization of women's missionary societies was one among many developments that made the nineteenth century, in the words of Montgomery, the *Woman's Century.*

The period from 1836, when the American Baptist first started their mission in NEI, to 1870 can be referred to as the period of the pioneers. During this, period, there were altogether 18 women missionaries who served in NEI.[2] Out of these, 15 were wives of male missionaries, and only two were single women missionaries. It is interesting to note that of these two single women missionaries - one was the sister of Miles Bronson – Rhoda Bronson, and the other Maria Bronson Cotes, the daughter of Miles Bronson. The early missionary wives shared with their husbands the theological background of New England during the Second Great Awakening. They were also part of a Patriarchal culture in which it was expected that the primary concern of women was maintaining the home. The only way a woman could serve as a missionary was to marry a missionary. Thus, for some women, the choice of a mate in the ministry was a vocational one. Nowhere is the connection between marriage and vocation as clear as for the early missionary wives.[3]

Thus, for the early missionary wives, divine calling, education and marriage intersected in a female social context that paralleled that of the male missionaries. Husbands and wives found each other through a web of acquaintances that centred on church membership and attendance at an institution of higher education – college or theological seminary for women. Thus, the husbands and wives were united by mutual commitments

[1] Henen Barett Montgomery, *Western Women in Eastern Land: An Outline Study of Fifty Years of Woman 's work in Foreign Missions* (New York: The Macmillan Company, 1910), 3.

[2] Narola Imchen, *Remembering Our Foremothers: The Influence of the American Woman's Movement on American Baptist Women Missionaries in North East India* (Jorhat: Women Study Department, 2003), 135.

[3] Dana L. Roberts, *American Women in Mission: A Social History of their Thought and Practice* (Georgia: Mercer University Press, 1996), 18.

and supported by mutual friendship that emboldened them to undertake an enterprise that would take them away from their homeland, relatives and friends into a field of work that was often dangerous, discouraging and difficult.

The period from 1871-1913 may be referred to as the Later Period. This period was marked by new developments in the Assam Mission. Several new stations were established and for the first time missionaries of the newly formed Woman's Baptist Foreign Mission Society (WBFMS) began to serve there. From the time of its formation single women missionaries began to be sent to the mission fields, including the fields in NEI. Thus, the work of women missionaries in this period became more diversified. There were new opportunities for wives of male missionaries and single women both in the traditional plains fields and in the work beginning to be done among the hill tribes women.

During this period, 71 women missionaries served in NEI. 16 of them remained unmarried, while the rest either came out as wives of male missionaries or came out as singles but subsequently married missionaries whose wives died. Altogether 20 were officially appointed by the WBFMS. These women were better educated than those of the earlier period. They all had high school education of some kind. As was the case in the earlier period, the missionary women were as a group better educated than the average American women of that time. The American civil war provided a common background for the women missionaries who come to NEI during this period. The civil war was the main empowering force of women of this period in the US. During the awful struggle the women of both North and South received a baptism of power. They were driven to organize, and forced to co-operate in raising and distributing aid to the soldiers. In these activities they discovered abilities of which they themselves and the nation had been quite unconscious. It is no accident that during the decade following the close of the civil war scores of women's organizations, among them women's missionary societies were formed.

This was the context out of which the women missionaries serving in NEI in the 19th century came. They were all products of the woman's movement.

Women Missionaries: Their Work in North East India

As women's missionary groups in America began to promote their work through publications of various kinds, a common missiological theme began to emerge. It was: ***Woman's work for woman.*** The basic goal remained the same as in the missiology of early nineteenth century wives – to evangelize women and bring them to salvation. But, there was more to it than that. As Dana Robert puts it:

> The end of evangelization was not the establishment of three self churches: for heathen women, evangelization was intertwined with civilization, with being elevated by Christianity into social equality with western women and into positions of respect in their own societies.[4]

The work of American Baptist women missionaries in NEI became increasingly complex during this period. The work undertaken often grew out of special interests and abilities of individual missionaries, rather than out of a comprehensive plan. Yet, there are certain generalizations that can be made regarding the work of all. They were involved in running schools for children and women, in evangelistic work and developing literature, industries and philanthropies of various kinds.

It will not be possible to discuss the life and work of all the women missionaries. Hence, as stated in the introduction, I have decided to discuss the life and work of only one woman, whose work never fail to amaze me.

Anna Hasseltine Kay Scott: 1862-1914

She was born on April 20, 1838, in the village of Payson, Illinois. This village was named for Rev. Edward Payson, a celebrated New England minister. The early settlers of Payson were chiefly from New England, though her own father was from the South.

As we read the biographies of that time, we find many of them were filled with references to the network of women's benevolent activities. However, though the female benevolent network provided valuable opportunities for women, it stopped short of permitting them to preach or otherwise assume leadership positions in the churches. It simply kept them in the *rear of the army* as described by Dana Robert.[5] Such limitations created frustration and the desire to do more. Thus, for several women as in the case of Anna K. Scott, the opportunity to marry a missionary represented a step beyond the limitations imposed upon them by society because of their sex. She hoped that the mission could permit a larger role in the ministry.

But, the mission at the time was not prepared to send out single women missionaries. As she writes:

> ...My pastor's wife, living in Sherburne, N.Y, wrote the secretary of our society asking him if their rules permitted the sending out of unmarried ladies to the foreign mission field. The reply was that they were not sending single ladies and I must 'await the openings of providence'. This meant I must wait until a man asked me to go with him. It seemed rather a strange way to get a chance to go as a teacher to heathen girls...[6]

---

[4] Dana, *American Women in Mission,* 130.

[5] Dana, *American Women in Mission,* 10-14.

[6] Anna Kay Scott, *An Autobiography of Anna Kay Scott* (Chicago: NP., 1917), 11-25.

Thus, marriage to a missionary had important social implications for the missionary woman of the early nineteenth century. Leonard Sweet argues that, *the most common vocational fantasies of Evangelical women in nineteenth century America involved becoming a minister's or a missionary' wife.* Thus, marriage to a minister meant that a woman could virtually function as a minister by leading prayer meetings, visiting the sick, and exhorting. In fact, marriage to a missionary meant that a woman could work as a missionary. Nowhere is the connection between marriage and vocation as clear as for the early missionary wives.[7]

Reviewing the Life and Work of Anna Kay Scott

The life experiences and contributions of Anna Kay Scott for the Assam mission are remarkable and need to be recognized. In her life and work, we can easily discern the spirit of the nineteenth century American Woman's Movement. Through the study of her life and work, it is understood that, she has inspired many men and women in the past and continues to inspire us even today. The determination she had for the mission can be understood through the following works.

1. Determination to carry on the Lord's Work

She was the wife of Edward Payson Scott. They were assigned to work in Nowgong, Assam.

Unfortunately, her husband died leaving her alone with their three children. After the death of her husband, everybody expected her to leave the mission field along with her children. But, the records and writings proved that she was determined to carry on the work in the mission field. This came as a big surprise for the other missionaries as is evident from the following writings.

In the fifty-sixth annual report of the ABMU (1870), the work of Anna Kay Scott is thus described:

> Nowgong: By the death of her husband, Mrs. Scott was left in sole charge of the station, with the additional care of three children. The blow was fearful, and its effects for the moment stunning. But she soon recovered herself, took hold of the everlasting arm and rose up to duty and enjoyment in duty. With the remarkable degree of courage and firmness, she put her hands on the helm of affairs and from that day to this, all parts of the work, including the church, school, native helpers and financial matters have gone on successfully.

Mr. Ward further writes:

> The change of the Nowgong mission, from the hour of her husband's death until missionaries from home shall arrive, is sister Scott. The picture

[7] Dana, *American Women in Mission,* 18.

> of womanly devotion and heroism is unique and I would sooner have stayed away than that coming here for a short time should mar it. I shall touch nothing, meddle with nothing, dictate nothing, but let well done. Thank God for this exhibition of his grace which is so sustaining and strengthening our sister in such an emergency, even enabling her to decide to remain among her beloved Mikiris in a work for which her experienced capacity and surprising knowledge of the language of those under her charge. We had taken it for granted that she would accompany us home. It seemed rather strong doctrine, when she wrote that she proposed to remain and continue in the work saying, " I gave myself to the work of missions before I ever knew my precious husband". But, it now seems to me to be of the Lords; and with her good health and excellent domestic arrangement, I see no reason why she may not give much time to successful missionary labour in connection with the Mikir school for young men.[8]

Anna Kay Scott herself writes about her experiences during this crucial period of her life after the demise of her husband. She writes:

> When strength and life came back to me I gradually took up my husband's mission work, in addition to my own, and carried it on until the mission society sent other workers. Then I moved to Gowahaty and worked for the women's missionary society for four years.[9]

From these sources it is clear that Anna Kay Scott had the will and determination, unexpected of a widow at that time. Everyone expected her to pack up and leave the mission after the demise of her husband. But, contrary to the expectation of the people around, she decided to stay on. Not only did she stay on, but also she successfully carried on her husband's work. In this she closely resembled those women who carried on in their husband's absence or after their demise during the American civil war.

Little is said in the annual reports of the society about Anna's work in particular during the Assam years. Like many other missionary wives, who were seldom referred to as missionaries themselves, she shared in her husband's work of teaching and school supervision, as well as caring for their home and children. Yet her husband, Edward Scott, seems to have been more aware of the value of women's work than many of his colleagues. He wrote of the repair to the mission buildings that needed to be done during the cold season while he was on tour, which Anna would have to supervise in addition to overseeing the schools, teaching them, attending to visitors, and caring for the family. He writes:

> All this seems hardly within the sphere of women's labour, especially when the care of a house and family of children are continually calling

[8] "Fifty-Sixth Annual Report," in *N BMM,* Vol. L, July, 1870, 240-49.

[9] Anna Kay Scott, *Autobiography,* 41.

> for attention; yet this is in fact the work that our missionaries wives do much of. In fact choose to do rather than have their husbands kept from the school and precious harvest in the jungle. This is Mrs. Scott's program for the cold season in addition to superintending the religious services, which cater with attention to the spiritual wants of the mission, in general constitutes the chief burden of her work.[10]

2. Interest in Women's Welfare

Anna Kay Scott seemed to have great interest to uplift the status of women in North East India. This is made explicit by the special concern she had for the women. In one instance she writes:

> I think our people in America can hardly realize what a good work there is to be done among the women and girls of India by educated, Christian ladies. Fully to realize the importance and magnitude of this work one must live in India and know the social status of East Indian life. I could not believe, until I entered the hi-caste home and saw how the women were treated, that human beings brought up in the 19th century could think it right to treat women so cruelly.[11]

For such ill treatment of women in India, Anna felt the Brahmin Shastras are largely to blame. Her conviction that there is nothing so unreasonable and stubborn as a false religion, and a corrupt priesthood which can give almost any meaning to a command which in itself may be harmless, was typical of her time. She also noted that if a Hindu woman suffers much in giving birth to her child, her husband and all of her family take that as positive evidence that she has not been a virtuous woman, and they will beat her, demanding to know who her lover was. More than once Anna Scott said she had known a woman under such circumstances to confess to a sin of which she has never been guilty. No male physician was ever allowed to see these high-caste women in their times of suffering. Hence the great need for women doctors who could minister to them.

3. Evangelism

Anna Kay Scott was one who often went on missionary tours to various places, spending many days in camp. In a letter she describes the experiences of camping at a place called No-Noi. She writes:

> About a week ago I came to this place to spend a fortnight. Our native preacher, Charles, is stationed here and I am much pleased with the

---

[10] Alice Findlay, "A Worthy Woman who can Find? Anna Kay Scott," in *American Baptist Quarterly,* Vol. XII, Sept. 1983, No. 3. 226-27.

[11] Mildred Marston, Korno Siga, *The Mountain Chief or Life in Assam*, Philadelphia: American Baptist Publication Society, 1900.

> thoughtful arrangements he has made for my comfort. I have my three children with me, and leaving them during the days and their nurse, I have gone sometimes on foot and sometimes on horseback, through the country, visiting our mission-schools, and fifteen miles in the day, with very little fatigue. This amount of physical exertion talking to the people of Jesus and the way of salvation. In this way I have travelled would have laid me up for a week when I first came to this country. I congratulate myself upon having become thoroughly acclaimed now. As the schools in the station are having a month vacation, the pupils who are Christians are also out in the villages and on the hills distributing tracts and talking "of this same Jesus". This sick and the afflicted gathered in number at my tent door every day, begging for medicine for their several diseases. Would that they would seek as eagerly for a cure for their sin-sick souls.[12]

Anna Scott was one who had special concern for women in India. I believe this must have been reinforced as she saw the real living conditions of women on her several tours. In her book Korno Sigas, *The Mountain Chief or Life in Assam*, she recalls an interesting incident during one of her tours. In it one clearly sees the relationship between evangelism and social transformation for women.

Here she describes a night when she was encamped in a Hindu village and heard at midnight the wailing of a woman. Taking one of the Christian man with her, she set out to ascertain the cause of her suffering. She found one of the low-caste Hindu woman seated on the ground with a dead baby clasped to her breast, while she rocked herself to and fro. These were the words of her lamentations:

> Oh Ram, Khrishna, Shiva and all Hindu gods, can you not tell me where my child is gone? It smiles no more upon me, when I call it, it answers me not again. Whither has its spirit fled? Into what form of beast or reptile has its spirit entered? Is there no power, good or evil? That can tell me where to search now for my child? Has it entered into a toad or a snake, with this last question she shuddered with fear and beat upon her breast and tore her hair in agony and despair.[13]

Anna sat down beside her and told her of the Christian women's belief that when their little ones die, they thought of them as forever happy, as being in a lovely home where a father more tender and loving than any mother on earth could be, who provided for their every want: where they would hunger no more, neither thirst any more, and where the intense heat of the sun shall never more trouble them. She further told her of the Christian women's faith that she would meet her child, who is called dead, in that beautiful country.

---

[12] "Letter from Mrs. Scott", in *BMM,* Vol. LI, June 1871, 178.

[13] Marston, *Korno Siga, 173-77*

Anna then told the woman what Christ's religion had done for women – how Christ had called her daughter, and gave her positive assurance that she had a place in the paradise of the good where they neither marry nor are given in marriage, but are as the angels.

Thus, the women missionaries including Anna Kay Scott, gave much emphasis to evangelism. As we can understand from the above discussion, she had so much passion to preach the gospel to the non-Christian women. This aspect of their work clearly indicates that they were truly the products of the missionary societies of the early nineteenth century.

Concluding Remarks

- As noted, this woman – Anna Kay Scott could do so much during the short period she worked as a missionary in Assam.
- This remarkable woman spent eleven years of her life in Assam and twenty-five years in China.
- She alone raised and educated three children to professional status as a single mother, and lived to see both her daughter and grand-daughter follow her in missionary service in China.
- In spite of numerous bouts of illness, constant exhaustion from heavy works, and seriously unsettled political conditions, she persevered and generally managed to ignore the adverse circumstances as she pursued her goal of physical and spiritual healing.
- She was an innovator, able to see what was needed before others saw it, and bold enough to go ahead and make a start on it.
- She took the long view into the future and made plans to meet the needs she knew would arise.
- She spent her life focusing on leadership development among the people she worked with. She trained them. She commissioned them to do a task. She trusted them and in return, she was deeply respected by all her co-workers.
- Alice Findlay,[14] describes her, in the words of Proverbs 31:10 – *A Worthy woman who can find? Her price is far above rubies.*

[14] Alice Findlay, *A Worthy Woman,* 232.

7

The Participation of Women in the Society with Special Reference to Chakhesang Community: A Holistic-Missiological Approach

Mekronyi-U Thele

Introduction

Chakhesang women are placed in the margin in spite of their great participation towards the society. In the pre-Christian era women were excluded and subjugated in the socio-cultural, religious and political structure as the Chakhesang society follows patriarchal system. In spite of the rigid patriarchal culture, women continue to make significant contribution in the society. The study also highlights the present significant participations of Chakhesang women in the family management, different organizations, education, politics etc. Therefore, this paper is an attempt to bring out women's participation and to examine the various hindrances so that the society will accept them as equal partners rather than suppress them. The motif of applying this methodology is to clearly analyze the significance of women's role and participation. The researcher employs a holistic-missiological approach in order that people change their attitude towards women and accept them as equal partners participating in the society.

Methodology

The word "*holistic*" is derived from the philosophical notion of holism which means "the whole is greater than the sum of its parts." Holism (Ὅλος, *holos,* a Greek meaning *all, whole, entire, total*) should be viewed as a whole, not as collections of parts. The Hebrew word closest to *holos* is possibly *shalom.*[1] Valson Thampu further explains holism with three other corollaries - the whole determines the nature of its parts, parts cannot be understood if considered in isolation from the whole and the part of an organic whole are dynamically inter-related or inter-dependent.[2] 'The model of relationship' which was developed by F. Hrangkhuma is one of the methods that falls under holistic missiological approach. For Hrangkhuma, humanity exists in three dimensional relationships, namely in relationship to God, with one another, and with creation.[3] The holistic concept is used to emphasize the inseparability of word and deed or of evangelism and social responsibility. Holistic mission is concerned with ministry to the whole person through the transforming power of the Gospel. Holistic approach cannot neglect necessity of women's equal participation with men in the society. Based on this approach the research will discover and expose the valuable participation of Chakhesang women in the society.

1. Participation of Chakhesang Women in the Pre-Christian Society

The Chakhesang society practices a patriarchal system where women were debarred and discriminated in the socio-cultural, religious and political structure. In spite of the rigid patriarchal culture, women continue to contribute significant role in the society. However, their participations were often overpowered by the existing patriarchal culture. Let us observe how women participate towards the family life, Socio-Economic Life, Socio-Cultural Life, Religious Life, Political Life in the society before Christianity.

1.1. The Participation of Women in Family Life

Mothers were valued for their child-bearing role but consecutive birth of a female child was not so welcomed and barren women were stigmatized. Majority of the domestic affairs are in the hands of women. The women in

---

[1] John Steward, "Holism, Biblical" in *Evangelical Dictionary of World Missions*, edited by A. Scott Moreau, Harold Netland and Charles Van Engen (Grand Rapids: Baker Books, 2000), 448.

[2] Valson Thampu, *Rediscovering Mission: Towards a Non-Western Missiological Paradigm* (New Delhi: TRACI, 1995), 4, cited by Andrew Lalhmagnaiha, *Holistic Mission and the Serampore Trio* (Delhi: ISPCK, 2010), 16.

[3] F. Hrangkhuma, 'Mission and Evangelism Today,' *B.C.M Compendium: In Honor of BCM Mission in Mizoram 1903-2003* (Lunglei: Baptist Church of Mizoram, 2003), 43, 44, cited by Lalhmangaiha, *Holistic Mission...,* 16, 17.

the Chakhesang society were honored and praised for their role in the family only because of her ability in fulfilling her household chores like cooking, washing, fetching water and firewood, minding the children and the domestic animals, working in the fields, weaving, spinning, pounding paddy etc. Thus, a woman's worth and value is measured by the amount of work that she performs. Therefore, women often find themselves trying to live up to the expectation and favor of the society.[4] At the same time, even women themselves simply considered all these manual works as women's duty.[5] At the time of marriage, her consent is sought by her parents for her life partner as marriage being one of the chief duties of filial piety.[6] A woman is required to have a shaven head till she marries.[7]

1.2. Socio-Economic Life

Women usually works harder and longer time than men do in the family because after working in the field for the whole day together with her husband, the wife has to carry fire-wood, vegetables, the baby, along with all the tools. The wife continues her domestic works in addition to raising livestock. It is unusual for a husband or father to help with the wife's responsibilities at home because deep-rooted in men's mind is that domestic work is only for women.[8] Women grow cotton, spin threat and weave diverse designs of clothes for their family and for trade purposes. Women make various designs and colors by boiling leaves and berries.[9] Weaving of various kinds, embroidery and design works were taught to young women by the older women in *Luke/Cethicie* (a dormitory type).[10] Usually men visit the women's dormitory bringing meat and rice beer with them. Strict social codes control these dormitories whereby boys and girls are nurtured with decent attitudes.[11]

---

[4] Lovely Awomi James, *Tribal Theology: Reviewing the Naga Traditional Worldview* (New Delhi: Christian World Imprints, 2017), 36.

[5] Adani Ngullie, "Status of Women in Naga Society," *Women in North East India: Status, Empowerment and Development Perspective*, edited by Harendra Sinha, Sanjay Sinha (New Delhi: Akansha Publication House, 2013), 75, 76.

[6] M. Horam, *Nagas Old Ways and New Trend* (New Delhi: Cosmo Publications, 1988), 61.

[7] J. H. Hutton, *The Angami Nagas: With Some Notes on Neighboring Tribes,* 2nd ed. (London: Oxford University Press [1921], 1969), 168.

[8] Kewepfuzu Lohe, *Socio-Cultural Heritage of Kuzhami Chakhesang Nagas* (Pfutsero: Kuzhale Zawe, 2010), 6.

[9] Interview with Zhiekhwelhi-u Nuh, Former Women Leader of Mesulumi Village, 3 January 2015.

[10] Vezuhu Keyho, "Culture, Traditions and Festivals of the Chakhesang," *The Years Commemorating Golden Jubilee CSU (1947-1997): Souvenir* (Dimapur: CSU, 1997), 10, 11.

[11] Interview with Zhiekhwelhi-u Nuh..., 3 January 2015.

1.3. Socio-Cultural Life

Headhunting made life intricate for the family of a defeated warrior. History reveals that during that long nonappearance of the men in the homes and villages, it was the women who shouldered the workload and carried out all the chores for the function of the homes. A woman in reality does more work than the man.[12] The wife is forced to undergo the burden of having to look after the children with the stigma of being a widow and overworking to provide for the children. These were the invisible side and sorrow of women in one era that exposes the male-centeredness.[13]

1.4. Religious Life

Metimi (foreteller) is the one who claims to have contact with the spirits. In general, *Metimi* acts as the mediator between human being and spirits.[14] Lhoupezü-u Nuh, act as a diviner in Thetsümi village. After encountering with the spirit she started healing people. The village began to implement the instructions[15] given by spirit through her directions. She mentioned the names of the spirit as "*Nihova*," "*Yisu*," and "*Meshilo*."[16] Then, in 1930, she told that the British soldiers were coming to their village to stay on the hillock. Therefore, all the neighboring villages were also asked to come and level the site. The hillock was leveled to be occupied by the soldiers. Hence, it was declared by the Government as common land. Then, in 1966, her predictions were fulfilled as the Thetsümi Baptist Church building was constructed in that leveled hillock. Thus, she played the role of *metimi* (foreteller) and has greatly contributed to the village and prepared the way for Christianity.[17]

The *Mawopi* (Village Priestess) enjoyed a very comfortable place as the wife of the *Mawo-o* (Village Priest). For instance, when the *Mawo-o* died leaving behind a minor, the *Mawopi* assumed all the charges of the *Mawo-o*. A renowned *Mawopi* worth mentioning is that of Chi-o *Mawopi* wife of

---

[12] Lovely Awomi James, *Tribal Theology: Reviewing the Naga Traditional Worldview…* 48.

[13] Eyingbeni Hümtsoe-Nienu, "Women's Experience of "Sorrow": Ending the Saga of "Headhunting"," *Nagas: Essays for Responsible Change,* edited by Eyingbeni Hümtsoe-Nienu, Paul Pimomo, and Venüsa Tünyi (Dimapur: Heritage publishing House, 2012), 70, 71.

[14] Lohe, *Naga Village: A Sociological Study…*, 118.

[15] The instructions given by the spirit are: Unmarried ladies began to keep their hair long which was forbidden earlier. Six days people were to work and have a genna-day (meni) on the seventh day.

[16] Interview with Veprechu Nuh, Thetsümi Village, 16 February 2015.

[17] K. Lasuh, "About Pfütsepa", *Thetsümi Baptist Church 75th Gospel Anniversary (1940-2015): Souvenir* (December 29-30, 2015), 24, 25.

Ngope *Mawo-o*.[18] Zehol also observes that among the Chakhesang Nagas, the wife of the traditional village priest wielded a lot of power and respect.[19] In Chakhesang tribe, a woman is selected as the first sower called *mushopü*[20] to perform rituals for the new crops. She will go to the field before anyone plucks the paddy and bring home.[21]

1.5. Political Life

Headhunting between inter-villages was a very common feature in the past. Therefore, some outstanding women were chosen as mediators called 'Demi' to mediate and call for peace between the warring villages. Apart from the above role, *Demis* were the only ones to carry the head of the slain one to the bereaved family. Their role was so important that it was tabooed to slain a *Demi*.[22] She was the only one for peace talks between two warring villages. Some of the *Demis* were: Kaponie-o,[23] Tariinie-o,[24] and She-o.[25] These women mediated between Khezhakeno and neighbouring villages.[26]

Women contributed much to the family and in the society and there were no marked difference in their worth to that of male counterparts. Similarly, the following section will study the participation of women after Christianity and the unequal treatment in the patriarchal structure of the society.

2. Participation of Chakhesang Women in the Society after Christianity

With the coming of Christianity, women had begun to open up to modern education where women had in the past been thought of as only suited to manage home. Number of women became officers in different fields. They began to take up leadership roles in the society as well. Women had formed

[18] Kevekha Zehol, and Lucy Zehol, "Women in the Chakhesang (Chokri & Khezha) Society." *Women in Naga Society.* Edited by Lucy Zehol (New Delhi: Regency Publications, 1998), 70-71.

[19] Zehol, "Women in the Chakhesang (Chokri&Khezha) Society,"..., 70.

[20] Vezuhu Keyho, "Culture, Tradition and Festivals of the Chakhesangs," *The years Commemorating Golden Jubilee, CSU (1947-1997): Souvenir,* edited by Yiepetso, Wepe and Vaprümu (Dimapur: CSU, 1997), 8, cited by Sashikaba Kechutzar, "The Role of Women in the Indigenous People's Religion of North East India," *Women's issues in the 21st Century,* edited by Narola Imchen (Jorhat: Women Study Centre ETC, 2001), 97.

[21] Kechutzar, "The Role of Women in the Indigenous People's Religion of North East India,"..., 97.

[22] "Demi Pi-o Yiekiinyii" (i.e., It is tabooed to slain a Demi).

[23] She mediated between Khezhakeno and Mao-Maram Villages.

[24] She mediated between Khezhakeno and Poumai Villages.

[25] She mediated between Khezhakeno and Lanumi or Nenumi (i.e., Poumai villages).

[26] Zehol, "Women in the Chakhesang (Chokri & Khezha) Society"..., 70.

different societies and organizations in partnership with Government and Non-Governmental agencies for the upliftment of women in particular and also for the welfare of society in general.

2.1. Family Institution

The multiple role women play often goes unnoticed, for the simple fact that people have gotten used to their services that seem to come naturally.[27] All the household works are expected to be done by women even if they are working women and majority of the husbands would not even know that it is their responsibility too as fathers to care for their children. However, there are some exceptional cases where men even do most of the household work more than their wives do.[28] Wife's opinion was highly respected in the important decision-making at home. Nevertheless, when it comes to the society a woman's opinion was ignored. A healthy marriage needs decisions made together.[29] The belief that a daughter takes away educational and health assets from her birth family to her marital family, causes discrimination against girls in education, health, and family decision-making. It leads to discrimination even to the food on the plate between brothers and sisters even in Christian homes in this high-tech, globalized world and in poorer families contributing to female malnutrition.[30]

2.2. Chakhesang Women Welfare Society (CWWS)

The Chakhesang Women Welfare Society (CWWS) was formed in 1976, with a view to uplift the position of women in the Chakhesang community.[31] The Welfare Programs were run and looked after by the Chakhesang Baptist Churches Council (CBCC) Women department from the inception till 1980. However, due to the increase of the workload of Welfare activities, it was resolved to give autonomy to the CWWS.[32] The aim and objective of CWWS is to work for the welfare of Chakhesang community through addressing the needs of women, create opportunities of trade and undertake social welfare activities to support children, women and the weak, underprivileged, promotion

---

[27] Vishü Rita Krocha, "Empowering Women," *Secheku Women Welfare Society 25th Anniversary (1987-2012): Souvenir* (September 28-29, 2012), 28.

[28] Lalnghakthuami, "A Critical Re-Look at the Tribal Heritage from a Feminist Perspectives," in *Theologizing Tribal Heritage: A Critical Re-look,* edited by Hrangthan Chhungi (Delhi: ISPCK, 2008), 217.

[29] Beulah Wood, "Can we Learn from St. Paul," *Side by Side: Gender from a Christian Perspective*, edited by Beulah Wood (Bangalore: SAIACS, 2007), 237-238.

[30] Wood, "Can we Learn from St. Paul," *Side by Side*..., 238-239.

[31] "Chakhesang Women Welfare Society-Then and Now," *Chakhesang Women Welfare Society 25th Anniversary (1976-2001): Souvenir* (October12-14, 2001), 3.

[32] "CWWS as Separate Development under CBCCWD," *Chakhesang Women Welfare Society 25th Anniversary (1976-2001): Souvenir* (October12-14, 2001), 6.

of traditional crafts and textiles etc.[33] Some of the activities which CWWS have taken up are: Self Help Group, Seminars and Workshops, Weaving & Tailoring, Preserving Traditional Attires, Fruit Processing and Preservation Unit etc.[34]

2.3. Chakhesang Mothers' Association

Chakhesang Mothers' Association (CMA) was formed in the year 1986. Zaposhelu Venuh is the present President of Chakhesang Mothers' Association (CMA). She said: "It's high time for the womenfolk to voice out that gender equality is being enforced worldwide. Thereby, the status of women will never be inferior to that of men."[35] It aims to improve the social life and to enhance cultural life of the Chakhesang society. The activities of CMA are conducting seminars, CMA take initiative for liquor and drug prohibition, condemning the rape cases, involve in peace talks, fight against social evils in the society, etc. Every mother in a family is a member of CMA; hence they collect Rs.10 from each member.[36]

2.4. Women and Education

Chakhesang society began to recognize the participations that the educated women were making. Women began to hold important posts in government offices, NGOs and in various other fields.[37] Accordingly, Chakhesang women in the modern and post-modern period own land, houses and moveable properties, as a result of earning considerable salaries.[38] Education empowers both men and women to earn better income, participate in decision making and contribute to the standard of living.[39] Chakhesang women have played a key role, individually and collectively, in helping their communities survive and in enabling human development. In spite of rapid increase in the number of educational institutions in the region, it is seen that there is still a veiled bias towards boys. This needs to be looked into in order to avoid lopsided progress in education.[40]

---

[33] Interview with Neikhwepe-u Khalo, Former President of CWWS, 19 December 2014.

[34] Interview with Vechülou Kanuo, Director of CWWS, 6 December 2014.

[35] "Seminar on women development held at Phek Village," http://www.morungexpress.com/local/93830.html (9 Feb 2015).

[36] Interview with Zaposhelü Venuh, President of CMA, 6June 2015.

[37] Interview with Zacive Thele, retired Additional Secretary. 14 January 2015.

[38] Interview with Meniele K. Nuh..., 19 December 2014.

[39] *Gender Budgeting Manual, Government of Nagaland* (Kohima: Department of Planning and Coordination Government of Nagaland, 2011), 110.

[40] Chotisuh Sazo, "Parliamentary Secretary, Social Welfare and Women Development, Nagaland," *Kangla Online*(March 22, 2011), http://kanglaonline.com/2011/03/speech-of-shri-

2.5. Women and Politics

Among the Chakhesang tribe, so far no real space is given for women to contest. The votes of women are appreciated equally with that of men. However, when it comes to the choice of candidates preferences are given to men whereas people feel hesitant to choose women candidate.[41] It is clear that the traditional attitude continues to influence, regarding the participation of women in politics. In every political society political power is often assumed that women are "uninterested" in politics.[42] Sano Vamuzo called upon the women to keep themselves updated and well informed of their rights effecting them and stressed on the importance of gender equality.[43]

In spite of Christian faith and organized governmental system and modern education which brought about changing attitudes and new perspectives, still there exist traditional attitudes of domination among the Chakhesang people. To have holistic and inclusive community, the next section will be an implication for the society in order to understand women partnership in different spheres of life.

3. Guiding Principles for Creating Holistic and Inclusive Community for the Society

Women are yet to be fully empowered because of the various hindrances in women's participation in society. Patriarchal culture has mainly influenced male dominated reading of the Bible which seriously distorts the image of women and their position in the society. Women are treated as inferior and they themselves have the self understanding of being so. This concept has so long chained them that it hinders them from full and active participation in different spheres of life. For that reason, holistic mission for inclusive community is considered necessary. The following concerns will be discussed: partnership of women and men, restructuring some traditional practices and society's response in uplifting women in the society.

3.1. Holistic Mission for Inclusive Community

3.1.1. The Need for Partnership of both Women and Men

There are many instances where woman are advised to resign from their jobs if their husband can earn enough to maintain the family as most of the works that

---

chotisuh-sazo-parliamentary-secretary-social-welfare-and-women-development-nagaland/ (9 Feb 2015).

[41] Interview with Sano Vamuzo, NSCW Chairperson, 3 March 2015.

[42] Brinda Newman, "Women in Politics," *Women and Society: A Reader in Women's Studies*, edited by Nirmala Jeyaraj (Delhi: ISPCK, 2008), 130.

[43] "Women Commission stresses on awareness of rights," *The Shillong Times* (April 29, 2012), http://www.theshillongtimes.com/2012/04/29/nagaland-women-commission-stresses-on-awareness-of-rights/ (24 Feb 2015).

women are engaged in are considered supplementary and complementary to men.[44] Vimeno Lasetso remarks that most of the mothers are undergoing great pressure managing between home and ministry responsibilities. Therefore, men should understand the demands of the changing times and give helping hand to their wives in household tasks and childcare responsibilities so that she women can balance their ministries and careers.[45]

3.1.2. Restructuring Some Traditional Practices

In the past men had to be physically fit in order to defend the village therefore women performed almost all the works at home.[46] The practice of patriarchy is the root cause of women's discrimination, exploitation and marginalization in the society.[47] The Church reminds her falsely that she is physiologically "unclean" to be a Pastor, to serve the body and blood of Jesus, to conduct baptism etc. Deacon Board, the main body of a local church is managed by men, who are neither aware nor bothered that there are no women in the meeting. Churches today greatly need women's participation in its planning and programs if they wish to provide holistic service to the people of God.[48]

3.1.3. Society's Response in Uplifting Women

The Nagaland State has adopted a Policy for Women empowerment to ensure women in their rightful place in society as equal partners with men.[49] Vechisalu Nukhu,[50] articulated that restriction on women's mobility, exclusion of women to participate in political spheres, domestic violence etc are also a violation of human rights, because women's rights are human rights.[51] NSCW[52] chairperson Sano Vamuzo highlighted provisions and rights

---

[44] "Gender and Related Concept," *Gender Budgeting Manual, Government of Nagaland* (Kohima: Department of Planning and Coordination, Government of Nagaland, 2011), n.p.

[45] Interview with Vimeno Lasetso, SATHRI Research Scholar, Jorhat, 21 August 2017.

[46] Adino Vitso, *Customary Law and Women: The Chakhesang Nagas* (New Delhi: Regency Publications, 2003), 82, 83.

[47] Lalnghakthuami, *Understanding Jesus - Indigenous Women's Perspective* (Delhi: ISPCK, 2014), 146.

[48] Eyingbeni Hümtsoe–Nienu, "Theological Perspectives on Select Concerns," *Nagas: Essays for Responsible Change,* edited by Eyingbeni Hümtsoe–Nienu, Paul Pimomo, Venüsa Tünyi (Dimapur: Heritage Publishing House, 2012), 71-72.

[49] Chotisuh Sazo, "Parliamentary Secretary, Social Welfare and Women Development, Nagaland," *Kangla Online* (March 22, 2011), http://kanglaonline.com/2011/03/speech-of-shri-chotisuh-sazo-parliamentary-secretary-social-welfare-and-women-development-nagaland/ (9 Feb 2015).

[50] She was the former President of Chakhesang Women Welfare Society (CWWS).

[51] "Women's Rights are Human Rights," *Morung Express* (December 11, 2013), http://www.morungexpress.com/local/108052.txt (9 Feb 2015).

[52] Nagaland State Commission for Women.

of women under Protection of Women from Domestic Violence Act 2005.[53] In Numbers 27:1-8, the daughters of Zelophehad fought for their rights.[54] Thus, women have their rights just as the men.

Conclusion

Chakhesang women occupied a comparatively leading position in the family relating to household affairs. Despite the fact that women participate significantly in all spheres of life they were not regarded in the society. In spite of all that, there were also some prominent women who took up leadership roles in religious life and society such as the role of *Metimi* (foreteller), *Mawopi* (priestess), *Demi* (mediator) etc. In a patriarchal society like Chakhesang, priesthood is mainly confined to males and yet there were instances of women exercising priestly function like the *Mawopi* (priestess). Thus, women should not be hindered because of biological differences and the ideology of the inferiority of women needs to be changed. Dedication, commitment and sacrifice of women must be utilized at the maximum level in the society just as the *Mawopi* (priestess) have the same status with the *Mawo* (priest). It is found that in spite of women greatly participating in the society, their status is still inferior to the male counterparts in the Chakhesang community. The holistic missiological approach in this research indicates that the Trinitarian nature of community makes it possible for the people to look up to God as the one who causes relationship and who continues to unite humanity as men and women in the world of dignified equals. The Triune God in partnership has achieved that for the world through Christ. Just as man was not complete when created, until joined by a woman, so also the current leadership will not be whole until women take their rightful place alongside with men.

---

[53] Sano Vamuzo"Alcohol a Major Cause for Domestic Violence,"http://www.nagalandpost.com/channelnews/state/StateNews.aspx?news=TkVXUzEwMDAwOTgwOA%3D%3D-h0PjD4e2Z6k%3D (3 March 2015).

[54] Winifred Irene Paul, *Women's Walk* (Delhi: ISPCK, 1999), 23.

8

Reading the Nexus between the Domination of Women and the Domination of Nature

Lovely Awomi James

Introduction

It was in the 1990s that the ecological crisis hit our attention so hard and demanded our critical response. Prior to that there were also several consciousness voiced by various individuals and groups, but it did not gain the global attention. Elizabeth Janeway succinctly stated that, "when things are stable, the world can run on the basis of limited input; not when the skies are falling."[1] We now have no other choice than to strenuously work in order to restore and recover the balance of the entire ecosystem. While there have been various efforts and movements toward developing an integral eco philosophy and eco spirituality, the most recent and promising attempt seems to be coming from the women's perspective all the world over. Feminism is an umbrella concept that permits meaningful talk of a variety of feminisms such as, Liberal feminism, Marxist feminism, Radical feminism, Social feminist, Black and Third World feminism and so on. Despite important differences among these feminisms, all feminisms are committed to the elimination of sexism

---

[1] Elizabeth Janeway, *Powers of the Weak* (New York: Alfred A. Knopf, 1980), 185. (Hereafter cited as Janeway, *Powers of the Weak*).

– the power and privilege of men over women. Feminism is a movement and theory that aimed at ending male-gender power and privilege, wherever and whenever it occurs, and creating practices and theories, which are, not male-gender powered and privileged.[2] The key element in their eco philosophy is the reclaiming of the feminine in women, in the earth, and in the divinity. This is so because they believed that the present ecological crisis has at its root, the male/patriarchal devaluation of the feminine aspect and anything that is non-male. Vandana Shiva writes: "The violence to nature as symptomatized by the ecological crisis, and the violence to women, as symptomatized by their subjugation and exploitation, arise from this subjugation of the feminine principle."[3] Feminists thus see the interconnectedness between the male domination of female and the human domination of the mother Earth, as arising out of the same root namely, the patriarchal understanding of the world, and of God.

The present paper is an attempt to present the feminist roots of eco philosophy. This will be done so by first briefly defining feminism in connection with ecology, then, it will focus on ecofeminism, which is the main strand under feminism that deals with the theology of the total ecosystem's relation – humans and the natural world. This will be followed by the various issues that come under its critique – woman/nature connection, instrumentalism, varied forms of dualism(s); next, under our study comes the Gaia tradition as one of the main traditional sources from which ecofeminism draws its insights, its critique of Christianity and Western philosophy, and patriarchy. Finally, we shall look at how ecofeminism develops its spirituality out of all these. Then the paper will close with a brief evaluation and conclusion.

Feminism and Ecology

With the fact that there are various types of feminism, we need to define very specifically what type of feminism we are talking about at present, in relation to its connection with ecology. Since time immemorial, women have been connected with nature. Both women and nature are seen as passive, matter, body, and therefore without any intrinsic worth of their own, except for instrumental purpose and value, under the male (who is said to be active, who possessed the spirit, intellect and reason) domination. Both women and nature were thus categorized as the inferior beings whose only purpose of being created is to serve the needs of the higher beings i.e., men. As a

[2] Karen J. Warren, "A Feminist Philosophical Perspective on Ecofeminist Spiritualities," in *Ecofeminism and the Sacred,* edited by Carol J. Adams (New York: Continuum, 1993), 121-122. (Hereafter cited as Warren, *A Feminist Philosophical Perspective*).

[3] Vandana Shiva, "Development, Ecology, and Women," in *Healing the Wounds: The Promise of Ecofeminism,* edited by Judith Plant (Philadelphia: New Society Publishers, 1989), 84.

result, the feminism in question can be defined as a refusal. It is "a refusal by the original 'other' in hierarchical human society, woman, to be reduced to silence or to be the 'other' any longer."[4] It is a commitment to recognize women as autonomous persons, valued for their diversity of gifts, and to free them to speak on their own behalf. Moreover, ecology in relation to women in this respect can be defined as "a consistent refusal to fragment the world into separate and independently existing parts."[5] It refuses to fragment the world by separating human beings from inert matter and other living organisms in such a way that distances them "above", "apart from" or "beyond" the natural systems of which they are a part. It considers the world as a whole, interconnecting non-hierarchical system containing diverse as well as cooperating equalities.

Feminism linked to ecology thus, is committed to challenge both these sets of assumptions that arise from men's social domination of sex, race and class, and to reveal that there is interconnectedness of both these twin oppressions. It refuses to accept the hierarchical fragmentation of the world that distances powerful men from subordinate women. It refuses to settle for any social or theological system that is patriarchal, which in turn programme both men and women to regard themselves as in control of the rest of the natural world.

Ecofeminism

Radical/cultural feminists, who saw the link between the domination of women and the domination of nature, developed what we now call as 'ecofeminism'. It is the coming together of ecology and feminism. The linkage results from the striking parallels, which exist between the treatment of the Earth and the treatment of women. For instance, the traditional role of both is seen as an instrumental one, where both are viewed only in terms of having usefulness rather than as having any intrinsic worth of their own. Moreover, each of them occupies a sharply differentiated place in the hierarchical system. As a result, feminist roots of eco philosophy can best be explained through the contributions of the ecofeminists. According to Carolyn Merchant, the term *ecofeminism* was first used by Francoise d'Eaubonne in 1974, in order to signify women's potential for bringing about an ecological resolution to ensure human survival on the planet.[6] This praxis of feminism and ecology together may be viewed as a natural development where both share common goals. Both of them see

---

[4] Anne Primavesi, *From Apocalypse to Genesis: Ecology, Feminism and Christianity* (Kent: Burns & Oates, 1991), 25. (Hereafter cited as Primavesi, *From Apocalypse to Genesis*).

[5] Primavesi, *From Apocalypse to Genesis*, 25.

[6] Carolyn Merchant, "Ecofeminism and Feminist Theory," in *Reweaving the World: The Emergence of Ecofeminism,* edited by Irene Diamond and Gloria Orenstein (San Francisco: Sierra Club Books, 1990), 100.

that all parts of the system, whether the human or the nature, have equal value. Whenever there is ethical conflict in the system, it must be resolved from the perspective of the good of the whole as well as from the perspective of the interconnectedness of all of the parts. Both regard the Earth's house and the human's house as habitats to be cherished, and to regard these habitats as life-sustaining rather than as life-destroying. Moreover, both regard process as primary–all process takes place within the understanding that the total amount of energy leaving and entering the Earth is a constant, that all parts are engaged in a dynamic process of growth and development, death and decay, and their input into this process needs to be valued.[7] This insight calls for cooperation and reciprocity rather than useless expended energy. All must return as much as possible to a system out of which they have taken.[8]

Ecofeminism grew out of radical, or cultural, feminism, which holds that identifying the dynamics–largely fear and resentment–behind the dominance of male over female is the key to comprehending every expression of patriarchal culture with its hierarchical, militaristic, mechanistic, industrialist forms.[9] There are many paths that led to the emergence of ecofeminism. One path into ecofeminism was the study of political theory and history. Radical/cultural feminists who had been exposed to Marxist analysis in the 1960s as well as those who had gone to study critical theory and social ecology in the early 1970s built upon the framework of dominance theory. They rejected the Marxist assertion that domination is based mainly on money and class, and argued that if there is a universally dominated class, then surely it is the women. Such radical/cultural feminists, who through experiencing and naming the inadequacies of classical dominance theory that ignore nature as well as women, moved in the direction of ecofeminism.

The second path into ecofeminsm is exposure to nature-based religion, usually that of the Goddess. It was in the middle of 1970s that many radical/cultural feminists discovered through historic and archaeological sources, a religion that honored the female and one that revered the nature itself. Here they found something that was cosmologically wholesome and healing. They discovered the Divine as immanent in and around us. The most intriguing was the discovery of the sacred link between the Goddess in her many guises and totemic animals and plants, sacred groves, and womblike caves, in the moon-rhythm blood of menses, the ecstatic dance – the experience of knowing Gaia,

---

[7] Eleanor Rae, *Women, the Earth, the Divine* (New York: Orbis Books, 1994), 24. (Hereafter cited as Rae, *Women, the Earth, the Divine*).

[8] Carolyn Merchant, "Feminism and Ecology," in *Deep Ecology: Living as if Nature Mattered*, edited by Bill Devall and George Sessions (Layton, UT: Gibbs M. Smith, 1985), 231.

[9] Charlene Spretnak, "Ecofeminism: Our Roots and Flowering," in *Reweaving The World: The Emergence of Ecofeminism,* edited by Irene Diamond and Gloria Feman Orenstein (San Francisco: Sierra Club Books, 1990), 5. (Hereafter cited as Spretnak, *Ecofeminism*).

her voluptuous contours and fertile plains, her flowing waters that give life, her animal teachers.[10]

The third path into ecofeminsm comes from the environmentalism. For many women with careers in public policy, science and technology, public-interest environmental organizations, and environmental studies programs in universities, their initial connection with feminism was the liberal-feminist attention to how and why their progress on the career ladder was blocked. Eventually they encountered a book, an article, or a lecture with ecofeminist analysis, and then suddenly their career work was framed with a radically different meaning. Similarly, women and men who become involved with Green politics for environmental reasons discover ecofeminism and deep ecology there. Moreover, college students, male and female, who enroll in an environmental studies course are also exposed to ecofeminist analysis and recognize a depth that was not present in their prescribed text books.

According to Karen J. Warren, there are four insights that serve as the foundation for ecofeminism. They are: One, that the oppression of women and the oppression of nature are deeply connected issues; Two, that an adequate understanding of these twin oppressions calls for an understanding of the nature of these connections; Three, that feminist theory and practice call for an ecological perspective; and four, that ecological problems can be solved only if they include a feminist perspective.[11] Ynestra King also holds these four beliefs on which ecofeminist principles are based, but in an expanded form-the interconnectedness of all of life and the critical need for diversity.[12] Within the boundaries of ecofeminism there are certain things which could not be included such as any of the "isms" of domination of sexism, naturism, racism, classism, heterosexism etc. What it includes is that, which treats women's moral experiences respectfully, and the interaction of the human and the non-human worlds.

Ecofeminism's ability to address the issue of power in its negative form of "power over" entails more than its ability to question the status quo and to develop coalitions around issues. Its strength also is in it being a way of thinking; a philosophy that offers an alternative vision. Moreover, its means and its end are identical; it increases the well-being of its adherents, and it

---

[10] For instance, a snake coiled around the arms of an ancient Goddess statue, teaching lessons of cyclic renewal and regeneration with its shedding of skins, as merely a member of the ophidian order in the reptilian class of the vertebrate phylum. Cf. Spretnak, *Ecofeminism*, 5.

[11] Karen J. Warren, "Feminism and Ecology: Making Connections," *Environmental Ethics* 9/1 (1987): 3, cited in Rae, *Women, the Earth, the Divine,* 24.

[12] Ynestra King, "The Ecology of Feminism and Feminism of Ecology," in *Healing the Wound: The Promise of Ecofeminism*, edited by Judith Plant (Philadelphia: New Society Publishers, 1989), 19-20. (Hereafter cited as King, *The Ecology of Feminism*).

operates out of the present virtues of joy, community, and integrity.[13] What is most distinctive in ecofeminism is that it extends the various feminist critiques of social systems of human domination to include domination of non-human nature.[14]

Ecofeminism and Its Issues

We will now look at some of the pertinent issues that have emerged as important to ecofeminism in the context of its being a philosophy. The issues include the relationship between women and nature, and the issues of instrumentalism, and dualism.

The Issue of Women/Nature Nexus

One of the main thrusts of ecofeminism is that there is a natural nexus between women and nature. Such nexus is expressed in various spheres like art, culture, literature, theology etc. Ecofeminists hold the view that since the beginning of the human species, women have been very closely associated with nature. When the attitude toward nature is one of reverence and awe,[15] this association benefits women as well. However when the attitude toward nature is one of rape and plunder,[16] as it is today, this association does not benefit women.[17] This contemporary articulation of the women/nature nexus goes back at least to the 1940s for example, when, Simone de Beauvoir "mentioned in

[13] Marilyn French, *Beyond Power: On Women, Men, and Morals* (London: Jonathan Cape, 1985), 445. (Hereafter cited as French, *Beyond Power*). Though French is referring here to feminism, the extension of her thinking into ecofeminism is well warranted.

[14] Ecofeminists claim that *naturism*, the unjustified domination, exploitation, or destruction of non-human nature, is wrong and ought to be eliminated. Cf. Warren, *A Feminist Philosophical Perspective*, 122.

[15] As ecological feminists claim through the immense contribution of archaeological and historical scientific discoveries that there was truly a period when the feminine was revered and worshipped in the nature-based and female honoring religion of the Goddess in Europe, the Near East, Persia, and India. Cf. Charlene Spretnak, *Lost Goddesses of Early Greece: A Collection of Pre-Hellinic Mythology* (Ann Arbor, MI.: Moon Books, 1978); James Lovelock, *Gaia: A New Look at Life on Earth* (New York: Oxford, 1979); Lovelock, *The Ages of Gaia: A Biography of Our Living Earth* (New York: Bantam Books, 1988).

[16] Ecofeminists, in contrast to deep ecologists who hold that our estrangement from nature began with classic Greek humanism and the rise of a Judeo-Christian culture, writes that it actually began around 4500 B.C. with the Indo-European invasions of nomadic tribes from the Eurasian steppes, who replaced the nature-based and female-honoring religion of the Goddess, with their thunderbolt God, removing that which is held sacred and revered from the life processes of the Earth to the distant realm of an omnipotent, male Sky-God. Hence it is in the Indo-European Revolution, and not in the Scientific Revolution of the sixteenth and seventeenth centuries, that one finds the earliest sources of desacralized nature, the foundation of a mechanistic worldview. Cf. Spretnak, *Ecofeminism*, 11.

[17] Rae, *Women, the Earth, the Divine*, 25.

passing the attitudes of men (under patriarchy) to nature and women and the connection between the two."[18] In the Indian tradition also this conflation of women and nature is seen. In the ancient scriptures of India, one can see nature portrayed in feminine categories. Aruna Gnanadason has argued that this conceptual framework of nature as the embodiment of the female principle should form the core of a feminist theology in India.[19] This link as seen in the Indian tradition is done on the basis of sexual and biological considerations, on the assumption that both nature and women have the power of fertility. Two presuppositions arise in India out of this: One, it serves as a natural model to legitimize the male's domination and control of the common female, and, two, it confers sacredness to nature and attribute power (shakti) to both women and the earth. However, it has been noted that the women/nature conflation has very often been used mainly to subjugate women and nature by the ruling male class in India as it is in the West.[20]

The writings around the women/nature nexus fall into two categories: those who respond directly, either negatively or positively; and there are those who question the validity of the analogy itself as well as the validity of the question itself. Those who respond in the negative call for the severance of the women/nature connection and the integration of women into culture.[21] Then, those who respond in the positive have chosen to reinforce and celebrate the women/nature connection. However, we need to note that this reinforcement may either take place in the context of an adversarial position toward men and patriarchal culture, or it may be in consciously choosing the women/nature connection as the basis for creating a whole new kind of culture.[22] Next, those who question the validity of the analogy itself would suggest that the use of "power over" (control) would provide a better measurement of the diminished

---

[18] For further reading see, Spretnak, *Ecofeminism*, 8.

[19] George Mathew Nalunnakkal, *Green Liberation: Towards an Integral Ecotheology* (Delhi: ISPCK/NCCI, 1999), 146.

[20] Janet Chawla, "Gendered Representations of Seed, Earth and Grain: A Woman Centered Perspective on the Conflation of Women and Earth," *Journal of Dharma*, Vol. XVIII/3 (July-Sept, 1993), 237.

[21] Simone de Beauvoir, who is considered as the mother of modern feminism represents this position. According to her, equating ecology (*nature*) with feminine (*women*) is something that irritates her; that they are not automatically one and the same thing at all. Cf. Alice Schwarzer, *After the Second Sex: Conversations with Simone de Beauvoir* (New York: Pantheon, 1984), 103. Moreover, Sherry B. Ortner also holds this position. Cf. Sherry B. Ortner, "Is Female to Male as Nature Is to Culture?," in *Woman, Culture and Society*, edited by Michele Zimbalist Rosaldo and Louis Lamphere (Stanford, CA: Stanford University Press, 1974).

[22] Ynestra King comes under this response. Cf. King, *The Ecology of Feminism*, 22-23; See also Ynestra King, "Healing the Wounds: Feminism, Ecology, and the Nature/Culture Dualism," in *Reweaving the World*, edited by Diamond and Orenstein (San Francisco: Sierra Club Books, 1990), 106-121. (Hereafter cited as King, *Healing the Wounds*).

status of women and nature in societies. They see this diminishment as highest where control is valued the most – even in those societies where men are associated with the wild (nature) and women with the tame (culture).[23] Moreover, there are others who have not only questioned the validity of the analogy but also the validity of the question itself. According to Catherine Roach, the question itself is wrong because of two reasons. One, no beings can be closer to nature than any other beings, since everything is part of nature. Second, the question perpetuates an environmentally unsound nature/culture dualism. To this, Eleanor Rae, adds another point, i.e., the validity of the analogy can be called into question because culture itself cannot exist outside of nature.[24] All these diverse responses are called for, as the paths to ecofeminism are diverse just as there are many kinds of feminisms.

Judith Plant summarizes the positive contribution of ecofeminism, stating that Ecofeminism, by speaking for both the original others, seeks to understand the interconnected roots of all domination as well as ways to resist and change. The ecofeminist's task is one of developing the ability to take the place of the other when considering the consequences of possible actions and ensuring that we do not forget that we are all part of one another.[25] Hence, the post-patriarchal society would be based on the understanding that all are a part of nature. It is also observed that it is not only the ecofeminists who have this encompassing worldview, but the 'deep ecologists'[26] as well, with whom ecofeminists are said to have much in common. Despite many convergences between them, there are also divergences. For example, deep ecologists would cite anthropocentrism, dualism, atomism, hierarchalism, rigid autonomy, and abstract rationalism as the structures and beliefs responsible for the present destruction of our biosphere.[27] On the other hand, ecofeminists would add to the above list, androcentrism (man-centeredness) rather than anthropocentrism (human-centeredness) as the key to the current destruction. Ecofeminists thus sees patriarchy as the foundation for the other categories. They furthermore

---

[23] Marilyn French is one who comes under this position. For further reading on the issue, see French, *Beyond Power*, 70.

[24] Rae, *Women, the Earth, the Divine*, 27.

[25] Judith Plant, "Searching for Common Ground: Ecofeminism and Bioregionalism," in *Reweaving the World*, edited by Diamond and Orenstein, 156.

[26] The phrase *deep ecology* was framed by the Norwegian philosopher Arne Naess, in contrast to what he saw as the band-aid approach of "shallow environmentalism."

[27] As a result, deep ecologists would argue that only a revolution in humanity's understanding of itself and its place within nature will bring about the dramatic changes in human behavior that are necessary at this critical juncture in human and terrestrial history. Cf. Michael E. Zimmerman, "Deep Ecology and Ecofeminism: The Emerging Dialogue," in *Reweaving the World: The Emergence of Ecofeminism,* edited by Diamond and Orenstein, 138-141. (Hereafter cited as Zimmerman, *Deep Ecology*).

argued that deep ecology has been hampered by the lack of women's voices in its development.[28]

The sources and consequences of cultural conceptions about women and nature arose in and have been perpetuated by a male-oriented culture. So, far male attitudes toward nature and women have been accepted as the law itself, as universally adequate. However, as seen, today feminists of both the sexes have called them into question. Ecologically speaking, we need to see them in the context of women's perception and experience of what it means to be defined in every sense, by the dominant partner in a relationship. We are aware that images are forever in dialogue with action. Therefore, ecofeminism, as it brings about an ecological paradigm into the picture from a feminist perspective, it discloses the intrinsic link in a male-dominated culture between how one speaks about women and nature and how one behaves towards them.[29]

Ecofeminism and Instrumentalism

Ecofeminists state that one of the striking parallels between the treatment of nature and the treatment of women is that the traditional role of both is seen as an instrumental one. In other words, both are seen in terms of their usefulness to others rather than as having intrinsic worth in their own right.[30] Instrumentalism: is seen as strongly connected to a theory of discontinuity; its existence depends on a recognition of a sharp distinction between the sphere of means and the sphere of ends; and, also there is an understanding that that which is being treated instrumentally (women and nature) is passive and therefore lacking in ends of its own, which leaves the superior side free to impose its own ends.[31] The expression "market values" including such data as the Gross National Product, dominates our culture and our power politics, which is the shorthand for all the factors involved in an instrumental view of the earth. When we talk about the "value" of the rainforest, it is based on its potential as timber, as a source of usable drugs, as land for ranching cattle, as a source of minerals, as a quantifiable factor in the destruction/retention of the ozone layer, as a gene pool for countless valuable (rare/unknown) species, and so on. All these economic indicators of value are based on utilitarian motives. In classic utilitarianism, actions are right when they maximize human pleasure, or when they minimize human pain. This is a "consequentialist" doctrine, which focuses on the consequences or outcomes of actions in determining

---

[28] Zimmerman, *Deep Ecology*, 142.

[29] Primavesi, *From Apocalypse to Genesis*, 35-36.

[30] Val Plumwood, "Ecofeminism: An Overview and Discussion of Positions and Arguments," in *Women and Philosophy*, edited by Jana L. Thompson (*Australian Journal of Philosophy*, supplement to vol. 64, 1986), 120, cited in Rae, *Women, the Earth, the Divine*, 30.

[31] Rae, *Women, the Earth, the Divine*, 30.

their value for humanity.[32] Ecofeminists trace this kind of rationalization back to the beginnings of the patriarchal age when people decided to use metal for weapons, for the purpose of aggression rather than for self-defense. At the same time, it has also been noted that the creation myth adopted by Christianity puts down not only women but also children (by their exclusion) and animals, plants, and nature itself. According to the scripture, men, and the male god are free, to mistreat, sell, violate, sacrifice or kill women, children, plants, animals, and nature.[33] This instrumental way of thinking and living accelerated down through the centuries until recently when the world seem to have woken up to realize its mistakes.[34]

Ecofeminists sees this crisis of instrumentalism as a result of our failure to define ourselves in relational terms. Hence, they suggest a redefinition of the human as the only way toward any solution. And in this redefinition, both the distinctness and the connectedness of the human, as well as of all of the other participants of creation, must be held together in creative tension. Subsequently, in their search for a model that embodies this new consciousness, they argue that it must be outside of this consciousness that has created the crisis in the first place. It would therefore mean those populations, individuals, who have participated less in fostering in the present crisis. And those populations are none other than the poor, indigenous people, and women.

Ecofeminism and Dualism

The principle of dualism is another important issue that comes under the critical scrutiny of ecofeminist literature. Dualism can be defined as the "theory which admits in any given domain, two independent and mutually irreducible substances."[35] Central to the ecofeminist understanding of dualism is the placing of the substances in a hierarchical system, where one term would be regarded as normative and the other as derivative or even defective. Dualism on the basis of gender has been identified as the root cause of oppression of women and nature by ecofeminists. Under their study come various levels

---

[32] Primavesi, *From Apocalypse to Genesis*, 55.

[33] Elizabeth Dodson Gray, *Green Paradise Lost* (Wellesley, MA: Roundtable Press, 1981), 5-6.

[34] Some ecofeminists see eating of animals (non-vegetarianism) as a form of instrumentalism. For example, Carol J. Adams considers eating of animals as a participation in an ideology of dominance and power over, a failure to define the self in relational terms. She argued that instead of romanticizing about the Native American peoples who hunted animals, we should be honoring those Native Americans who were basically horticulturalists and vegetarians. Cf. Rae, *Women*, the Earth, the Divine, 31, f.n. 40.

[35] Dagobert D. Runes ed., *The Dictionary of Philosophy* (New York: Philosophical Library, 1942), 84.

of dualism: dualism between God and the world; body and spirit; male and female; humans and nature etc.

Cosmic Dualism

Ecofeminists hold that dualism is predominantly a Western feature, influenced by Greek metaphysics, which was later upheld and incorporated by Christianity. According to them, the basic theological dualism is the cosmic dualism, the split between God and the world. It sees God as a God of ultimate value and a material universe as having no intrinsic worth. This cosmic dualism is believed to have emerged from our doctrine of creation ex nihilo, a doctrine that ecofeminists says is not in the Bible, because, the Bible rather shows that the Divine spirit formed the cosmos out of chaos. As a result they trace this dualism between God and the world to the philosophical traditions like that of Plato, to the time of Descartes, and to the theological traditions of Origen and Augustine, who held that man's creation in God's image pertained to his mind alone and not to his body.[36] According to Grace Jantzen, this primary dualism of God/World (creation *ex nihilo*) was itself constructed as a theological justification for patriarchy.[37] This kind of dualism makes us go against the reality that we are all parts of the universe, and creates an unbridgeable chasm not just between us and the rest of the universe, but also within our very selves.[38]

Dualism between Creation and Redemption

Another set of dualism that ecofeminists argue against is, the dualism as seen in Christian history, where it appears as a conflict between the patriarchal order of creation and the egalitarian order of redemption. However, this Christian historical dualism was broken by the Enlightenment, which severed the connection between patriarchalism and the theology of creation. It was replaced by a theology of creation based on an understanding of all humans as being created in the imago Dei. Thus, all Christians were freed to establish the just social order rather than waiting for heaven.[39] Ecofeminists would further include in this egalitarian community not only human but the non-human as well.

---

[36] Rae, *Women, the Earth, the Divine*, 32.

[37] Grace Jantzen, "Healing our Brokenness: The Spirit and Creation," *The Ecumenical Review* 42/2 (1990): 137. She argues that the dominant group of ruling class males constructed a worldview which set them apart as normative humanity, over against the "other" – women, other races, the poor, the earth – and then fashioned in their own image a God of ultimate value, power, and rationality over against the disvalue, passivity and irrationality of the opposite side of the duality.

[38] Jantzen, *God's World, God's Body* (Philadelphia: The Westminster Press, 1984), 148.

[39] Rosemary Radford Ruether, "Christianity," in *Women in World Religions*, edited by Sharma (New Delhi: South Asia Books, 1995), 228-29. (Hereafter cited as Ruether, *Christianity*).

Male/Female Polarities

The third set of dualism within the Christian history is seen in the male-female relationship. Rosemary Radford Ruether observed that throughout its history, the dominant and official view has been that of a theology of subordination. It is a theology based on the notion of male headship of the order of creation. This notion basically identifies patriarchal social order with the natural or divinely created order. Male headship is thus regarded as rooted in the intrinsic nature of things and willed by God. Any effort to upset this order by giving women autonomy or equal rights would constitute a rebellion against God and would result in moral and social chaos in human society. This notion that male headship is the order of creation usually carries with it the hidden or explicit assumption that God is male or at least properly represented by symbols of paternal authority.[40] Women were thus considered as the moral, ontological, and intellectual inferiors of men. Feminist scholars like Ruether and Fiorenza would argue that such theology of subordination is not true to its Christian origin, as we see from the writings of Christian scriptures. They trace this Christian dualism back to the ancient Greek philosophy[41] where women are the primary symbols of the lower moral and ontological sphere which is to be repressed and subjugated. Plato's creation story, **Timaeus**, is an abstract and metaphysical story. The primal dualism underlines the reality – dichotomy between the invisible and the eternal sphere of thought and the visible realms of corporeality. The creator, Demiurgos, the cosmic artisan, creates by **making**. Demiurgos, first shapes the space into primal elements of fire, air, water and earth (cosmic body) and shapes the world soul and infuses it into the cosmic body as its principle of life and motion. The creator then goes on to shape human souls from the same elements from which he had mixed the world soul, but in a more diluted form. He then infuses the souls with celestial truth, which are incarnated into the male bodies. Hence, the male souls are entrusted with the job of controlling the chaotic sensations that arise from the body. Here, if the souls are successful, they return to their celestial home; if they are not successful, then they will be reincarnated as lower beings – women. Still more, their failure will result in being born as an animal. The social messages of this Greek creation myth are: dichotomy between mind and body; and the supremacy of mind over the body that extends to the hierarchy of male over female, and humans over animals.[42]

---

[40] Ruether, *Christianity*, 208.

[41] Most particularly Plato and Aristotle advocated the male-female polarities in terms of form-matter, rational-irrational dualism. Women were to be considered as semi-humans and a deformity.

[42] George Mathew Nalunnakkal, *Green Liberation*, 161-162. See also Ruether, "Ecofeminism: Symbolic and Social Connections of the Oppression of Women and the

The key to the historic agency of women with respect to the nature/culture dualism lies in the fact that the traditional activities of women such as mothering, cooking, healing, farming, foraging etc., are as social as they are natural. As a result, the task of an ecological feminism[43] is the organic forging of a genuinely antidualistic, or dialectical, theory and practice. Instead of succumbing to nihilism, pessimism, and an end to reason and history, ecofeminism seeks to enter into history, to a genuinely ethical thinking – where one uses mind and history to reason from the "is" to the "ought" and to reconcile humanity with nature, within and without.[44]

Domination of Our Natural Bodies

Another central area that ecological feminism employs as their concern in overcoming misogynist dualism is that of body consciousness. Accepting our bodies as they are, and learning to work with them to become healthier is a basis for cultural and political liberation. It is noted that in many patriarchal cultures, women are complicit in the domination of our natural bodies, seeking to please men at any cost.[45] Ynestra King made a critical examination that even the Western feminists despite their condemnation of others, they will do anything to their bodies – sunbathing, submission of our bodies to dangerous surgical procedures, using of deodorants, dieting etc., – making our natural bodies our mortal enemies. Thus women submit themselves to participate in the domination of nature under this patriarchal age of science and technology. Ecofeminists therefore suggest that we need to develop an appropriately mediated relationship to our own natures, we need to learn to work with the restorative powers of our bodies, using medical technologies and drugs sparingly. Health therefore should also be fully understood as an ecological and social rather than as an individual problem.

Ecofeminism and the Gaia Tradition

Ecofeminism draws its sources also from the ancient traditions with the help from a revolution in archaeology. It makes it possible to document the way people lived and thought in prehistoric times. These traditions go back thousands of years. One such fascinating discovery was about our past – for millennia[46] prehistoric societies worshipped the Goddess of nature and

---

Domination of Nature," in Adams, *Ecofeminism*, 21.

[43] Ecological feminism and ecofeminism are used here interchangeably.

[44] King, *Healing the Wounds*, 116.

[45] For instance, the Chinese foot binding, performed by women, is a widely cited example of misogynist domination of women's bodies.

[46] A span of time many times longer than the 5,000 years conventionally counted as history.

spirituality, our great Mother, the giver of life and creator of all. In addition to that these societies were structured very much like the peaceful and just society that we are now trying to construct.[47] However, this does not mean that these were ideal societies, but that they were not warlike like ours today. Their societies do not portray women's subordination to men, and they did not regard the Earth as an object for exploitation and domination. They were sound ecological societies that had an awareness to treat the Earth with reverence and respect. This reverence for the life-giving and life-sustained powers of the Earth was rooted in a social structure that does not subjugate women and "feminine' values such as caring, compassion, and non-violence, under the men and the so-called masculine. The life-giving powers incarnated in women's bodies were given the highest social value.[48]

The Gaia Tradition Re-discovered and Redefined

Gaia is the Greek name for the Earth.[49] Ecological feminists endeavor to reclaim Gaia as Mother-Earth in order to create a new earth-based spirituality rooted in ancient traditions that revered both the earth and the female deities. They bring under their critical re-examination the accounts of Western civilization that describes anything and everything prior to Judeo-Christian as "pagan." In contrast to the impression these accounts gives (that these prior societies were both technologically and morally "primitive"), recently found knowledge from archaeology shows that such view is a highly misleading one.

The Paleolithic Period

The Paleolithic period, 2.6 million years back, is generally considered to mark the beginning of the Western civilization. According to the conventional view of this period, the art as the story of "man the hunter and warrior," the hundreds of highly stylized carvings of large-hipped, often pregnant women found in the caves were dubbed as "Venus figurines" – ancient obscene objects, "fertility cult." They were often viewed as obese, distorted erotic symbols, probably prehistoric counterparts of pornos. However, a careful unbiased study of these strange figures shows that they are representations of the life-giving powers of

---

[47] Riane Eisler, "The Gaia Tradition And The Partnership Future: An Ecofeminist Manifesto," in *Reweaving The World: The Emergence of Ecofeminism*, edited by Diamond and Orenstein, 23. (Hereafter cited as Eisler, *The Gaia Tradition*).

[48] In the words of Greek archaeologist Nicolas Platon, who for 50 years excavated the civilization of Minoan Crete where this type of social organization survived until approximately 3,300 years ago, it was a social organization where "the whole of life was pervaded by an ardent faith in the goddess Nature, the source of all creation and harmony." Cf. Eisler, *The Gaia Tradition*, 24.

[49] Gaia is the ancient earth-mother who brought forth the world and the human race from the gaping void, chaos. See, Carolyn Merchant, *Earth Care: Women and the Environment*,

the world. They are the precursors of the Great Goddess still revered in historic times as Isis in Egypt, Ishtar in Canaan, Demeter in Greece, and later, as the Magna Mater of Rome and the Catholic Virgin Mary, the Mother of God.[50]

Another hitherto misinterpreted area was on the Paleolithic drawings and stone and bone engravings. They were interpreted as barbed weapons. The earlier scholars could not figure out why in these pictures the arrowheads or barbs were all going the wrong way. It was only when these pictures were re-examined by an outsider did it become clear that these were not pictures of weapons at all. Rather they were the images of vegetation: trees and plants with their branches going exactly the right way.[51]

The Neolithic/Agrarian Age

The next phase of human culture (8000-1500 B.C.) also comes under re-examination. The conventional view is that the most important human invention – the development of the technology to domesticate plants – was also the beginning of male dominance, warfare, and slavery. In other words, with "man's" invention of agriculture came not only male dominance but also warfare and a generally hierarchic social structure. Once again the evidence contrasted the conventional view. Anthropologists today believe that the domestication of plants was probably invented by women, and not by men. A closer look at the new data about the first agrarian or Neolithic societies reveal that all the basic technologies on which civilization is based were developed in societies that were not male dominated and warlike.

Hence, with the help of scientific and extensive archaeological excavations, it is revealed that in these highly creative societies women were held in high esteem and they also held important positions as priestesses, craftspeople, and elders of matrilineal clans. Contrary to what we had been taught about these societies,[52] these were generally peaceful societies where women and men lived in harmony with one another and with nature.

Therefore the striking feature about the Gaia hypothesis[53] is that in essence it is a scientific update of the belief system of Goddess-worshipping prehistoric societies. In these societies the world was viewed as the great Mother, a living entity who in both her temporal and spiritual manifestations creates and nurtures all forms of life.[54] Ecofeminists sees this consciousness

---

[50] This was pointed out by UCLA archaeologist MarijaGimbutas and other archaeologists.

[51] Eisler, *The Gaia Tradition*, 24-25.

[52] As male-dominated and highly violent.

[53] A new scientific theory proposed by biologists Lynn Margulis and James Lovelock that our planet is a living system designed to maintain and nurture life. See Eisler, *The Gaia Tradition*, 26. See also Rae, *Women, The Earth, The Divine*, 68.

[54] Eisler, *The Gaia Tradition*, 26.

of the essential unity of all forms of life in modern times preserved in the numerous tribal cultures that revere the Earth as our Mother. They discover that these cultures, which have often been described as "primitive" by anthropologists, were in fact very rich with sound ecological insights for us the so-called "civilized" people of today.

Therefore the rediscovery of these ancient traditions paves the way for us to break free from our alienation from one another and from nature. The reclamation of these traditions is considered to be the basis for restructuring our present crisis-ridden society. However, an uncritical suggestion to reverse the structure of society is not what is being intended. Rather it simply means that we need to reclaim those life-affirming elements and insights which could offer much positive remedies to help usher in healing touches to our diseased world of today.

Critique on Christianity and Western Philosophy

Today there is a widespread view that the present eco-crisis is undoubtedly the result of the attitude towards the environment, which is 'Western' in origin. It is a product of Semetic religions – Judaism, Islam, and, particularly, Christianity – and Western philosophy. According to this view, the understanding of nature, of human destiny, and even of the human body that we find in Western religion and philosophy, led us to an indifference towards exploitation, even animosity towards nature.[55] The Western Christianity developed its creation story out of the synthesis of the Hebrew account of creation (Gen. 1 and 2), the Greek and the scientific-philosophical perspectives reflected in Plato. It retains the symbolism of the 'rational soul' as 'masculine' and the 'irrational' body, passions and emotions as 'feminine.' This gave birth to the division between equality of souls in relation to God and inequality of bodies and status across gender and class hierarchy.[56]

The question whether it is really true that the Western thought and Christianity propagated a negative attitude toward the environment, had been mostly answered in the positive. Our Christian heritage largely draws on the teachings of our so-called great teachers like Thomas Aquinas. Though he did not extensively deal with the humanity's relation to the natural world as a whole, sufficient answers can be drawn out from his views concerning our treatment of the non-human creatures. In the *Summa Contra Gentiles*, he opined that by the natural order of divine providence the passive non-human creatures are

[55] William Street, "Christianity, Western Philosophy, and the Environment," in *Eco-dynamics of Religion: Thoughts for the Third Millennium,* edited by Augustine Thottakara (Bangalore: Journal of Dharma & Dharmaram Publications, 2000), 179.

[56] Nalunnakkal, *Green Liberation*, 162.

there for the use of the active rational humans.[57] Thus, the humans who have immortal soulsare justified for ill-treating the non-humans who do not have. So, also Immanuel Kant argues that there are universal and absolute moral principles that govern the relation of rational beings toward each other, yet they do not include any direct duties or obligations toward the natural world. Hence, it is plausible to hold that Kant who advocates that as long as the non-human creatures serve humans' benefit any infliction upon them is justified, also fall in the same line with Aquinas, that legitimizes humans' supremacy over the natural world, and men's superiority over the natural females of the human society.

Thus, feminists critical evaluation of such traditions brought to light that we need to critically re-read our religious and philosophical teachings and identify what is good and what is harmful. They point out that the traditional Christian doctrine of creation is hierarchical, anthropocentric and androcentric. They challenge these traditions that have for quite too long done far more harm than good, and calls for change in our attitude, in our theology, faith and practice.

Patriarchy: The Father of All Dominations

Ecofeminists see Patriarchy as the root cause of fostering all kinds of dominations in the society. Patriarchy can be simply defined as *male supremacy or domination over, and of anything and everything that is not male.* Particularly, it defines man as the intelligent rational being and woman as the emotional, irrational being, thus legitimizing male superiority over the female. It places women and nature under the same inferior category, whose basic purpose of existence is to please and serve the higher good of men. This definition of the male excludes women from their full humanness; men were seen as fully human, whereas women were seen as semi-human. Patriarchy divides humanity into two rigid sexes, which grants men greater power than, and over women.[58]

It further sees women as being closer to nature and that they possess innate powers which men sees as threatening. This power of women and nature is seen as malevolent and therefore, had to be diminished and subjugated by the men's divinely vested benevolent power. The interdependency of men and women and of all forms of life is cut off by the perpetration of Patriarchy. It places all rights in the male, granting males almost all of the economic and political power in the society. Thus it transforms the women into helpless dependent minors in the hands of the adult males,[59] leaving the destiny of women in their custody.

[57] *Summa Contra Gentiles* III, 112.

[58] French, *Beyond Power*, 79.

[59] French, *Beyond Power*, 83.

Another significant finding in the work of ecofeminists was that development is considered as a project of the West. It viewed "Development" largely from the perspective of economic growth, and from the perspective of the "winners" in our societies.[60] It undermines the knowledge, wisdom, labour of the women and other traditional tribal societies. Vandana Shiva succinctly pointed out that Development is Western Patriarchal project because it has emerged from centers of Western capitalist patriarchy, and it produces those patriarchal structures within the family, in community and throughout the fabric of Third World societies. Patriarchal prejudice colours the structures of knowledge, as well as structures of production and work, that shape and are in turn shaped by "development" activity. Women's knowledge and work as integrally linked to nature is marginalized or displaced, and in its place are introduced patterns of thought and patterns of work that devalue the worth of women's knowledge and women's activities and thus fragment both nature and society.[61]

Shiva further states that maldevelopment is the new source of male-female inequality. Maldevelopment militates against the equality in diversity of men and women in the society. The interdependence and complementarity of the male and female domains are to be understood as equality in diversity and not as inequality. The dominant mode of perception that creates maldevelopment is reductionism, duality, and linearity, which cannot understand equality in diversity. It cannot understand how forms and activities can be equally significant and valid even though different.[62] Subsequently it results in the violation of the integrity and harmony of all life – between people and nature and between men and women. Maldevelopment is thus stripped off of the creative life force and power of the feminine principle, viewing women and nature as the "other," as the passive worthless self. Hence, ecofeminists challenges such fragmenting structures and calls for the re-affirmation of the lost feminine principles that include both women and nature, thus making connections between all forms of life into one harmonious whole.

---

[60] Aruna Gnanadason, "An Eco-Feminist Theology," in *Quest for Gender Justice: A Critique of the Status of Women In India*, ed., Sebasti L. Raj, S. J. (Madras: T. R. Publications, 1993), 197.

[61] Vandana Shiva, *Staying Alive: Women, Ecology and Survival in India* (New Delhi: Kali For Women, 1988), 3-13. See also Vandana Shiva, "Development as a New Project of Western Patriarchy," in *Reweaving the World*, edited by Diamond & Orenstein, 198-200. (Hereafter cited as Shiva, *Development as a New Project*).

[62] Shiva, *Development as a New Project*, 192.

Ecofeminist Spirituality: An Earth-Based Spirituality

Ecofeminist spirituality is an earth-based spirituality.[63] It is rooted in three basic concepts – immanence, interconnection, and community. Immanence is the understanding that the Earth is alive which is a part of the living cosmos. It means that "spirit, sacred, Goddess, God, is not found outside the world somewhere" but "in the world", because "it is the world, it is us."[64] This understanding of the universe as a living entity then removes the breach between religion and science as opposed to one another. Rather it unites them as complementary to each other as someone has said that science without religion is "lame" and religion without science is "blind."

Next, our understanding of the Earth as active living being leads us to understand that everything is interconnected.[65] Nothing is independent of another. We are all connected to one another as in a web-like existence. Interdependence is central for everything in this universe of ours. This interconnection becomes the second principle in ecofeminist spirituality. Thirdly and finally, these interconnections bring us to the conclusion that we are all part of a living community, the Earth. Our spirituality, our politics of life, are all rooted in community and not somewhere outside it. The goal of our existence is not individual salvation or enlightenment, but rather "the creation of a community that becomes a place in which we can be empowered and in which we can be connected to the Earth and take action together to heal the Earth."[66]

> All of these principles call for a challenge to be taken up immediately – to live a life of preservation. And this act of preservation can be done only through compassion, the ability to really feel for all beings on the Earth. It emphasizes "life" in everything. It challenges the limited views of development that measures the value of God's creation only in profit perspective. It thus affirms the sacredness of all of God's creation – both animate and inanimate. It rejects the anthropocentric, androcentric worldview that legitimizes the belief that the Bible sanctioned the random

---

[63] Although there might be some who would disagree that an earth-based spirituality promotes harmful gender-stereotypical views of women as "closer to nature than men," less rational, detached, and objective or more emotional, attached, intuitive, and subjective than men; and also whether it mystify and romanticize nature etc. See Karen J. Warren, "A Feminist Philosophical Perspective on Ecofeminist Spiritualities" in Adams, ed., *Ecofeminism and the Sacred*, 124.

[64] Starhawk, "Power, Authority, and Mystery: Eofeminism And Earth-Based Spirituality," in *Reweaving the World*, edited by Diamond & Orenstein, 73: (Hereafter cited as Starhawk, *Power, Authority, and Mystery*).

[65] Starhawk gives the example of our human body, how what happens to one part of our body effects other parts also.

[66] Starhawk, *Power, Authority, and Mystery*, 74.

extraction of the Earth's resources for humans' benefit and legitimizes man's exploitative power over women and nature.

Furthermore, ecofeminists re-affirms the Earth as "Mother." It emerges from the alternative model Genesis story of creation propagated by the ecofeminists like Sallie McFague – procreation model, against the production model. Symbolically, it denotes that creation is a physical act where the universe is bodied forth from God's womb. This model relates all reality in a dynamic way. McFague therefore states that the dynamic, changing, evolving body - that is, all reality do not grow from God, but in, through and toward God.[67] This model becomes ecological as it relates all reality to God. McFague continues to explicate the concept of sin in a wider perspective. She views sin from three arenas, which we commit – between human beings, between humans and animals, and between humans and nature. She defines this as – Us versus Us: Living a Lie in Relation to Other Human Beings; Us versus Them: Living a Lie in Relation to Other Animals; and, Us versus It: Living a Lie in Relation to Nature.[68] Thus, it calls for us to stop living a lie but to right the wrong that we have for so long been committing. It calls for the total restoration of relationships between and within the web of life on earth.

Ecofeminists proposes a worldview that truly honors the differences in a complementarity attitude and praxis. At the same time they also propose that we furthermore need to have a sense of unity alongside the honoring of differences.[69] As a result, it brings forth the issue of diversity and unity within the total ecosystem. It celebrates life in its beauty of diversity, and in its unbroken unity. An ecofeminist ethic is therefore a critique of the male domination of both women and nature. It recognizes the varied forms of women's voices across all race, class, and age, and it builds upon these voices to bring out positive changes within the entire home on earth.

An ecofeminist spirituality therefore invites us to live life with integrity. Knowing that we are all part of this living body – the Earth – makes the world the terrain where we each, and all, live out our spiritual growth and development. It challenges all forms of dominations. It is not interested in who holds power, but in how power is being wielded. It strives for the transformation of power itself. This is so because, for too long and for many, power is understood only in a negative light. It is not power in itself that is negative but that how power is used which gives it either positive or negative meaning. Power becomes

---

[67] Sallie McFague, *The Body Of God: An Ecological Theology* (Minneapolis: Fortress Press, 1993), 153. (Hereafter cited as McFague, *The Body of God*).

[68] McFague, *The Body of God*,116-124.

[69] Rae, *Women, the Earth, the Divine*, 35-37.

negative when it is used as "control over,"[70] and ecofeminists pointed out that this new value of "control over" replaced the traditional values of fertility, continuation, and sharing. Therefore, ecofeminists posit that we can replace this harmful "power over" concept with "power for" – that which enables, which enhances and gives life, which co-creates with the Spirit.[71] Upon this power of transformation we are called to celebrate, to use, and to be changed by it.

Thus, ecofeminism and its spirituality call us for transforming our theology, thought patterns and our actions in relation to nature and to one another. It calls us to rethink and reformulate our understanding that there is an ontological chain of being; that spirit and matter are to be seen as the inside and outside of being. And despite our drawing of rich valuable resources from the prehistoric past, the answer to our present ecological crisis does not lie in our return to matri-centric society (reversing the order). What we need today is neither matri-centric nor patri-centric worldview, but rather an omni-centric one – a true honoring of unity in diversity in all of the Creation.[72]

Evaluation

Feminism, with its broad wings challenges and fights against all oppressive elements in the society. One particular strand of feminism that has gained much recognition and appreciation is in their involvement and contribution toward the philosophy and theology of nature. Feminist eco-philosophy calls us to the recognition that there is an ontological chain of being within the entire ecosystem – between humans, between humans and the rest of creation. It challenges the age-old philosophies based on hierarchical, dualistic principles that have contributed toward the normatization of the male over the female alongside nature. It calls for a new theology of all relationships – God and the world; humans and nature; and, humans and humans particularly men and women.

---

[70] Marilyn French argues that this has become the dominant value of the Western world. See French, *Beyond Power*, 75.

[71] They cite their basis from the scriptures viz., Micah 3:8; I Thess. 1:5; Rom 15:19; Lk 1:35, 4:14; Acts 1:18, 10:38. Elizabeth Janeway gives a very interesting explanation: that the ability to question the strong is the basis for the power of the weak. And our power is based on the fact that it is the weak who give the strong legitimacy. Power is an interdependent relationship between the governors and the governed. As a result it is a process and not a thing. She also says that the governors are answerable, not to a Divine authority, but to the governed alone. This is so because power is based in the community. See Janeway, *Powers of the Weak*, 108-22, 157-67. Nevertheless, the present writer would argue that any and every governing body is answerable to both God and the governed people or community – vertical as well as horizontal.

[72] Thomas Berry, *The Dream of the Earth* (San Francisco: Sierra Club Books, 1988), 138-39.

Ecofeminists view the ecological crisis as inextricably linked with the problem of women, under the patriarchal structures of society. They believe that ecological problems cannot be solved in separation from women's issues. This is so because they unearthed the twin oppression of nature and women as being perpetrated under the same oppressive structures and norms of patriarchy. Therefore they emphasize that women's voice or participation is a must if at all we hope to bring out viable results. They believed that the reclamation of the feminine principles in both women and nature will be able to contribute far better implications and practices for our nearly collapsed eco system.

Ecofeminist spirituality centers on the concepts of immanence, interconnection, interdependence, and, community. They view the Earth as 'Mother'- the living and life-giving entity – one that encompasses all forms of life within her, in a web-like existence. It upholds complementarity and unity, equality in diversity. It sees all, human and non-human alike as having their own intrinsic worth. It therefore resists all concepts and ideologies that perpetuate polarities and dichotomies between humans and the rest of creation. And it calls for all to participate in developing this kind of home – pluralistic, inclusive and non-sexist.

Finally, one could make few critical observations on the feminist eco philosophy. Despite the value of drawing on the prehistoric traditional societies that was non-violent and matri-centric, there is the danger of radical romanticizing about a very distant past, which could either remain an unrealizable dream, or, which could if over emphasized, present itself as a wrestling of power against patriarchy – which then would defy all of its (feminist eco philosophy) claims for building a non-sexist and life-affirming society. Moreover, in its attack on the male power over the female and nature (both feminine), over emphasis on the feminine issues and its liberation, against everything male or masculine, could then also result in an establishment of a reversed order of hierarchical, dualistic worldview. Therefore, these observations, though which may seem unlikely to them, should be kept in mind as one continue to work for developing aneco-philosophy through the reading of women.

Conclusion

Ecological feminism or ecofeminism has much to contribute toward the solution for our present eco crisis. It converts our human consciousness toward the Earth – to recognize our interconnectedness and interdependency in the web of life. It calls each and every individual, men and women alike to wake up from our long stupor, and fight for the environmental justice, which includes both human and non-human (nature) justice. It challenges us to rethink and reformulate our theology about God, world, and about life in general. We are called to a new form of intelligence that is non-dualistic and Earth-centered. It calls for both human and non-human to work together as friends, as family members in one home (Earth).

9

Reclaiming Women's Spirituality

Esther Jish Rengma

1. Introduction

What would happen if a woman tells the truth about her life? Women today are daring to tell their truth, to break open the silence in which their lives have for generations been shrouded. More and more of them are using the language of spirituality as they name their new sense of themselves, of the world, of God and of their own Godlikeness. Women's Spirituality is the spiritual essence within each woman. This can be experienced as a unique sense of serenity, joy and fulfillment. This is the presence of the Sacred Feminine, or the Goddess. When women come together in a spiritual group, the Sacred Feminine can be felt very strongly. Women's Spirituality Circles provide a sanctuary for women to uncover the truth of who they really are, inherently powerful and free. The subject on spirituality is a diversified theme that can be addressed from various viewpoints. Therefore, it is important that we focus our attention to a particular concern. Therefore this article deals with the nitty-gritty of women's spirituality; the paper begins with how one views women's spirituality; it explores the beginning of reclaiming women's spirituality, answering the question, "why do we need to reclaim women's spirituality?", it also informs about the concept of goddess and questions what the world would look like if God were still imagined in feminine image today? It further discusses

Christian woman and spirituality, the emerging Asian women's spirituality, and the paper concludes with a reflection from Tribal women's understanding of spirituality, so as to reclaim women spirituality that has long been neglected and sidelined.

2. How does one View Women's Spirituality?

Spirituality can be described as a process of transformation and growth, an organic and dynamic part to human development, of both individual and society.[1] Spirituality is about wholeness, holiness and alignment with the emotional, intellectual, psychic and physical self. And Women's Spirituality is that which comes of being within the body of a woman. It values life, creativity, empathy, receptivity, diversity and the natural cycles that ensure constant change. It values the ordinary daily rhythms of living. Above all, as with the nature of a women's body, the most valued and important focal point, the source of all power and life, is HIDDEN deep within.[2] Women who take part in Women's Spirituality Circles describe them as energizing, a truly safe space, and deeply sacred.[3] For this very reason Women's Spirituality brings a totally different perspective from that of all the mainstream spiritualities. As women, we need to reclaim what has always been our birthright - our own spirituality. As we reclaim this we can envision a world where we bring a way of being that redresses the balance in a very out of balance world.

3. The Beginning of Reclaiming Women Spirituality

The institution of Monasticism offered women real opportunities for professional ministry during the Middle Ages. After the fifth century, Monasticism began to flourish which became an important outlet for women who desire to commit their lives to the fullness of spiritual endeavors. In the west Monasticism for women began in A.D. 512 when Bishop Caesarius of Aries established a convent that was ruled by his sister Caesaria. The convent was permitted only to women and virgins because they need a lifetime commitment and have to renounce all claims to material wealth. The purpose of this convent seems to have been primarily focused on personal spirituality. According to Eckenstin, Monasticism from its beginning lay outside the established order of the church.[4]

---

[1] Ursula King, *Women and Spirituality: Voices of Protest and Promise* (London: Macmillan Education, 1989), 5.

[2] *http://www.yoni.com/cronef/womens_spirituality.shtml* (05.01.2018).

[3] *https://www.centreforwomensspirituality.com/* (02.02.2018).

[4] Narola Imchen, *Women in the History of Christianity* (Jorhat: TDCC, 2014), 76-77.

4. Why Do We Need To Reclaim Women's Spirituality?

Reclaiming is an organization of feminist modern witchcraft, aiming to combine the Goddess movement with political activism (in the peace and anti-nuclear movements). Reclaiming was founded in 1979, in the context of the *Reclaiming Collective* (1978–1997), by two Neopagan[5] women of Jewish descent, Starhawk and Diane Baker, in order to explore and develop feminist Neopagan emancipatory rituals. Today, the organization focuses on progressive social, political, environmental and economic activism. The current interest in feminine perceptions of the ultimate stems from a widespread sensing that many women's stories have not been adequately told at all and kept in silence. Of Mary, Luke wrote "But Mary kept all these things, pondering them in her heart" (Luke 2:19). Her word never became flesh and dwelt among us. Perhaps she never heard stories which could give her words for her own experience. Women find that self-identification with the sons and other male images and symbols in the language of the Bible and the tradition.[6] The Women movement of the late-nineteenth and mid-twentieth century provided Annie McGrew Bennet with a lens to explore how Christianity made Women subordinate. Annie rewrites some of the history with an eye towards inclusion of women whose names and stories have been passed over.[7]

---

[5] Modern paganism also known as contemporary Paganism and Neopaganism, is collective term for new religious movements influence by or claiming to be derived from the various historical pagan beliefs.

[6] Carol Christ, "Spiritual Quest and Women's Experience," in *Woman Spirit Rising: A Feminist Reader in Religion*, edited by Carol P. Christ and Judith Plaskow (New York: Harper Collins Publishers, 1979), 228-230.

[7] Annie McGrew Bennet, *From Woman-Pain to Woman-Vision: Writings in Feminist Theology* (Minneapolis: Fortress Press, 1975), 3-4.

5. In the Beginning There Was the Goddess

Some of the popular Goddesses were *Isis,*[8] *Durga,*[9] *Danu,*[10] *Tonantzen,*[11] *Gaia,*[12] *Artemis of Ephesus,*[13] and *Asherah.*[14] These names were once held with great reverence, and carried unimaginable power. They are the names of the Earth Goddesses throughout time in varying cultures, and if the list were to be complete, it would be very, very long. To worship the divine as feminine was a foregone conclusion. Women and the Earth had much in common. They still do. They were ruled by the cycles of the moon, they grew new life from within their bodies; they fed and sustained life with the abundance that flowed from their breasts. Women were magic and women still are.[15] There is a common notion in almost every society that women are considered as life-sustainers alongside their male counterparts. Some of the tribal Christians address the Creator God in neuter gender connotation. The Rengma Nagas believe in the creator God called *Sunggigu or Anyiza*. The word *Sun* means "hatch", *Gi* means "female" and *Gu* means "male."[16] There is an element of both male and female in the etymological word *Sunggigu.* According to the Angami Naga folklore, *Ukepenuopfii*, the mother goddess was the mother who gave birth to

---

[8] Isis is part of the Ennead of Heliopolis, a family of nine gods descended from the creator god, Atum or Ra. She and her siblings – Orsit, Set, and Nephthys-are the last generation of the Ennead, born to Geb, god of the earth, and Nut, goddess of the sky.

[9] A fierce goddess, wife of Shiva, often identified with Kali. She is usually depicted riding a tiger or lion and slaying the buffalo demon, and with eight or ten arms.

[10] In Irish mythology Danu is a hypothetical mother goddess of the Tuatha De' Dannan (Old Irish: "The people of the goddess Danu"), though primarily seen as an ancestral figure, some Victorian sources associate her with the land.

[11] In classical Aztec mythology and among present day Hahuas, Tonantzin is the title of an Aztec mother goddess.

[12] In Greek mythology gaia was the mother goddess who presided over the earth. She was the mate of Uranus and the mother of the Titans and the Cyclones.

[13] The Ephesians Artimes, the great mother goddess, also mentioned in Act. 19, was extremely popular in the ancient world, as we might deduce from the fact that copies of her cult statue have been excavated in many parts of the Roman Empire.

[14] Ashera was also given the title *chawat* from which the name *Haww*ah in Aramaic and the biblical name Eve are derived. Ashera poles, which were sacred trees or poles, are mentioned many times in the Hebrew Bible.

[15] https://searchingforeve.com/2016/06/24/in-the-beginning-there-was-the-goddess/ accessed on 24/01/2018.

[16] Khontele Seb, "The Religious Practices and Belief of the Rengma Nagas," in *Tribal Christian Theology: Methods and Sources for Constructing a Relevant Theology for the Indigenous People of North East India*, edited by Razouselie Lasetso and Yangkahao Vashum (Jorhat: ETC Programme Coordination, 2007), 190.

her two sons.[17] Subsequently the concept of mother goddess and neuter gender about God is not alien or unknown to the tribals in the context, which could be further developed in the process of reclaiming women spirituality.

6. What Would the World look like if Today God were Still a Woman?

What would the experience of women and men be had they grown up inside a culture where the divine was feminine, mothering, nurturing, powerful, and abundant? Where cooperation and unity were valued over individualism, where each decision was based on how it would affect the children, and their children, and their children's Children, seven generations down the line. It is not hard to imagine that the people who grew up steeped in such a culture might have values that were reflective of the feminine - values that favoured life, balance, equanimity, and inclusion rather than war, power-over, division and exclusion.

What such a world would look like is almost impossible to imagine. The dominant theology in the west has been masculine, and with it the eradication of the feminine. Even when there were Goddesses mentioned, they were subjugated and at the mercy of the Gods that took their place. The story that informs our culture is that God is a male, and his earthly representative and our Saviour is also a man. Through his holy spirit, God spoke to men on earth, and told them to write down his laws and edicts; by men, for men, to distribute as they saw fit. Women, under the rule of Yahweh, were property, much like goats and land. They were not permitted to teach, were encouraged to be meek, mild, and obedient to the men. This teaching is still found inside the walls of the majority of churches. In most denominations of Christianity, Islam, and Judaism, women are not permitted to hold positions of Pastor, Preacher, Priest, Deacon or Rabbi. Think about that. 50% of the populations are told they cannot hold positions of spiritual leadership based upon their gender.[18]

We can talk about progress, about feminism, about gender equality all that we want, but we must remember that we are talking about it *inside* of a paradigm where the masculine is valued as greater, is considered the "norm", and where anything outside of that norm is considered less-than, suspicious, and in need of being controlled.

---

[17] Riimatho Nyusou, "Nyi Nyieza Kiijiwa: The Concept of the Supreme Being from the Pochury Naga Perspective," in *Tribal Christian Theology: Methods and Sources for Constructing a Relevant Theology for the Indigenous People of North East India*, edited by Razouselie Lasetso and Yangkahao Vashum (Jorhat: ETC Programme Coordination, 2007), 304-305.

[18] https://searchingforeve.com/2016/06/24/in-the-beginning-there-was-the-goddess/ accessed on 24/01/2018.

7. Christian Women and Spirituality

Several years ago, noted feminist scholars wrote that, after centuries of 'spiritual colonization' by men, women had not yet found a language to describe the spirituality which they were beginning to live. That observation may already be outdated, judging by the growing volume of written and spoken material on the theme. First, what are women saying about spirituality in general? Most would see it holistically, linking it with the whole range of human development. For Joann Wolski Conn, Christian spirituality "involves the human capacity of self-transcending knowledge, love, and commitment as it is actualized through the experience of God, in Jesus, the Christ, by the gift of the Spirit."[19] Holism and self-transcendence also play a central role in the work of Denise Lardner Carmody. In her feminist spirituality, an upward spiral symbolizes the human impulse to stretch beyond ourselves, and 'Lady Wisdom' stands for the wholeness toward which we all aspire. The language of 'transcending' rather than 'denying' the self is significant for several reasons. Both Conn and Carmody, acknowledging their debt to Rahner, intend to evoke the image of the person as a being open to, and capable of communion with, ultimate Mystery. As such, the self to be transcended is good, graced, not evil. But, to maintain that movement beyond the self to others and to God is not only possible but necessary presumes that there is a self to move beyond. Herein lies a major problematic for women: socialized to place the needs of others before their own, women often repress awareness of their own rightful needs, or feel guilty and 'selfish' for even having them. So, the task of spiritual self-transcendence for a woman demands that she first grow into and claim her conscious and responsible selfhood.

Women's spirituality must be developed as a deep inner resource which shapes and sustains outward action-first for women themselves, then for others, for community building. Elisabeth Schussler Fiorenza stated that women's religious communities have always existed in the Catholic tradition, but they were practically all under male hierarchical control. Christian Feminist spirituality claims these communities of women and their history as our heritage and history seeks to transform them into *ekklesia* of women by claiming of their own spiritual powers and gifts,[20] which as a result would benefit the community at large.

Anne Carr makes an important distinction between 'women's' spirituality and 'feminist' spirituality. The former term refers to the ways in which women, in contrast to men, relate to the ultimate dimension of life, ways as distinctive

---

[19] Elisabeth Schussler Fiorenza, *In Memory of Her: A Feminist Theological Reconstruction of Christian Origins* (New York: The Crossroad Publishing Company, 1988), 347.

[20] Ursula, King, *Women and Spirituality: Voices of Protest and Promise* (London: Macmillan Education, 1989), 94.

as women themselves. Underneath the distinctions, we might notice some aspects common to women's experience, in contrast to men's: women seem more related to nature and to other people, more concrete, more heart-than head-centred, for example. On the other hand, feminists - described as 'those who are deeply aware of the historical and cultural restriction of women to a narrowly defined "place" within the wider human (male) "world" live a spirituality shaped by this consciousness.[21] Claiming firm Christian as well as cultural foundations, feminist spirituality is critical of the reality of women's subordination and committed to changing attitudes and structures which reinforce that evil.[22]

8. Emerging Asian Women's Spirituality

Women's struggle is part and parcel of the historical struggle for the holistic salvation of all humanity. Women can make a unique contribution toward this goal based on their spirituality, which is formulated through their concrete pro-life way of living and experiences. All the disastrous dimensions of patriarchal culture are typically exemplified in its demeaning, ignoring, and despising the very spirituality of women that is oriented toward, and sustaining life in, love. The spirituality affirming womanhood, reaching out for liberation of all women and all humanity, is emerging in all parts of the world, and Asia is not exempt.

8.1. Asian Women's Reality

Asian women share the domestic, economic, political, and religious oppression that their sisters all over the world suffer. However, the concretization of the oppression varies. The image of the subservient, servile Asian woman is behind the varied forms of trafficking in Asian women ranging from male order brides to prostitution. Because of the economic crisis, women in Asia suffer a double burden at work (low wages and sexual harassment) and in the case of rural women, a triple burden (field work, domestic work, and marketing of goods).[23] The Asian Women rejected and challenged the old notion of spirituality which is individualistic and away from the concerns of this world as practiced by mystics, monks, priests and religious individuals. They proposed a paradigm shift by defining their own understanding of spirituality which empowers them since it originates from the actual life experiences of women.

On the other hand, if we invest so much and the other party doesn't, we'll just feel cheated. "Spirituality is really a whole attitude. The essential

---

[21] https://www.theway.org.uk/Back/28Bechtle.pdf (15 January 2018).

[22] https://www.theway.org.uk/Back/28Bechtle.pdf (15 January 2018).

[23] Chung Hyun Kyung, *Struggle to be the Sun Again: Introducing Asian Women's Theology* (Mary Knoll: Orbis Book, 1990), 85.

element of authentic spirituality is being relaxed. If we are so tense, then there is something wrong." Spirituality, says Sr. Mary John, is "surrendering oneself to God. There is nothing more empowering than believing that within us lie the source of our power and strength."[24]

8.2. Interfaith Dialogue and Asian Women

Interfaith dialogue is an important part of the discussion of the emerging Asian women's spirituality. Ecumenical spirituality seeks unity of humankind in humility and reverence toward all life and all belief systems. Should Christian women condone all the structural and systemic evils Christian civilization has brought and concentrate only on securing privileged posts in a rotten structure? While it is important to fight for power positions when one is discriminated against for being a woman, it is as important to remain committed to bringing about radically new values that are people-oriented and concerned for life and a truly humane community.

In Asian women's emerging spirituality, God is one who unites, not one who divides people by creedal dogmas, happiness of the people of God in (God's) presence and company. ***Buddhism:*** The key word for the affirmation of the wholeness of life is to walk on. When one is a weakling, one is afraid of death and suffering and cannot walk on. Once we understand the Dharma, then we can adjust our inner condition to have a detached view of the world, less greed, hatred and delusion. ***Islam:*** All creation and humankind is one single whole, living through genesis, leading to the perfection of the person, i.e., the complete expression of one's creativity in terms of reaching towards two essential aims: (a) the relation between person and environment, and (b) the relation between person and God, i.e., the inner being. ***Hinduism:*** That which holds is Dharma, i.e., the order. It is a totality, a holistic point of view towards life... It is a question of an order, a complete, total view of things in which things have to fall in place. When we talk of the so-called Hindu, in fact, we are talking civilization and not of religion or faith. This statement represents the common views of these four major religions in Asia as they seek the holistic salvation of humanity. However, knowing that deep-rooted misogynous ideologies and practices are the reality in all the region's major religions and cultures, one cannot help raise the question: No matter how beautiful the idea of wholeness might be, can a patriarchal culture be inclusive of women's aspirations? What Elisabeth Schussler Fiorenza says about feminist suspicion in hermeneutics is echoed by Asian women who see the reality of discrimination against women in the name of respect for the traditional culture and regions.

---

[24] Mary John Mananzan and Sun Ai Park, in Journal of *Women in Action* No 3, Emerging Asian Spirituality Culled from the "Emerging Spirituality of Asian Women". 1996. 14.

Women find themselves very often excluded even by the ideology of wholeness and holistic salvation. It is because patriarchy can never be holistic. Patriarchy is basically androcentric, and it can never include women and children in the center of its world as equals. Even love for women and children is motivated by men's own selfish needs. That is the reason why women and children are put at the periphery although mechanisms of make-believe are woven into their emotional and financial dependency. In the coming reign of God, Christ will put children in the center (Mt. 19:13-15). In Jesus' life and mission of counter culture, he befriended all the downtrodden, including women. If a growing people's movement all over Asia is a sign of our times, the demands made by the various women's movements are the torch lighting the way toward the true wholeness of life.[25]

8.3. Consciousness of the Woman Question

There is a growing awareness among Asian women of the ramifications of the women's question. Their personal and social experiences, as well as their common struggle, have shaped the particular form of spirituality emerging among them. This spirituality is nourished by their growing understanding of their self-image, which has been obscured by the roles assigned to them by patriarchal society. This self understanding, in turn, influences not only their interpersonal relationships with the significant people in their lives, like their husbands, but also their relationships with men in general. It also forms the collective consciousness growing among them as they struggle against exploitation and discrimination, and as they experience the triumphs they achieve in the course. It is therefore not just a vertical relationship with God but an integral spirituality shaped by prayer, by relational experiences and struggle— personal, interpersonal, and societal.[26]

9. Tribal Women's Understanding of Spirituality

Narrowing down to the tribal context, they have so much to offer on the concept about women's spirituality that could enrich the contemporary understanding of women's spirituality. Tribal life spirituality could be seen from the ecological view in which people esteem and worship the Supreme Being as their God. For tribal their existence itself is sacred, it is their creed and scripture itself. Their spirituality can be understood from their life which is found in the form of oral traditions and in their daily activities. Women from dawn to dusk are involved in spiritual activities; she starts the day with

---

[25] Mary John Mananzan and Sun Ai, in *Journal of Women in Action* No. 3, Emerging Asian Spirituality Culled from the "Emerging Spirituality of Asian Women", 1996. 15-17.

[26] Mary John Mananzan and Sun Ai Park, in *Journal of Women in Action* No. 3, Emerging Asian Spirituality Culled from the "Emerging Spirituality of Asian Women" 1996. 17-18.

sincere prayer for the entire family, asking God's blessing before any members of her family gets up. She served the morning meal (breakfast) with devoted prayers, all the activities of the day she blesses, and she also close the day with thanksgiving prayers. Eventually, there are no activities in the family that women (mothers) are not involved, especially where her prayers and blessing are concerned.

Various tribal scholars have defined spirituality. A Wati Longchar defines spirituality as "the deeper dimension of the socio-ethical principle that governs the life of a community."[27] People understand spirituality in different ways, for some it is a life of contemplation and meditation, for others self sake of gospel and still others believe that it is a commitment to struggle for justice. While an anthropocentric spirituality is strongly emphasized in other traditions, the indigenous peoples share a common spiritual heritage and the most striking feature of this is their cosmic-centric perception of spirituality. Similarly, in recent times, theological thinkers among the tribals find a sense of cosmic oneness in the tribals' worldview. Thus tribal people spirituality is unique, wholly, holistic and realistic which is cosmic-oneness centred on the nature, land and creation.[28] This oneness and holistic concept of tribal spirituality could be further developed where man and woman may perhaps enjoy a higher sense of their spirituality. Another tribal scholar like Yangkahao Vashum while describing spirituality stated that "Spirituality for the Indigenous people is a way of living in the constant consciousness of the presence of God. It has to do with the way they live, act and related with God, fellow human being and the whole creation of God's creation."[29] Here the concept of relatedness with fellow beings could be a striking point where tribal spirituality could be taken to higher and deeper level. Somehow our relationship with the whole creation and with the creator God has been understand and easily comprehensible. Nevertheless when it comes to inclusiveness and gender spirituality tribal were not very open and sensitive to women. Present day tribal theologians and the emerging tribal theologians are very accommodative and considerate particularly to women's issues. Hopefully with the present trends there is a great scope to accentuate the issue of tribal women's spirituality.

---

[27] Wati Longchar, *Returning to Mother Earth: Theology, Christian Witness and Theological Education: An Indigenous Perspective* (Taiwan/Kolkatta: PTCA/SCEPTRE, 2012), 20.

[28] N. Tialemba Phom, "Affirming Indigenous Spirituality and Life for Climate Justice: From Women Perspective," in *Doing Theology with Indigenous People's Spirituality*, edited by R. Sashikaba Kechutzar and Zulunungsang Lemtur, (Kolkatta: Tribal Study Centre, ETC, Jorhat, Clark Centre for Peace Research & Action, CTC Mokokchung & SCEPTRE, 2016), 204-205.

[29] Yangkahao Vashum, "Space, Creation and Land: Indigenous Peoples' Spirituality," A Paper Presented at the Asian Theological Forum, Thiruvananthapuram, Kerala, 24th to 26th July 2014, 1-2.

Few tribal women and their views on tribal spirituality have helped us to understand the subject much deeper. According to Lovely Awomi James, tribal women were and are always to be found devotedly strong and unmoving in their relationship with God, whether it be at home or outside of the home. Tribal women and mothers were closely attached to their trust, belief and devotion in God in their daily lives. God, for tribal women, is a very "dear" Being, an intimate subject and object of devotion, trust and worship. Tribal women's image of God as the "Supreme Spirit and Author of Life; the Eternal Parent; the Most Trusted Friend and Confidant; the Provider of Resources for Sustenance of Life; and, Jesus as the Saviour and Liberator, should all be considered and understood in the light of their significance in the lives of tribal women in particular and in the context of the tribals in general."[30]

According to Narola Imchen, it has often been observed that, "the church is strong where the women group is strong and weak where the women group is weak... they are among the most regular worshippers in all the different church services."[31] Therefore, when we consider the participation and contribution of tribal women, it is tremendous and these are all part of women's contribution to community spirituality among the tribals. Unconsciously or consciously tribal women are actively involved in the entire spiritual affairs of the family, church and the community, however much recognition has not been accorded to them in proportion to the amount of time they invest upon it. This is an area we need to seriously look into, if we want to develop tribal spirituality more comprehensively by reclaiming women's spirituality.

Whilst the past can never provide a blueprint for the shaping of the present, it contains many spiritual treasures which can help us in living today. Many people began to be aware about the rich spiritual heritage of women which must be recovered from the past. This entails the time has come to uncover which has been hidden, left out; and have to remake, rewrite and reinterpret much that has gone for history of our religious traditions.[32] To this end the present day theologians and researcher are implicated to strive harder and make positive contribution in the making of spirituality as a common enterprise. Spirituality is which abides life for all. It is the way persons live out their lives in the Spirit as expressed in their thoughts, words and deeds. It is a thoughtful reflection and application of divine sense into practical, human,

---

[30] Lovely Awomi James, "Re-Imaging God from Tribal Women's Perspective," in *Inspiring Change: Tribal Women and Men Reading the Bible and Doing Theology,* edited by Marlene Ch. Marak (Jorhat: Women Study Centre, 2015), 64-65.

[31] Narola Imchen, "A Brief History of Women in the Church in North East India," in *Inspiring Change: Tribal Women and Men Reading the Bible and Doing Theology,* edited by Marlene Ch. Marak, (Jorhat: Women Study Centre, 2015), 91.

[32] Zubeno Kithan, comp., *Women in Church and Society* (Kolkata: SCEPTRE, 2014), 312-313.

material sense.[33] Spirituality should embrace all humanity, young and old, man and woman, literate and illiterate alike.

We can further understand the women's contribution to spirituality when we look deeper into the concept of *Women and the Life Giving Spirituality*. The importance of the Holy Spirit as a Mother who fulfills and completes the divine community in partnership can be fully recognized when God is seen in relation to the whole created order of the universe. The creation story in the book of Genesis shows that order of the universe was the result of the Spirit of God hovering over the waters of chaos. The spirit's presence was an indispensible element in the whole creative process of God. The role of the spirit in creation was given the supreme importance in Psalm 104:30, the tendency to view the spirit as a distinct person whose main role is to create life is further strengthened in the New Testament times where she is seen as giving life in a spiritual sense which is found in John 6:63. A woman is also the one who bestows and protects life in the human progeny rather than the man, for which she may be also called as "Eve" because she is "the mother of all living". The Hebrews believed that there is a Spirit in every human person; an element woman corresponds to the divine Ruach which comes into the womb of the woman. Therefore there is a close relation between the Holy Spirit and woman in regards to life, the Holy Spirit is the Lord and Giver of Life and woman cooperates with her in that she plays a major role in bringing forth the image of God.[34] Similarly, even in the tribal concept a woman is the one who bears witness of God's presence in the continuity of human race. Tribals regard and value life as very precious gift of God, and it is through woman that life comes to the world, though through the contribution of man. Therefore during the entire period of pregnancy and nurturing of children a mother is fully devoted to strict rituals, as a result her spirituality is maintained. Both in the traditional belief and even after embracing Christianity, the entire family and community continue to support the woman spiritually and physically to make sure that her child bearing and nurturing is healthy without any disturbances.[35] Ultimately a tribal woman understands spirituality as the core of her existence as she continues to pass on her rich spiritual heritage to the next generation.

Conclusion

We need to bring back the honoring of women; we need places for women inside of the center of spirituality where they can usher in a feminine view of

---

[33] Elizabeth S Tapia, "Earth Spirituality and the People's Struggle for Life; Reflections from the perspectives of Indigenous Peoples," *Ecumenical Review* 54/3 (2002), 220.

[34] Leelamma Athyal, "Pneumatology and Women," in *A Reader in Feminist Theology*, edited by Prasanna Kumari (Madras: Department of Research and Publications, 1993), 84-88.

[35] Joseph S. Thong, *Glimpses of Naga Legacy and Culture*, edited by Phanenmo Kath (Kerala: Society for Naga Students' Welfare, 1997), 84-86.

the world. Reclaiming the Spirituality of women have made women realize their voices of spiritual power that they are not inferior to men but they also have their own spiritual power which was hidden. It has also strengthened women in their struggle against oppression. The emergence of Asian women spirituality empowers them to fight injustices and bring awareness that emerge from their experiences. Women are to be given a space where they can appreciate themselves for being women and also regain their full humanity as persons. This spirituality of women can correct the errors of the male-dominated theology which has been prevailing for so long that we have inherited from the past, so as to make it equal irrespective of gender differences because in the eyes of God everyone is equal. To God, men and women both bear His image, as recorded in Genesis chapter 1:27 "So God created humankind in his image, in the image of God he created them, male and female he created them." Therefore, we are to honour him and serve him with the unique identity and image he has created us as male and female with our unique identity and characteristics. More importantly the concept of Asian women and tribal Christian women's spirituality would make the subject of spirituality more comprehensive and holistic.

10

Towards a Substantive Role of Women in the Naga Society

Akatoli Chishi

Introduction

I would like to begin with a statement of Haimendorf quoted by Lucy Zehol "...many women in the more civilized parts of India may well envy the women of the Naga Hills, their high status and their free and happy life and if you measure the cultural level of the people by the social position and personal freedom of its women you will think twice before looking down on the Nagas as savages."[1] Is this observation a reality? It is indeed not an easy question to answer because at present we find different opinions with regard to the position of women in the Naga society. Some would say that the Naga society generally assign a high status to women while others would opine that women are no better than a mere sex object or otherwise an inferior sex. Women on one hand have made lot of progress and have touched greater heights. On the other hand, there is moral and character deterioration in the churches as well as the social field, the values having disappeared giving way to corruption. Presently, the world is also passing through financial recessions besides being

[1] Quoted by Lucy Zehol, *Women in Naga Society* (New Delhi: Regency Publications, 1998), 1.

faced with the problem of world terrorism. In the present time of crisis, without awakening of women as well as their co-operation, transformation seems to be impossible. Women are supposed to be better than men from moral point of view. Therefore, a society where human and moral values are required, it is impossible without the co-operation of women. There is a need for the women to understand the present scenario and should be conscious of their duty. So, far they have extended their fullest co-operation and it is hoped, they will continue to do in every field more rigidly. With this aim and object, this paper attempts to bring out some roles that women can play to enhance women's capabilities as they shoulder the responsibility in the church as well as the society within the framework of Patriarchy/patriarchal structures and the customary laws of the traditional and the present Naga Society.

1. Patriarchy

Patriarchy is a culture in which men exercise control over women and restrict women's freedom in a position of subservient and dependent on men.[2] The term *patriarchy* is derived from two Greek words *Pater* meaning father and *arche* meaning beginning or first-thus refers to a form of social organization in which the father has the first place.[3] The whole of the social institutions in the patriarchal societies are being controlled by the men folk. The lineage is traced through the father/male line, where properties and inheritance are passed on from father to sons. Male dominance is maintained in such society where the male members are unquestionably considered as the "head, owner, administrator and protector of the family and society."[4] Thus, patriarchy denotes and connotes the rule of male and male hegemony with absolute power and dominion. Normally women's productive or Labour power[5], women's

---

[2] N. Limala Lkr, "Rediscovering Women's Role and Status in Society," in *Doing Theology with Tribal Resources,* edited by Wati Longchar & Larry E. Davis (Jorhat: Tribal Study Centre ETC, 1999), 77.

[3] Aliece L. Laffey, *An Introduction to the Old Testament: A Feminist perspective* (Philadelphia: Fortress press, 1988), 8.

[4] G. Khegholi Zhimomi, "Violence Against Women in Naga Society: A Feminist Theological Response" (M.Th Thesis: Senate of Serampore College, 2003), 34.

[5] Men control over women's productivity both within the household and outside, in paid work. Men also control women's labour outside the home in several ways. This control over and exploitation of women's labour means that men benefit materially from patriarchy; they derive concrete economic gains from the subordination of women. In other words, there is a material basis for patriarchy.

reproduction,[6] women's sexuality[7] and mobility,[8] property and other economic resources[9] are said to be under patriarchal control.[10] Such is the common feature found among all the tribes of the Nagas. Naga society following the patrilineal and patriarchal system has the norms and attitudes of patriarchy which affects the status of women. Institution and traditions are inspired by the belief in male dominance and female inferiority. Hence although patriarchy persists in all contemporary societies, its impact varies from tribe to tribe among the Naga Society.

2. Customary Law and Custom

The customary law of any given society emanates out of a body of observations, norms, tradition and usage of customs since the dawn of human civilization. The traditional laws and customs are informal sanctions, which require some degree of conformity from a member of a society. The social behaviour, which is strengthened by recurrence ultimately gives rise to an enforcing authority, which in its structure and system continues as trends of customs transmitted from one generation to another and becomes the source of customary law.

[6] Men also control over women's reproductive power not only as individual male but also as male dominated institutions like the church or state (Institutionalised control). According to radical feminists women are subjugated mainly because the burden of mothering and nurturing is forced on to them, and only on them, by patriarchal societies. They asserted that patriarchy limits abortion and often seeks to deny them entirely, but at the same time subjects women to intense and unremitting pressure to engage in sexual relations. Thus, patriarchy not only forces women to be mothers, it also determines the conditions of their motherhood and it restricts women's mobility and growth and reproduces male dominance.

[7] A radical feminist analysis said that women under patriarchy are not only mothers, they are also sexual slaves, and patriarchal ideology typically opposes women as sexual beings to women as mothers. In order to control women's sexuality their dress, behaviour and mobility are carefully monitored by familial, social, cultural and religious codes of behaviour. Rape and the threat of rape is another way in which women's sexuality is dominated through an invocation of "shame" and "honour". A radical feminist analysis said that women under patriarchy are not only mothers, they are also sexual slaves, and patriarchal ideology typically opposes women as sexual beings to women as mothers.

[8] In order to control women's sexuality, production and reproduction, men control women's mobility. The restrictions on leaving the domestic space, a strict separation of private and public, limits on interaction between the sexes etc., all control women's mobility and freedom in ways that are unique to them – that is, they are gender-specific, because men are not subjected to the same constraints.

[9] Most property and other productive resources are controlled by men and they pass from one man to another, usually from father to son. Even where women have the legal rights to inherit such assets, a whole array of customary practices, emotional pressures, social sanctions and sometimes, plain violence, prevent them from acquiring actual control over them. In other cases, personal laws curtail their rights rather than enhance them. In all cases, women are disadvantaged.

[10] KamlaBhasin, *What is Patriarchy?* (New Delhi: Kali for Women, 1993), 6.

According to Khatoli Khala, Custom is not a law but it controls the code of conduct and becomes a binding force for the members of the society.[11]

In olden times each village or clan developed their own customary law to pursue their local genius, local conditions, local politics, local temperament and peculiar tribal needs. But, today Nagas are within one democratic set up and judicial system of laws and the procedures have traversed a long way towards enlightening civil society and thus the customary law should conform to the changing needs. An alleged law can be abrogated by consensus of common opinion among the members of the said community. A new goal based on an equal justice will ensure removing uncertainty, confusion and ignorance; the practical customs must be sufficiently guarded for its application. It should be composed of rules and conducts which the society itself feels bound to be observed to legalise the behaviour of the people.[12]

The tribal customary laws and codes do not provide any legal protection for women.[13] The existing social injustice combined with inequality of women is a continuous cause of struggle. The authority structure under the customary law, where the male dominated unquestionable authority never gave equal opportunity; such structures are held together by the coercion and the structure is always functional for the socio-economical frontage. Ironically such struggle under the customary law continues right from colonial power, till the formation of Nagaland State. Since the formation of Nagaland State, the Article 371 of the Indian constitution maintains that no Acts shall apply in the state in respect of religious or social practices of Nagas. It is also noted in the 5th and 6th Schedule of the Indian Constitution that preserving the unique cultures and society of tribal based greater autonomy.[14] However, in the case of Nagaland, it is observed that the autonomy, understanding of the state controlled policy, the law enforcement and the legislative are subjected to customary Law. The parallel legislation created bias and confusion; results are prone to violation of women's rights that is torn between the Laws. The women's rights scenario continues to be bleak and gender awareness is regrettably missing in society.[15]

3. Role of Women in the Traditional Naga Society

In the traditional societies, the roles and status of women were usually in relation to her family as a daughter, wife, sister and mother. In such a society,

---

[11] Khatoli Khala, *Women and Agriculture in Nagaland: A Gender Study of Sumi Customary Law and Custom* (Dimapur: Shikhu Scholastic Press, 2012), 22.

[12] Khatoli Khala, *Women and Agriculture in Nagaland*..., 23.

[13] Limatula Longkumer, "Our identity: Judges 19-21," in *Weaving New Patterns of Ministry for Women in NEI,* edited by NarolaImchen (Jorhat: ETC), 2004, 156.

[14] Khatoli Khala, *Women and Agriculture in Nagaland*..., 2.

[15] Khatoli Khala, *Women and Agriculture in Nagaland*..., 3.

men do not only enjoy authority but also enjoy inheritance of property. The fact that Naga society is patriarchal and patrilineal proves beyond any doubt that women are not equal to men in status concerning certain aspects of life. This may be also due to the biological constitution of women. Women are considered to be physically weaker than men which is why a Naga man feels responsible towards women.[16] Since women were considered to be weaker than men, they were not required to do any hard work. He is convinced that it is his duty to protect a woman as their society practices the patrilineal system where women are entitled not to get any share in the ancestral property.[17]

Though women did not have equal status as men in social as well as in family affairs, they played an important role in the domestic affairs. They were given full authority regarding the domestic affairs. Nagas by nature are self-respecting, just, loving and fair people. In all matters of social and religious importance, women were treated with respect and fair opportunities to express their personal opinions were given, even though they might have not played a dominant role.

4. Role of Women in the Socio-Economic and Political Arena of the Nagas

In the new emerging situation, a woman's status and role is described more in terms of her achievements in education, career, and position etc., in the society. Her role is not limited to the home but also outside the home. Unlike the traditional family, where a woman's place was only beside the hearth, now she can move outside and get herself socially involved. The scenario has taken a turn in the modern society. With the growth of literacy rate, the society's attitude in relation to women has broadened a great deal. She is no more given bias treatment for being a woman. Even the Western norm of equality has made a fissure in the tight compartments of male and female differences in our society. Education has made many mothers and wives earners, which has boosted up the women's moral and social standing. The wife or mother need not necessarily confine herself to the household drudgery, but she is free to engage herself in other social and economic matters as her competency and abilities render her fit. Today, education is encouraged for both sexes which has gone a long way in raising the status of women in general. However, the institutional inequality is reflected in the dominance in political sphere and also in the elementary fields of socio-economic life of women.

---

[16] Hunibou Newmai, "The Status of Women in Zeliangrong Society," in *Women in Naga Society*, edited by Lucy Zehol (New Delhi: Regency Publications, 1998), 43.

[17] Hunibou Newmai, "The Status of Women in Zeliangrong Society"..., 43.

4.1. Role of Women in Economics

Today when we evaluate women's economic participation many women are employed in Government services and more are joining civil services. They are taking part as administrators both at the State and National level. This reflects a new attitude towards roles appropriate to women among women themselves as well as the public. Contemporary Naga women have realized a new identity that they can hold any position not as assigned by traditional society but by virtue of their own merit through competitive examinations.

Looking at the present economy of women especially the active involvement of women in Government jobs and private businesses, one may conclude that the economic condition of women in Nagaland is satisfactory. However this does not reflect the true picture as it involves only a relatively few women. There are many more who are unemployed and which shows that unemployment is much higher among women than men.

4.2. Role of Women in Politics

The traditional Naga society did not provide any place for the public exercise of leadership for women, or even membership in any decision making bodies. Important decision was not proper role for women who in this respect were certainly regarded as inferior to men. The male dominated society thus imposed restrictions on the role that women could easily play, including their exclusion from a political life.

At the village level though the traditional exclusion of women from political involvement in the councils is somewhat subsiding to some extent yet at the same time in many cases it is continued as before. Women are still not members of any village council, nor can they take part in the decision making process at that level. Women are denied the right to play a political role in the legislative village Panchayats and councils and town committees etc. At the state level also the fact remains that all parties are dominated by male leadership and even when choosing their candidates, the parties favour males. Though there are few women who have involved themselves in state politics, their role is still very limited. Even the 33% reservation was denied with all known and unknown reasons. However, the question often asked these days is why women cannot play an important role in politics? The reason may be that the traditional attitudes are still continuing to influence attitudes concerning the involvement of women in politics. Politics is viewed as an area where only men can exercise power, authority and control. Actually politics in theory gives people freedom to select their own candidates, and vote for anyone of whatever sex. The votes of women are valued equally with those of men but when it comes to the selection of candidates people are reluctant to select women. People still find it difficult to permit women to exercise political power. Hence, the male dominated traditions still keep women in a second-class status.

4.3. Women's Contribution through Sports and Different Welfare Societies

It is noted that women have taken an active part in changing traditional society through participation in sports and other village developmental programmes of various kinds. In the field of sports we have Ms Chekrovolü Swüro as the first Naga Lady Olympian. She was also selected for the Arjuna Awards 2013, which is the highest civilian award in India. She is also the first Naga woman to be honoured with such prestigious award. In many villages there are women's welfare societies or women's organization working for village development. Many organisations like the Naga Mothers Association,[18] women societies at the district, area, village and tribe levels raise their voices against corruption and other evils that have entered society. While they are committed to the maintenance of high social values, they are at the same time committed to positive changes in situations where the traditional ways discriminate women.

5. Towards a Substantive Role of Women in the Naga Society

In order for women to play their role effectively in the church and society they need to be empowered. This power cannot be achieved by asking, demanding or complaining, it is rather achieved by claiming it. And to claim the power, women first need to make themselves powerful. Women in general have been weakened emotionally and intellectually by the relentless challenges of a 'partriarchal, misogynistic, and materialistic culture'. Women in general have been corrupted by materialism, vanity, loss of self-respect, dependence and subservience. Thus, Women (and men at some points), need to heal their spiritual and psychological wounds, cultivate their intellectual and professional abilities, by adopting some components of empowerment.

---

[18] The Naga Mothers Association (NMA) was formed in 1984. The main purpose of forming the NMA was to fight against social evils, especially the use of drugs and alcoholic drinks and corruption in Government. They have had a significant impact. All the women belonging to different tribes have taken an active role in the NMA as well as in other similar organisations. The women organisations in the Naga society are increasing and getting stronger. Their main aim and objectives are mainly to fight against immoralities, drug abuses and so on. They are striving not only for their better status in social, political and educational fields, but also striving their best to do away with all kinds of social stigmas that hinders the community without degrading their feminism. Cf: NarolaImchen, *Women in Church and Society: The Story of Ao Naga Women* (Jorhat: Eastern Theological college, 2001), 88; Salome Zhimomi, "The Status of Women in Sema Society" in Lucy Zehol, *Women in Naga Society …*, 52.

i) Self-Esteem

An empowered woman is proud of herself. She feels good about the fact that she is a woman. The prevailing cultural attitude, which many women absorb, is to feel ashamed and socialized to believe that she is not physically, emotionally or intellectually capable of doing many things that men can do. One of the slogans of the Women's movement is "My biology is not my Destiny."[19] While it is true that certain biological functions are performed only by women, in other human activities gender is not an issue. A woman need not feel sorry that she is a woman, or try to be like a man. In our society, if someone wishes to compliment a woman they often use a male reference point and say. 'You are different; you are just like a man'. Thus such negative compliments need to be challenged.

ii) Awareness

An empowered woman is aware and educated about her rights. This presupposes inner sensitivity and intellectual examination of her intuitive feelings, which she begins to articulate. She seeks out information, recognizes the value of discussion about relevant issues and follows matters up. When a woman knows and understands her rights and she is aware of her rights first as a person, and then as a woman, she can take further step. Awareness becomes a power when a person translates it into action.[20] Thus, this calls women to be aware of their own rights in the church and in society as well.

iii) Power of Choice

An empowered woman is free to make informed decisions and exercise her rights. This is the power of choice. Choice means a woman has control over her life and the freedom to make informed decisions relating to her body, as well as to all other aspects of her life. It does not mean that a woman has to do certain things to be labelled empowered. An empowered woman knows which choices she wishes to make and is free to exercise them. She does not do things only to please others. If a woman wants to stay at home, or work outside, or remain single she should be free to make those choices. An empowered woman is conscious of the gender inequalities in society. At every stage she resists them. She does not take for granted the way women are spoken about. An empowered woman is always conscious of gender biases hidden within language, attitudes and practices.

She identifies them and responds immediately and intelligently, that is, she demonstrates her ability to make choices based on understanding.

---

[19] B. K. Jagdish Chander, *Applied Spiritual Knowledge* (Mount Abu: Literature Dept., Brahma Kumaris Ishwariya Vishva Vidyalaya, 2000), 71.

[20] N.n, *Women's Empowerment* (Mt Abu: PBKIVV, women's wing, n.d.,), 70.

Gender biases are deeply ingrained in all aspects of our society. However, an empowered woman does not compromise or accept that gender bias is so prevalent that she cannot do anything rather, she takes decisions and responds wisely to those kinds of situations and biased thoughts of others which will ultimately create change on a wider scale.

Few women in our society have broken the barriers that constrained them, identified their goals and reached targets they set for themselves. Empowered women have usually had social, economic and educational advantages. The vision of women's liberation is realized when empowerment takes place on a large scale across all sections of society.

iv) Re-discovering Women's Role in the Naga Tradition

One of the means to empower women for a fuller participation in our society is through recovery of women's lost stories in our traditions. Through patriarchy, women's stories and roles are badly distorted, misinterpreted and almost wiped out from the mainstream of our history.[21] In most of the Naga tradition, there is a myth of the three Primeval Beings; a tiger, a Man and a spirit. They were all born from the same mother. When the mother died, her three children parted their ways and thus began to establish the spirit world, the human world, and the animal world. Here the mother is depicted as the ancestress and the supreme being of the supernatural beings, animal kingdom and human beings, who is worthy of all oblation and service from each of her creation.[22] Among the traditional Sumis, women's word was most of the time a point of reference in decision making, though they were not a part of decision making body which can also be interpreted as very encouraging and positive element in strengthening of our roles in the present day society. There are number of liberative elements in our traditional stories, poems, songs, myths which need to be reconstructed and rediscovered to make our society more inclusive. Reconstructing our history in an inclusive way can restore women's image and role.

v) Embracing Femininity[23]

The word feminine need not be confused with weak or inferior with the male members. Rather what we have to understand is that when we are feminine and

---

[21] Limala Longkumer, "Rediscovering women's role and status in society", in *Doing Theology with Tribal Resources,* edited by Wati Longchar & Larry E. Davis (Jorhat: Tribal Study Centre ETC, 1999), 78.

[22] Sashikabakechutzar, "A Discursive Reading of the Oral Traditions: A Tribal Women's Perspective", in *No More Sorrow in God's Garden of Justice,* edited by Limatula Longkumer (Jorhat: Eastern Theological college), 72.

[23] An idea borrowed from Michelle Hammond, *The Power of Femininity: Rediscovering the Art of Being a Woman* (Eugene, Oregon: Harvest House Publishers, 1999).

show our care and compassion not only for people, but also for all animals and nature as a whole, than that is the most powerful weapon a woman can possess - much more powerful than anyone who shows hate, deceit, competition, or violence.

The feminine style of leadership is co-operative, loving, peaceful and looking out for the best interests of everyone - not just the powerful or a select few. For me leadership has nothing to do with gender, but more to do with qualities on display and it is the feminine qualities of unconditional love, allowance, acceptance, softness, gentleness, compassion, understanding, caring, tolerance, calmness, serenity, nurturing, cooperation, quiet determination, perseverance, peacefulness, inner strength and many more which are the essence of truë leadership and which are not seen much in our present world leaders or leaders at most levels.

With these qualities, there is a genuine desire to serve the whole. The Feminine is the embodiment of heart energy. Her key qualities are compassion and the ability to accept and honor the process of whatever is happening. Contrary to the idea that women are overemotional, the Divine Feminine is well grounded emotionally and has the capacity to bring all of her energy to exactly where she is in the moment. Feminine energy accepts the paradoxes of life and has the ability to hold them within her heart simultaneously. Feminine energy connects deeply with the Earth and all of her children, feeling for and with them.

Recognizing these qualities as ones that we possess, or can aspire to possess, frequently helps us recognize and respect our innate talent to usher in to all situations the energy of love and acceptance. A revolution of love, a revolution of respect, a revolution of acceptance, tolerance, and inclusion. All of these values must first be nurtured in our own hearts and souls, and in our intimate social groups, if they are to be transformative for the whole. To begin this revolution of love, we need to brave our fears and honor who we truly are.

Conclusion

In the past years the women's liberation approach was based on the assertion of their rights and deconstruction of the existing structure. In the recent years, an attempt is made for re-discovering women's role in the tribal tradition which has been undermined and concealed due to the male bias interpretation of history and tradition. As our expression, experiences and forms are culturally conditioned, hence the task of reinterpreting and rediscovering its meaning, values, and role in our traditional heritage will help for the empowerment of women. Unless there is a healthy respect for the other fellow beings, no society can progress in the real sense of the term. There is no doubt that women and men have different biological functions to perform but these differences do not justify any discrimination against women. It is a well known fact that men are very particular about imposing rules and regulations on women but they are not willing to follow any code of conduct for themselves. If we are serious about progress, then both women and men must abide by certain principles. Both men and women have greater roles to play in the society. The difference in their role must be recognised and acknowledged and once it is done, there is no doubt that the Naga Society will also achieve the desired progress.

11

Construction of Gender Role in the Society

Vimeno Lasetso

Introduction

Gender identity can be defined by the way people act as male and female. Usually males have different mindset about something that females do not have, and vice versa. But, people learn about their gender identity through experiences from their childhood. Gender roles play a huge role in individuality and growth. It is a social construction, which means that it is fluid and cannot be confined by any boundaries. Keeping in mind that there are different understandings and perspectives in deriving gender issues from different branches of study, it is a humble attempt to define gender role from the sociological point of view. This study is pertinent because it is very important to know the difference between sex and gender, for this has confused many people in their understanding of gender issue. At the same time it is also important to look at gender because power and privilege is not equally distributed between the sexes. Men often gain privilege at the expense of women, and this is how injustice and inequality or discriminations take place. Gender role in the society creates discrimination among men and women, thus, providing information alone is not the answer, but to look at it critically and analyse it from different perspectives will shape our mind and thoughts.

Difference Between Sex and Gender

It is a common misconception that the words sex and gender are used to describe the same thing, when there are actually big differences between the two. Many people fail to realize that 'sex' and 'gender' refer to two things. According to Oxford A-Z of English Usage, even though "the words gender and sex both means the 'state of being male or female', they are typically used in slightly different ways: sex tends to refer to biological difference, while gender tends to refer to cultural or social ones."[1] Thus sex is more commonly used to refer to the biological anatomy of a person and is determined when a child is conceived and was born. The World Health Organization (WHO) defines sex as "biological and physiological characteristics that define men and women."[2]

On the other hand, gender is the role or differentiation that is created by the society. Gender is influenced by the culture and the society that a person is born in. It differs depending on the country, state, culture and religion etc. According to World Health Organization (WHO) gender is define as "the socially constructed roles, behaviors, activities and attributes that a given society considers appropriate for men and women. Thus, gender includes all norms that a society sets in order to separate the male and the female.[3]

Therefore sex and gender do not always align. The word **Cis-gender** describes people whose biological body they were born into matches their personal gender identity and the experiences is distinct from being transgender. **Transgender** people are those whose biological sexes do not align with their gender identity. They usually undergo a gender transition that may involve changing their dress and self-presentation. They may undergo hormone therapy to facilitate their process, but, yet not all transgender people will undertake surgery. **Intersexuality** describes Intersex person who is born with a combination of male and female biological characteristics, such as chromosomes or genitals. They are born with some biological characteristics that are considered "female" and that are considered "male." Thus, Transgender and Intersexual person are gender category and not sexuality. **Genderqueer** - people can also choose to be genderqueer, it is rather a new term used mostly among young adults. It is commonly used to describe a person who feels that his/her gender identity does not fit into the socially constructed norms associated with his/her biological sex. A person who is genderqueer

---

[1] Jeremy Butterfield, *Oxford A-Z of English Usage* (New York: Oxford University Press, 2007), 67.

[2] "Gender, Equity and Human Rights," *http://www.who.int/gender-equity-rights/en/* (9/7/2018).

[3] "Gender, Equity and Human Rights," *http://www.who.int/gender-equity-rights/en/* (July 7, 2018).

is not transgendered, they have no bearing on sexual identity or orientation.[4] Therefore the social scientists describe the third gender as cultures that accept non-binary gender positions.

Gender Construction from Sociological Perspectives

As discussed above, from the sociological point of view gender is defined as social construct, and that is something that we have to learn and perform, rather than what we are born with. It is how society constructs ideals of behavior which are fundamentally different from men and women. For example, even in the past as well as in the present days, childcare was seen to be woman's domain because of the conceptions that women and femininity associated with being more emotional and caring than men. The sociology of gender examines how society influences our understandings and perceptions of difference between masculinity and femininity. In turn it influences identity and social practices. Social constructionism is one of the key theories sociologist put gender into historical and cultural focus. It is about how meaning is created through social interaction, through the things that we do and say with other people. Therefore gender norms are learned from birth through childhood socialization, from parental teachings, from the schools or through religious or cultural teachings, as well as from various other social institutions. It evolves over a person's lifetime. Gender is always in flux therefore, "we see this through generational and intergenerational changes within families, as social, legal and technological changes influence social values on gender."[5] Gender socialization is where for instance children are taught to adopt appropriate gender role, where in the school girls are taught to wear skirts, and boys are taught to wear trousers. That cements their minds that there are differences between the sexes.

Understanding Gender Role in the Society

Gender refers to the socio-cultural definition of man and woman, the way the societies distinguish men and women and assign them gender or social roles and expect them to follow accordingly. Strong evidence around the world confirms that gender equality accelerates over economic growth and reduces poverty and insecurity and therefore promotes development and empowerment. On the other hand contrary to that, it rather promotes discrimination rather than development. In our society today man/males are ascribed the greatest or highest status, where men had legitimate power over women.[6] As soon

[4] Marisa, "Genderqueer," in *Urban Dictionary*. February 18, 2004, *https://www.urban.dictionary.com.* (July 7, 2018).

[5] "Sociology of Gender," *https://othrsociologist.com/sociology-of-gender/* (July 3, 2018).

[6] Y. Hotoni Yeptho, "Gender Construction in Naga Society," in *Morung Express*, February 17, 2017.

as a child is born families and society begin the process of gendering. Boys are to be masculine; they are to be tough, strong, active aggressive, daring, dominant protective and outgoing, whereas girls must be feminine-emotional, sweet and submissive. Boys are expected to play with trucks, tough toys, guns, blocks etc, while girls are expected to play with dolls, kitchens goods etc. As children grow more stereotype idea are involve regarding which subject are favorable and more suitable for each gender. For instance, subjects like math are probably the notion that boys are better in than girls. Therefore one could see that social influence affects perception about gender identity and roles.[7]

These traditional gender role patterns have been influential in the socialization of children. And it is the part of the adults who play critical role in guiding children in those gender roles deemed appropriate in the society. The society is constructed in such a way that we construct our behavior socially so as to create our exaggerated male-female differences. Our society focuses on masculine and feminine qualities, and evaluates men and women in those terms, thus continue to "do gender."

Gender Stereotype and Inequality

As Gender is a structural feature of the society, it is device by which society controls its members, thus like social class and race can be used to socially categorize people and even lead to prejudice and discrimination, towards members of the group. Discrimination occurs when there is differential treatment of people based on their sex and thus the term sexism defines this behavior. "Sexism refers to any bias against as individual or group based on the individual's or group's sex. Gender discrimination is another way one could define sexism and in particular is associated with discrimination and stereotype belief against women."[8] In most of the countries, particularly in India, it is still evident that women are still considered a minority and do not have equal access and rights in their own society as do males. This variation regarding gender around the world makes prominent that gender identity is influenced by social variables and has little to do with biological variables.[9]

The stereotype that we know today were not always present in the past, they are relatively new trends in the human society. This is because social expectations of each gender change over time, and often develop differently according to the cultural settings. According to *Sara Bobolts*, She describes

[7] J. Conzalez-Mena, *The Young Child in the Family and the Community*, 4th edition (Upper Saddle River, NJ: Pearson Merrill Prentice Hall, 2006), 78.

[8] Frank W. Schneider, Jamie A. Gruman, & Larry M.Coutts, (Eds), *Applied Social Psychology: Understanding and Addressing Social and Practical Problems* (Thousand Oaks, CA: Sage Publications, 2005), 340.

[9] J. H. Henslin. *Essential of Sociology: A Down-to-Earth Approach*, 6th edition (Boston: Pearson/Allyn and Bacon, 2006), 117.

how stereotypes, such as color blue being for boys and the color pink for girls, are of new concept. She further explained that in 1918 and 1940, pink was viewed as masculine color, while blue was seen as dainty and soft, making it best suited for females. She also stated that during the Middle Ages in Europe, high-heels were exclusively for men, rather than women, they were seen as a sign of masculinity, depending on their height.[10] This shows that gender categories are different only a few centuries ago and thus cannot be used as a reliable basis for establishing roles and influencing our society today.

Furthermore, it can also be stated that how gender roles vary based on the historical and cultural background of a society, as well as ethnicity. For example, traditionally in the Naga context, particularly the Angamis of Nagaland, women often played significant role in community life. They were the leaders, healers, sowers, peacemakers, of the village or community, and certain festivals or rituals cannot begin without the elderly women playing their roles.[11] Such very important roles were played by the women in the community. Yet in the present society all those significant roles are not been taken seriously or in other words, they have been eliminated from practice. Therefore depending on the time and period, gender role drastically changes. Even though many fits in the specific categories of masculinity or femininity, these generalizations are simply social constructs. As Nathaniel Givens observes, "Because Gender roles have always existed in the human society and because they were never invented or designed,"[12] but over time, they were developed, and therefore they cannot work as generalized distinction. Therefore cultural and religious beliefs and attitudes have a serious impact on gender identity and in many cases promote stereotype beliefs against women and lead to gender discrimination. Thus, social construction of gender could lead to discrimination about gender, particularly towards women. Women are treated differently than men in many ways, they are seen as weak and emotional through religious beliefs, which leads to certain type of gender identity.

Gender Role in the Bible

Despite the fact that gender traditionalist argue, for example, that ministry of the prophets included some functions that excluded women, yet both men and women were recognized as prophets in the ancient Israel. In fact we see that God switches the most culturally accepted gender norms throughout the

---

[10] Sara Bobolts, "9 Facts that Prove Traditional Gender Roles are Bullsh*t," *The Huffington Post,* Post online Addition on April 26th 2015 (July 3, 2018).

[11] Particularly one of the biggest festivals among the Angami's Naga called Syikrenyü where women take the active role in the traditional society, without women the festival will not take place.

[12] Nathaniels Givens, "What are Gender Roles Good for?" in *Time and Seasons* (July 5, 2018).

Bible. For instance, in the Old testament God calls Huldah and Deborah to be warriors for His glory (II Kings 22:14-19; Chronicles 34:23-27). God puts Esther in the leadership position over all Israelites. There are also passages in the New Testament telling of women who were called and blessed in ministries that entailed teaching and leading assemblies of both men and women. In Romans 18:7, Paul refers to male apostles Andronicus and female apostles Junia,[13] as outstanding among the apostles. In Acts 21:9 four young women are referred to as prophetesses. In the Bible women were not only apostles, but also preachers, deacons, evangelists and that they presided over Eucharist.[14] Therefore, "It is clear that women were active in various ministerial activities in the early church like administering, teaching, baptizing and also as disciples and ministers of Jesus."[15] Furthermore, there is instruction in the New Testament for all believers to relate to one another with humility, respect, to submit to each other as others' servants and not to be concerned with positions of status or authority. There are passages which urge believers to treat one another as they would like to be treated themselves (Luke 22:25-27, Mathew 7:12; 20:25-28, 23:8-12, Roman 12:3-10, Philippians 2:2-5).

In the gospels women occupy a place of dignity and freedom. Jesus Himself is the main force behind the emancipation of women. In the Pauline churches, the role of women was prominent, women as followers, apostles and proclaimers in the early church and their ministry. And thus there is no question as such of gender discrimination in the early church, because women have been equally contributing in the life and ministry of the church. Yet many of the prominent roles played by women are not acknowledged and recognized, mainly because the writers were men.[16] God gives both man and woman specializations both in a physical and spiritual sense. He gave us a framework for what matters most to Him and that is partnership. Likewise God desires the same for men and women in the context of society and in the family. No matter what, God's will and purpose of our lives reveal that we all are given roles to play without any discrimination.

Theological Implications

The theology of gender equality is built upon theological principles that enable participation and inclusion of both men and women in creating and sustaining communities that re-affirm, respect and celebrate that being male and female

[13] Junia is a woman's name though some editors have interpreted it as a man's name. Cf., Donald and John Collins (Eds), *Catholic Study Bible*, Second edition (Oxford: Oxford University, 2006), 1515.

[14] Suzan Rakoczy, *In Her Name: Women Doing Theology* (Pietermaritzburg: Cluster publication, 2004), 202-207.

[15] Narola Imchen, *Women in the History of Christianity* (Jorhat: TDCC, 2010), 25-26.

[16] Imchen, *Women in the History of Christianity,* 25.

are of divine gift. In genesis 1:27. "And so God created human beings in His own image... male and female He created them." And in the following verse 31, "God saw all that he had made, and it was very good." Few things that we need to ponder and take into consideration:

- Human dignity and equality are restored through the gospel. Faith in Christ Jesus is what makes each of us equal with each other as we find in Galatians 3:28, "There is neither Jew nor Gentile, neither slave nor free, neither male nor female, for you are all one in Christ Jesus." Thus every believer is the child of God and co-heir with Jesus Christ (Roman 8:15-17). Husbands and wives are equal heirs of all God's gift of life (I Peter 3:7). As equal heirs, men and women have equal rights and responsibilities, without discrimination on the ground of sex, age, race, social status or gender (Acts 2:17-18).
- Jesus declared his mission was to bring abundant life to humanity as we find in John 10:10, "...I have come that they may have life, and have it to the full."
- Through Jesus' radical compassion He challenged the traditions and practices that excluded the vulnerable and most marginalized. He exemplified and lived out the principles and values of the Kingdom of God. It is therefore within the very essence of God's ministry through the Christian community to continue to seek out and strive to empower the least and most vulnerable in society.

Conclusion

Gender roles are assigned by society or culture. Each man or woman, is given the expected role in the society. Thus, it is people who construct cultures and gender roles. It is also people who must change cultures that dehumanize and deny certain groups of people their God-given humanity, dignity and equality. It is therefore important to recognize that women, men, girls and boys are equal in the sight of God. UNICEF says, "Gender equality means women and men and girls and boys enjoy the same rights, resources, opportunities and protection. It does not require that girls and boys, or women and men, be the same, or that they be treated exactly alike."

Lastly, a question to ponder, "Are women and men equal?" In some ways we are and in some we are not. We all have our distinct role to play as men and women. We are given those roles by the divine God. Yet, we are not to gain privilege or discriminate at the expense of each other as men and women. God has chosen distinct role for both to complement each other and that it glorifies Him. If the world has problem in differentiating role and discriminate, take it to God who created us in His own image. It is essential that we work together for God's glory, each with distinct role, but for one common goal and that is, partnership and respect for one another as God intended.

12

Tribal Narrative Communication

Marlene Ch. Marak

Introduction

To be frank, I am not a very good storyteller. Actually, I am a bad storyteller and sometimes I forget the story before I can complete it. Sometimes, I get too excited half way through the story and I tend to mess up my punchline. But, I am a good listener and I am learning from others. Many good storytellers have a good voice. They are enthusiastic and funny when they tell humorous stories and they are sombre and even have a catch in their voice when they are telling a sad or touching story. Good storytellers do not waste time on unimportant details and even when they tell old stories they make you feel like you are hearing it for the first time.

As a young girl, I grew up listening to some stories narrated by one of my grandfathers (my mother's uncle). I used to look forward to his coming to our house every day. A small built man, with one of his legs amputated from his thigh, he had only a few of his front teeth and he wore Gandhi-like spectacles. He would sit on a short stool and so would I, near him, to listen to his stories. Sitting there together in the shade of a plum tree, he would start narrating stories as I listened with rapt attention. At the same time, we would look out for the birds and chickens that come to eat the paddy being dried in the hot sun. Sometimes he told me random stories of some of his life's experiences, war stories, stories about the Garo labour corps in France, events in his life, and stories about some relatives who were not familiar to me. At other times, he narrated popular Garo folk stories and fairy tales. One of the earliest fairy tale that I heard from him was the story of *King Thrushbeard.*

Another teller of tales during my childhood was my Garo language teacher in school when I was in my class six and seven. I remember she dressed elegantly, wearing the usual *dakmanda* (Garo *mekhela* – tribal women's wraparound) and *chaddar* (a stole). Sitting on her chair, she would narrate stories. It was from her that I heard some of the Bible stories that has remained with me throughout my life. I remember hearing from her about the story of friendship between Jonathan and David, about the battle of Jericho, the story of Deborah and Barak, and about Ehud the left-handed judge of the Israelites. She also enjoyed telling us stories from *A·chikgolporang* (Garo folklores) which I still remember and cherish so fondly.

Stories are easy to tell and remember. We hear many things every day. But, it is the stories that linger on in our memories. Narrative is the most natural way of communicating with each other.

Narrative Communication

Humans cannot exist without communicating. We communicate with one another about anything and everything. We learn about life and about each other from stories, and we are emotionally and intellectually affected by them. Arthur Asa Berger said that it is important for people to hear stories to lend colour and interest to their everyday lives. Human beings are not simply *Homo Sapiens*, which is man and woman the knower, but *Homo Narrans*, which is man and woman the storyteller, the teller of tales.[1] When humans communicate by way of telling stories, it is called narration. And the act of communicating stories by narration is known as narrative communication. Julia Chaitin in her article, "Narratives and Storytelling," writes this way, "People are storytellers—they tell narratives about their experiences and the meanings that these experiences have for their lives."[2]

According to *Webster's Dictionary*, a narrative is "a discourse, or an example of it, designed to connect a succession of happenings."[3] The *American Heritage Dictionary of the English Language* gives a definition of narrative as, "a story or description of actual or fictional events; or the act, technique

[1] Arthur Asa Berger, *Narratives in Popular Culture, Media, and Everyday Lives* (London/ New Delhi: Sage Publications, 1997), 174.

[2] Julia Chaitin, "Narratives and Storytelling" in *www.beyondintractability.org* (accessed on 22 October 2018).

[3] *Webster's Third International Dictionary* (1966), 1503.

or process of narrating."[4]Although, verbal narration is the primary form of communication, the written form is also said to be narration (because it tells events and stories through written form). Narratives or stories are often told or communicated in order to be recounted or retold to others.

Narratives are part of our everyday life. It is narrative when our mothers sang lullabies to us. It is narrative when we recited nursery rhymes and sang songs. It is narrative when we read novels and biographies. All the time, we hear, see, listen or read stories. From birth till death, humans swim in the sea of stories. In fact, Berger says that even "our deaths are recorded in narratives, also—for that's what obituaries are."[5] Hence; we cannot but accept the fact that our lives are but fabricated in the sea of narratives. Peter Brooks says that human life is "intertwined with narrative."[6] Berger defines Narrative or Narratives as "story or stories that tell about things that have happened or are happening to people, animals, aliens from outer space, insects—whatever. That is, a story contains a sequence of events, which means that narratives take place within or over to be more precise, some kind of time period."[7]

Narrative Communication and Tribal Culture

Most tribes did not have written literature but oral tradition. It is through storytelling that tribal culture, way of life, norms, beliefs, customs, practices, values, folksongs, stories and tales, proverbs, riddles and various sayings of the tribe are passed down from generation to generation. Tribal life and culture are unimaginable without storytelling or narration.

A. L. Kroeber, an anthropologist, says that there are no cultureless societies.[8] Culture is the creation of the human beings and something which we cannot find in the world of animals. In describing culture, we can say that it includes language or speech, knowledge, belief, custom, art, ideals and norms. These are traditionally learnt from others, particularly parents, relatives and elders, who in turn had learned them from previous generations through narrative communication. Kroeber notes that there is every possibility of each generation also adding and subtracting customs and ideas, thus modifying "social tradition" and "social heredity."[9] Clifford Geertz in his definition of the concept of culture says,

---

[4] *American Heritage Dictionary of the Language* (1966), 873.

[5] Berger, *Narratives in Popular Culture, Media and Everyday Lives*, 1.

[6] Peter Brooks, *Reading for the Plot: Design and Intention in Narrative* (New York: Knopf, 1984), 3.

[7] Berger, *Narratives in Popular Culture, Media and Everyday Lives*, 4.

[8] A. L. Kroeber, *Anthropology: Race. Language. Culture. Psychology. Prehistory* (New Delhi: Oxford and IBH Publishing Co., 1923), 252.

[9] Kroeber, *Anthropology: Race. Language. Culture. Psychology. Prehistory*, 253.

> The concept of culture I espouse...is essentially a semiotic one. Believing, with Max Weber, that man [sic] is an animal suspended in webs of significance he himself [sic] has spun, I take culture to be those webs, and the analysis of it to be therefore not an experimental science in search of law but an interpretative one in search of meaning.[10]

K. Chattopadhyay, the writer of the book *Tribalism in India*, talks about culture as the epitome or the very essence of tribal life.[11] Culture also plays a very significant part in the religious life of the tribal. Since there is no written creed in tribal societies, A. Wati Longchar says that narrative communication as the living creed of tribal people. It is contained in the hearts and minds of the people. Hence, narrative communication makes each member of the tribe in the family, clan and the village, a "living creed."[12]

Among the tribal communities, narrative communication takes place by way of storytelling. In the narration of tribal legends and lores, traditional beliefs are conveyed. Mythical stories of migration or origin of the tribe gives the tribe its identity. Feasts and festivals, incantations and prayers, rites and rituals are narrative performances that embody the social and religious expression of the tribe. Folk songs and dances can contain romantic stories or stories of war, they could narrate the cosmic act of the creation of the world and living beings, or they could portray natures beauty. Proverbs and riddles not only serve as entertainment to while away the time but also transmit the wisdom and values of the tribe. Then there is the tribal use of euphemisms—there are euphemisms for referring to things considered shameful to express openly and euphemisms for reprimanding or correcting one another. And so, there is a rich repertoire of narrative communication in tribal communities.

Since narrative communication in the tribal communities is verbal, it can only be passed on by word of mouth through narration. J. Goody calls this as an "intergenerational communication."[13] Had it not been for narrative communication, many of the cultural mores, customs and ethos would have been lost, our tribes would have lost their roots and not have their tribal identities as we know it today. Sadly, uncountable tribes around the world are losing their roots. Tribals lose their roots when modern development robs them of their land and disrupt their way of life. They lose their culture, traditions and indigenous knowledge as they are absorbed into modern civilization. Young people break the chain of oral traditions as they discard their traditional ways,

---

[10] Clifford Geertz, *The Interpretation of Cultures* (London: Fontana Press, 1973), 5.

[11] K. Chattopadhyay, *Tribalism in India* (New Delhi: Vikas Publishing House, 1978), 6.

[12] A. Wati Longchar, *The Traditional Tribal Worldview and Modernity: Focus on North East India* (Jorhat: N. Limala Longkumer, 1995), 5.

[13] J. Goody, "Oral Culture," in G. Gerbner (et. al), *International Encyclopedia of Communications*, vol. 2 (New York: University of Pennsylvania, 1989), 226-229.

considering them to be backward and based on superstitions. According to a study, 3,000 of the world's 6,000 languages are going to disappear as they are spoken only by adults. In an article on *Time* magazine, Eugene Linden states, "the most immediate tragedy in the loss of knowledge and traditions is for the tribes themselves. They do not always die out, but the soul of their culture withers away."[14]

Among the different forms of oral or narrative communication, it is said that storytelling or stories are the oldest form of structured and purposeful communication. Storytelling is considered to be the most effective and important form of communication because the traditional stories have been used to store, organise and communicate. Much of what is communicated or narrated is practised as a tribe's cultural practices and it is possible because of the collective memory of the members of the tribe.

If we look at the genre of the stories as told by our parents and grandparents, we will find that the story contents are usually about plants, trees, and shrubs (such as banana plants and simul trees); insects (such as ants and spiders); animals (such as squirrels, snakes, tigers, langurs, foxes, rabbits, elephants, frogs, hoolocks, turtles, leopards, deer, and monkeys); birds (such as crows, owls, pigeons, doves, peacocks, parrots, eagles, and sparrows too). There are also stories about mountains, peaks, rivers and streams, lakes and ponds. Another category of stories is about the celestial beings and supernatural things. Then we have legendary epics and mythical stories of heroes and battles fought during migration. For the Garo tribe, it is important to have a migration story. The story is not very clear and lack precise data but people like to narrate it with authority and ultimately it became the foundational story of the origin and history of the tribe. Another important group of stories that helps the members of the tribe recognise and relate to each other are the relational stories such as maternal or paternal relations.

A good or clever narrator is spontaneous. She is gifted with presence of mind and can make up stories on the spot, while going to the market or by observing an incident. She can weave the story even while in the process of narrating it. Listening to storytelling can be entertaining, informing and soothing or relaxing (such as bedtime stories). Stories also persuade, making the listeners believe what is said or told. There is a bond between the narrator and the listeners and a fondness develops especially where children are concerned. Stories are told in order to comfort or bring joy to the mourning hearts as well. Narrating the stories of a loved one who has passed away can bring some kind of healing. Remembering in story is an expression of love.

---

[14] Eugene Linden, "Lost Tribes, Lost Knowledge," *Time* (23 September 1991): 46-54, http://www.ciesin.org/docs/002-268/002-268.html (accessed on 16 August 2019).

Tribal stories have no real or known author. Their historical origins are obscure and unknown. Stories belong to the village, clan or tribe. The tellers and narrators of the tales and stories can be anyone. However, looking at its characteristics or style of telling and the fact that it is passed on from generation to generation, it can easily be understood that it is a communication from the older generation to the younger ones. The Garos call the proverbial or wisdom sayings as *Aganme·apa*. In *Aganme·apa* we find their deep thoughts which serve as the guiding principles for the community members. The members are expected to understand that these sayings are meant to be instructions for the members to live a good and peaceable life. Guided by such wisdom, they are expected to live a good, harmonious and convivial life.[15]

Garo sayings contain simple instructions as well as teachings and admonitions to educate one another of how to live as a tribe or as people living in one village. For example, there is a Garo saying that goes like this:

A·totko so·o a·makokama
Do·siko goo do·makosananga[16]

This saying is related to jhum cultivation. Literally, it means that if one is careless while burning a small hillock it could burn the whole mountain; and while trying to shoot a small bird like a parrot one could hit a very big bird. The idea or main teaching behind this saying is that if one is not careful or if one is unmindful in small matters, bigger troubles may come. The cultural ethos which are embedded in the stories, songs, proverbs, tales and other narratives are expected to help the tribal to understand "self," live a good life and be a good human being.

Women as Primary Storytellers in Tribal Communities

In the narrative communication of the tribal communities, there is no specific narrator. It is always attributed to the grandparents or the elders of the tribe. B. B. Kumar quotes J. P. Mills who wrote about the Ao Nagas and lamented that the past traditions are slowly eroding although the old men of the tribe continue to tell stories.[17] I would like to say that it is not only men who tell stories. My own mother told me stories about our clan and the place of origin from where our grandparents came from. When I was small, she told me the names of the morning star and evening star in Garo. My mother-in-law is a very good storyteller. Her narrative communication is based on her ability to remember and retell the stories that she has heard, seen, or experienced as a

[15] B. K. Sangma. *Aganme·apako Dokbadale Seani* (Tura: Author, 1996), 1.

[16] B. K. Sangma. *Aganme·apako Dokbadale Seani*, 6.

[17] B. B. Kumar, *Folk-Lores and Folk-Motifs*, 7-8.

child and while growing up in the village. She is able to tell various stories that are related to the Angami worldview.

The Garos do not have a particular name for tales told by the grandparents. Stories are simply known as *Golpo* and usually it is the grandparents who tell tales. There is no particular place or time for a narration of stories to take place. Among the Manipuris, the activity when the children listen to their grandmother's tales or stories while waiting for their meal is known as *Chakngai-wari*.[18] The Manipuri term used for tales told around by grandparents to their grandchildren around the kitchen fireis *phunga-wari*, which means tales of the hearth.[19] The fireplace is a private space in most tribal cultures where the family not only share food but where the elders, usually the grandparents, narrate stories to the younger generation.

Many cultures and tribes often talk about tribe's stories as grandfather's tales and some attribute their stories to both grandparents. This is not because grandfathers tell better stories. In one of the articles in *The Hindu*, Rani Devalla quotes a Tamil writer, Kutti Revati, who said that "women are better story tellers." Revati opines that "every woman should explore the creative domain as she has better visualisation and can express her thoughts more candidly."[20]

Women's telling of stories is not by oral narration alone. They use other creative means to give life and vividness to stories. They narrate stories through songs and dance forms. For example, in one of the dance forms of the *Wangala* the Garo women dance a step called *Ajema Roa*, which mimics the dancing of the wagtail bird in the streams. There are other steps which depict the works being done in the jhum or paddy fields—steps illustrating the sowing or planting of paddy, harvesting, chasing the monkeys away, plucking citrus fruit called *chambil* and such other activities.

Women are the primary storytellers in the family. They tell stories especially to their children right from a very young age. Garo women are fond of singing lullabies and telling things to their toddlers while playfully and lovingly lifting their children in admiration. This lullaby singing is known as *mumua*, and the playful lifting of the infant by putting both hands in between the two arms of the infant and making the infant comfortable is known as

---

[18] M. Kirti Singh, *Folk Culture of Manipur* (Delhi: Manas Publications, 1993), 2.

[19] Singh, *Folk Culture of Manipur*, 2. This particular setting of telling tales near the hearth is found in other tribal cultures also but I have not known any particular name. But in the Garo culture it is often called as *Wal·timoagangipagolporang*, meaning stories or tales told by the fireside.

[20] Rani Devalla,"Women are Better Storytellers," reporting on the Tamil writer Kutti Revati, *The Hindu*, 31 March 2014, https://www.thehindu.com/news/cities/Visakhapatnam/women-are-better-storytellers/article5855343.ece (accessed on 16 August 2019).

dingdinga.[21] While doing *dingdinga*, the mother can narrate small stories or sayings and make the child comfortable. Jamie Marak shares one such saying where a mother while doing *dingdinga* says – "*Do·magitabilangbo.*" It means that the mother is wishing the best and offers her blessing to her little one to soar high and go far in life.[22] Dokatchi Marak also talks about how women are fond of telling stories during their leisure time. They tell stories while in the jhum field, while collecting firewood and vegetables and also while sitting and relaxing by the fireside. She also expresses that most of the stories that women narrate are: "full of moral lessons, rightful living, and character moulding." According to her, women live in close connection with nature and through stories they teach their children to love and care for the environment also.[23]

Most tribal women are hardworking. They have to fetch water from far distances in rivers or village ponds or springs. At such times, women take chance to narrate the stories of events in the village to each other. They also like to talk about things available in the market, family life, their responsibilities as a mother or about clan matters. Women also like to talk about food and share recipes with each other even if it is their own tribe's cuisine. The other place that women like to talk and share stories is at the funerals, especially because it is the women who usually wait with the dead body before the funeral.

As I was writing this paper, I received an advertisement of some traditional clothes belonging to the Mizo tribe sent on a WhatsApp group. They were all different patterns with beautiful colours. The traditional clothes of the tribes can easily be identified through the motifs, designs, and symbols in the tapestry of shawls or *mekhelas*. Each tribe's clothes are expertly and intricately woven, thus communicating the identity of the tribe.[24]

In a programme called *Siyahi*,[25] which is organised to talk about different tribes' traditional shawls and *mekhalas*, different speakers were invited to talk

---

[21] This information was given to me by Dokatchi Ch. Marak, through a conversation on 23 October 2018. She is a professor in the Department of Garo Linguistics, NEHU, Tura.

[22] Even while the baby is in the womb, women are known to tell beautiful stories so that the babies are born well and healthy. Not only that but it is believed that this helps the babies develop good bonding with their mothers. In conversation with Jamie Ch. Marak, PhD student in Garo Linguistics, NEHU, Tura, on 23 October 2018. She also says that *Do·ma*is a very strong bird that can fly very far.

[23] In conversation with Dokatchi Ch. Marak, on 23 October 2018.

[24] In North East India, most of the time, apart from the language that we speak, the tribe is significantly identified as people belonging to a particular tribe, because of the traditional clothes that the women weave.

[25] Siyahi, as a literary consultancy is associating with World Learning India to create a lecture series to fulfill the aim of Culture and Development Seminar. It is a programme run by World Learning India and the School for International Training (SIT), http://siyahi.in/2011/06/programme-2/ (accessed on 16August 2018).

about how the clothes of different tribes tells us stories. The Sumi tribe of Nagaland sing a narrative song called *Aye Kuzu Le.* The song is performed by the women depicting various stages of weaving the traditional shawl—planting cotton seeds, plucking the cotton, deseeding, spinning, and weaving. So, the song is not just a song but a means for telling the story of weaving and passing on the knowledge and skill of weaving to the next generation. In Manipur, Naga men and women wear a woollen sarong called the *kashan*. The *Luingamla Kashan* is a red Tangkhul Nagawraparound, which is an elegy for a friend. The patterns of the cloth tell the story of the vivacious joy of a young girl, the brutality meted to her for resisting rape by two army officers, how she was shot dead and the route to justice, represented by the wings of a butterfly.

The Garo *mekhelas* which is known as the *dakmanda*, has mostly the floral motifs and geometrical designs. The shawls are woven usually with a *boring* (treehouse), *milam* (two-edged sword), and *danil* (a shield). The patterns of the *dakmanda* communicate the close affinity that the people have with nature as well as a reminder of their own tribe as headhunters.

The Place of Tribal Narrative in Christian Life

I believe it is important for tribal theology to be story theology. Story theology would tell of our life's struggles and triumphs, the plight of women, children and underprivileged people. Story theology would tell women's stories—stories of brave women like Jael, raped women like Tamar, faithful women like Hannah. Story theology would tell of those women who witnessed the horror of the cross and heard Jesus crying out to God, "My God, My God, why have you forsaken me?" It would recount how tribal women too have been branded as sinners and prevented from following Jesus' call to serve him and those whom he loves. Have tribal women not suffered for years and years under male tyranny and all they could do was cry out to God, "My God, My God, why have you forsaken me?"

Tribal narrative communication is also needed in tribal worship. God is a storyteller. We are living the story that God is still telling us. In worship, we retell God's story. And our worship is also our story about what God means to us, how we meet Jesus, and how we live as a community. Our stories will be flawed if only a male preacher is allowed to be narrator. Every one of us has a story. We ought to tell our stories. For as long as we can remember, most of us have attended worship services. If we are honest, most of the hours spent in church were boring, lifeless, and did nothing much to us except maybe a vague sense of goodness that we have attended church and performed our religious duty. Our stories can save us.

Story worship cannot happen so long as we go on worshipping in our conventional ways. Brief narrative sermons, life stories/testimonies, story songs, arts and crafts that tell the stories of the artists, and other creative ways of relating to God may be used in worship. Story worship is contextual because every story is told from the narrator's perspective.

There are many stories to tell. Let us begin with a few.

13

Liberative Symbolism of the Spirit/s: A Tribal Feminist Pneumatology

*Eyingbẹni Hümtsoe-Nienu**

Tribal perspective on the doctrine of the Holy Spirit seems to be comparatively less discussed; much lesser on tribal feminist pneumatology. The paucity of tribal discourses on the Holy Spirit, as compared to Christology,[1] does not reflect an absence of sources. It can be largely attributed to an overall neglect of pneumatology in Christian theology in general and feminist theology in particular.[2] Brief Christian essays relating to the ancestral tribal belief in the spirits have reproduced a (colonial) narrative informed by prejudicial perspectives on local traditions by either rendering absolutely negative

* Dr Eyingbeni teaches Christian Doctrines and feminist theologies at Clark Theological College, Aolijen, Mokokchung.

[1] There are considerable number of essays and volumes on tribal Christology. Recent books on the topic are Bendanglemla Longkumer, *Christ the Healer* (New Delhi: CWI, 2018); Yangkahao Vashum, *Christology in Context* (New Delhi: CWI, 2017); Lalnghakthuami, *Understanding Jesus: Indigenous Women Perspective* (New Delhi: ISPCK, 2014); L.H. Lalpekhlua, *Contextual Christology* (New Delhi: ISPCK, 2007).

[2] Nicola Slee indentifies various reasons for the neglect. See Nicola Slee, "The Holy Spirit and Spirituality" in *The Cambridge Companion to Feminist Theology*, Ed., Susan Frank Parsons (Cambridge, UK: CUP, 2004), 171-72.

interpretations of the spirits[3] or by emphasizing largely on the victorious defeat of them in Christ.[4] Despite its educative nature, in terms of a theological treatise such an approach has two flaws. First, it perpetuates a symbolism of feminine emasculation by masculine powers ultimately embodied in the victorious (foreign) monarch – Jesus Christ. Second, it leaves unanswered the perceptible connection between the workings of the spirits in ancestral belief and the Holy Spirit in tribal Christian thought. Both need attention for appropriating contextual Christian theology, belief, and practice in general and in understanding the person and work of the Holy Spirit in general, particularly in relation to women and their spirituality.

What a spirit-centered symbolism of feminine liberation and the functional continuum[5] of the Spirit/s achieve for women's faith and spirituality will establish the significance of the Holy Spirit in the life and witness of modern tribal Christians. Of interest in this essay is to articulate the way that the Holy Spirit works to empower women, without gender bias. I've taken a liberative approach in interpreting the work of the Holy Spirit derived from a three-way conversation between ancestral tribal traditions, biblical, and contextual phenomena. The thesis is to argue that the nature and function of the spirits in the ancient world and of the Holy Spirit in the biblical world are instructive to subvert patriarchal control over women's free expression of Christian faith, including in worship, today. Thus, the spirits then and the Holy Spirit now is a symbol of women's liberation from any oppressive and suppressive theology and practice in the church and community.

The Animated World of the Ancestors: Liberative Space

Tribals are familiar with legends and myths surrounding the animated characteristic of the natural world. Our ancestors spoke of rocks that were inhabited by ghosts[6] and that could move and grow in size.[7] They spoke of

---

[3] Cf., Najekhu Yepthomi, "early History of the Nagas," *From Darkness to Light* (Kohima, NL: NBCC, 1997), 16-17.

[4] Cf., Elungkiebe Zeliang, "Nagas' Triumph over Evil Spirits through Christ," *Journal of Tribal Studies* VI/2 (June-Dec 2002), 96-101.

[5] For a discussion on the ontological continuity and distinctiveness between the spirits, Holy Spirit and Supreme Being, refer, Eyingbeni Hümtsoe-Nienu, *God of the Tribes: Christian Perspective on the Naga Ancestral Idea of the Supreme Being* (Mokokchung, NL: CTC, 2014), 213-233.

[6] In Lotha language, the word *omon* is used to imply both the English meaning of ghost/s and spirit/s. it can have reference to both helpful, harmful and neutral spirits. Demons were considered inherently evil and called *Tsünghram*. Christianity uses this word to name Satan.

[7] J.P. Mills, *The Lhota(sic) Nagas* (London: MacMillan Co, 1922[1980]), 166-68.

tales that trees, fields, forests and rivers were inspirited by spirits[8] and that heavenly objects were human relatives.[9] There are guardians for each living body – including the waters and the forests.[10] P. Dozo clearly underlines that "...objects were not worshipped but were believed to be possessed and controlled by the spirits...Parents alerted or advised their children to avoid going near [to] those suspected mountains, rivers, trees, rocks or stones."[11] It seems that the whole 'universe' of the tribals was one big spirited sphere. The spiritedness forms a commonality across created beings, linking also to the Supreme Spirit/Being – from whom all lives are drawn.[12]

The space where spirits lived and functioned was comparatively freer than the established religious institutions. A case in hand is that of the office of the village priest/*pvüti*. One of the criteria for priesthood was the specification of gender; he should be a man, a "son of proper and legitimate parentage."[13] Such male-centric religious authority, appointed by a host of village male elders, is a patriarchal space, where female are tabooed or deliberately excluded. In contrast, the space of intermediaries between the spirit/s and human are gender inclusive. A shaman, whether practicing divination, sacrifices, dream interpretation, or traditional medicine, can be either female or male.[14] This clearly indicates that the spirits are non-prejudicial in responding to the diviners. For female shamans, then, where organized institutions refuse participation they receive unrestricted access to the world of the spirits. The common people likewise respond to their supernatural powers without casting aspersion on female competence, as they regrettably would in socio-political leadership and institutionalized religious arena.

---

[8] V. Nienu, *Naga Cultural Milieu: An Adaptation to Mountain Ecosystem* (SF, CA: Dorylus Pub. Gp, 2015), 143.

[9] Cf., Yangkahoa Vashum, "The Stars are our Relatives: Some Musing of Indigenous People's Stellar Theology," in *JTCA*, Vol. 6 (2007), 111-130.

[10] Cf., Mills, *The Lhota Nagas,* 115; Ezamo Murry, *Tribal Spirituality Reconsidered: A Psychological Study of Religion* (New Delhi: ISPCK, 1995), 61-62.

[11] Phuveyi Dozo, *The Cross Over Nagaland,* Revised (New Delhi: Zuve and Dozo, 1992), 11-12.

[12] Wati Longcahr, *The Traditional Tribal Worldview and Modernity* (Jorhat, AS: N. Limala Lkr, 1995), 42.

[13] Ezamo Murry, "Belief in a Supreme God among the Kyong Tribe of Nagaland" in *Tribal Christian Theology: Methods and Sources for Constructing a Relevant Theology for the Indigenous People of North East India*, Eds., Razouselie Lasetso and Yangkahao Vashum (Jorhat: ETC Program Coordination, 2007), 89.

[14] Bendanglemla Longkumer in the book *Christ the Healer: Exploring Indigenous People's Spirituality* (New Delhi: CWI, 2018) has developed a contextual Christology within the framework of the Ao traditional name of the shaman – *Arasantsur*. I would think that developing a contextual Pneumatology with the stated basis would be a far better alternative.

Interestingly, in some tribal narratives, the gender of spirits is popularly portrayed as masculine, though it is difficult to ascertain if they were actually seen or apparent. Also, the recipients of their favors or otherwise appear to directly fall on the menfolk. The Lotha Nagas speak of notable spirits with masculine connotations both in naming style and in tasks.[15] For e.g., Sükhyingo is believed to be a short man with twisted neck and takes charge of the animal world. It is his prerogative to grant success or failure to hunters. Likewise, another spirit of the waters by the name Jüpvüo – meaning "owner of the water" – is imaged as a "*man* with hair of enormous length, who lives at the bottom of deep pools and uses human skulls as hearth-stone."[16] As one having mastery over aquatic life, Jüpvüo "withholds or grants the fish of the waters to the fishers."[17] Community hunting and fishing being traditionally deemed as male sports, it is safe to conclude that both were perceived as male spirits who dealt primarily with men. Rengmas have a similar belief in Thyükhonyu – the ruler of the animal domain. He is nicknamed "the jungle man."[18]

Male-centric narratives maybe common but forming feminine narrative is essential for reclaiming the liberative spaces that also included feminine spirits and womenfolk. Much like the feminine connotations inherent in the biblical names of the Holy Spirit,[19] tribal belief in spirits is not bereft of feminine presence. Jümkaroni and Apisangla[20] are two spirit entities who are presiders at the deep end of the entrance to the land of the dead/*etchüi li*. They were responsible to determine the nature of death and act accordingly. Ezamo Murry attributes the principal spirit of the land of the dead to a woman known as Echulivantamvu.[21] Likewise, the Sümis speak of Kungulumi - the spirits of the sky - with reference to celestial feminine spirit beings. In the Ao tradition, Ongangla - Meyutsüng's wife - would obviously have to be considered a feminine spirit. The Rengmas also have female-centered stories. They tell of Nyesiginyu – the spirit of wealth – who is specifically associated with bountiful harvest (of paddy). In her honor, Rengma women would observe agricultural

[15] Ronsü and Ngazo, Jüpvüo, Sükhyingo and other spirits with specific authority over limited locale are structurally masculine. Their tasks are also stereo-typically masculine.

[16] J.P. Mills, *The Lhota Nagas*, 115.

[17] Ezamo Murry, *Tribal Spirituality Re-considered*, 62.

[18] Khontele Seb, "The Traditional Understanding of *Sunggigü* and its Relevance for Developing a Contextual Understanding of God for Rengma People," (Unpublished MTh thesis, Senate of Serampore, 2011), 39.

[19] We are thinking of names such as *Ruah*, *Sophia, Shekinah, Hokma.*

[20] Most Naga tribes like Lothas, Aos, Sangtams, and Sümis, to name some, believe that the dead go to the land of the dead, situated in Wokha. The former name sounds like Lotha and the latter Sangtam.

[21] Ezamo Murry, "Belief in a Supreme God among the Kyong Tribe," 87. The etymology of the name is *etchü* (dead), *li* (field), *Vantam* (Supremo).

rites and rituals.[22] Züriginyu – the spirit of the water creatures – seems to manifest in both female and male appearance depending on "the nature of the river and geographical settings."[23] But, it appears that the Rengmas generally revered her benevolence and had no issue with her femininity.[24]

The spirits cited above are named not merely to counter balance the masculine ideas and interpretations of the spirit world that have figured prominently in tribal theological discourses but also to rectify the invisibility of feminine powers in the spirit world. It is most probable that these supernatural beings functioned at the bidding of the divine authority - the Supreme Being – the source of the Holy Spirit.[25] To recognize the belief in the existence of both male and female spirits is a reaffirmation that like the Holy Spirit the spirits were characterized by egalitarianism in both nature and function. The gender inclusive narratives show that the spaces which the spirits occupy are just as liberative as the work they do and symbolism they conjure up (Cf John 4: 8), particularly for women.

The Empowering of the Spirit in Christianity: Liberative Spirituality

In Christianity as well, the Holy Spirit reveals its empowering authority in the most egalitarian fashion. In Nagaland, the basic ecclesial structure is hierarchically patriarchal. Leadership in the church, much like in the social sphere is dominated by men. In such a scenario, an emerging phenomenon is a witness to the enabling power of God in the Holy Spirit. In almost all churches, women form a large majority in worship services and also in the praying ministry of the church. I would like to focus on the latter aspect.

The praying ministry is undertaken by a group commonly known as "prayer warriors" – or simply prayer groups, prefixed by the church name or prayer home's name.[26] Almost all members are divinely endowed with charismatic gifts akin to the traditional powers of the shaman. Fasting, prophesying, speaking in tongues, seeing vision, exorcising, exhortations,

---

[22] Khontele, "The Traditional Understanding of Sunggigü," 35-37.

[23] Ibid., 38.

[24] Ibid., 37-39.

[25] Cf., Eyingbeni Hümtsoe-Nienu, *God of the Tribes: Christian Perspective on the Naga Ancestral Idea of the Supreme Being* (Mokokchung, NL: CTC, 2014), 213-214. Demonic activities were attributed to the Devil – Tsünghram – who was believed also to have gendered spirits at his beck and call.

[26] Prayer groups are common in most Baptist churches in Nagaland. The members consider themselves prayer-warriors. Prayer groups and Prayer centers are closely related and are mostly frequented by members of the prayer groups, and by those who seek physical, mental and psychological healing. Speaking in tongues, prophecies and healing are emphasized by both.

singing Revival songs[27] and intercessions are the common features of the prayer group meetings. Some groups carry out their task through the "prayer homes"[28] while some only meet in prayer halls or homes of its members on rotational basis. On some occasions, they visit homes of those assigned by God, as claimed by the group. The reasons for such visitation may range from praying against serious ailments to conveying a message of warning for impending doom. It is usually a weekly program in most instances.

One of the unique features of these prayer groups is the lopsided gender ratio; women are in clear majority. Also, a woman or women in the group are predominantly the recipients of God's message – "prophets". A cursory survey validates this claim. In one of the most notable prayer homes, Chathe prayer center, there are 21 prayer warriors. Among them 5 are men and the rest 16 are women. The "prophet" to whom God speaks in a major way is a woman by the name Apeno. Another group supported by the church is Lotha Baptist Church Kohima Randan (Prayer) Okho (group) (KLBC-RO); it has a total of 30 members. Of which 25 are women and 5 are men. Those who play major part in communicating God's messages are three women viz., Nchumbeni, Lanbeno and Penrolo.[29] There are two prayers homes/groups in Wokha town: Lothatsü prayer centers (LPC)–Zütanphen and LPC–Tsümang. Both centers have women in majority forming about 70% of the total membership.[30] This appears to be true across different tribes. The Satakha Town Baptist Church, Zunheboto, prayer group is recognized by the church. A total of 25 members form the group. Out of which 22 are women and 3 are men. There are 4 women who receive the message of God.[31] In the Ao Naga churches there are no organized prayer groups but there are members whose charismatic gifts are made best use of during Revivals[32] and church camps, particularly for

[27] Revival songs are very commonly sung by tribals in the region. They are popular during Revival events. Depending on the church, they are also sung in worship services accompanied by local drum. Most of them are original compositions, others are adaptation of western hymns. Ironically, the texts normally revolve around heaven and afterlife. Among the youth, the traditional revival songs are replaced by western "praise and worship" songs with full electronic instrumentation.

[28] Prayer homes are like spiritual retreat centers but with more functions. Such homes entertain people with different ailments and issues. They are usually manned by a group of persons who have gifts of healing, vision, tongues, prophecy and such.

[29] Interview with T. Zubeni Lotha, 70 years, Kohima, October 22, 2018. She has been a member of KLBC-RO since 1985.

[30] Interview with Nlumo Lotha, 75 years, Wokha Town. He's a member in the LPC–Zütanphen.

[31] Interview with Kuholi Z. Aye, 65 years, Satakha Town, Zunheboto. She is also member of the prayer group.

[32] Revivals are sporadic occurrences within the local Baptist Churches. Phuveyi Dozo, a Naga Church leader calls the revivals in Nagaland as "awakenings." He dates back the "First

youth and children. They are called "counselors" and women are in majority, at least 60% among them.[33] It is noteworthy that for the women who exercise the aforementioned spiritual gifts there is no resistance even when used within a staunchly patriarchal context. In fact, their gifting is openly acknowledged and at times sought after by those eager for intermediaries to speak, and be spoken, to by God.

Historical records on Nagaland prove that women and girls freely exercised their charismatic endowments during Revival events. Takatemjen writes of girls in the age of 12 and 16 making prophetic utterances and seeing vision respectively.[34] Perhaps, these are moments in which young girls are taken seriously in spiritual matters for once by the church. Luen also recounts events of the 70's Revivals in Nagaland in which women "filled by the Holy Spirit" exercised unprecedented and unrestrained authority. They could share testimonies of healing boldly; stop a car on the highway for miraculous deliverance;[35] send out a man to run divinely instructed errand;[36] see vision and be believed in, and make public declaration of personal desire.[37] Such exercises are unusual by normal standards but pleasantly quite liberative in terms of women's uninhibited participation in the spiritual matters. The manner in which God fulfills his promise: *Then afterward I will pour out my spirit on all flesh...your daughters shall prophesy....Even on...female slaves...I will pour out my spirit* (Joel 2: 28-29), to the early Christians and onto Christian women today is a vision *de facto* of the faithfulness of God. Migliore rightly opines that "the Spirit at work in the Christian community" is "first-fruit" (Rom 8:23) "first installment" or "guarantee" (2 Cor 1: 22; 5:5) of the future that God is bringing....for the completion of God's redemptive work...."[38] Of greater joy is the visible beginning of God's righteous work in the Holy Spirit that has begun in these women.

Wakening" to 1885, which was more evangelistic in nature. The second was in the late forties and early fifties. The "Third Awakening" happened in 1972. Charismatic features accompanied the later two "Awakenings." Cf., Phuveyi Dozo, *The Cross Over Nagaland,* 17-43. Cf., O. L. Snaitiang, *Churches Of Indigenous Origins in the Northeast India* (Delhi: ISPCK, 2000), 188-190.

[33] Interview with Dr Asongla Pongen, member of Alempang Baptist Church, Mokokchung, since childhood.

[34] Takatemjen, *Studies on Theology and Naga Culture* (Mokokchung: Author, 1997), 113-14.

[35] M. I. Luen, *The Fire of Revival* (Secunderabad, AP: Authentic Books, 2009), 36.

[36] Luen, *The Fire of Revival*, 111.

[37] Luen, *The Fire of Revival*, 101

[38] Daniel L. Migliore, *Faith Seeking Understanding: An Introduction to Christian Theology*, 2nd Ed. (Grand Rapids, MI: William B. Eerdmans Pub Co., 2004), 229.

The Enabling of the Inspirited: Liberative Living

It is significant to note that in the Ao belief *Tiaba* is considered as the one who "casts spirit of various kinds: man, animal and nature, and so some people are tiger-spirited, boar-spirited [and] fox spirited. *Some are not given any spirit so they remain dumb or dull* (emphasis added)."[39] This concept is important to impart the understanding the need of Spirit's empowering to exercise restraint over evil and injustices and nonconformity to righteous purposes of God. For a Christian, the absence of the Holy Spirit would mean that one is reduced to the state of being "dumb" and "dull" in aspects of life that must necessarily manifest the active presence and working of God. Any theology, belief, and practice that contradict God's working through the Holy Spirit is an affront against the domain that he seeks to establish. One of the essential characteristics of his domain is truthfulness. On the other hand, cultures that exhibit sexism in any form is a perpetuation of falsehood. To have the Holy Spirit is to be liberated from the bondage of falsehood (Jn 8: 32; 2 Cor 3:17) that assumes and treats one gender below par with the other.

Lovely is right in arguing, without euphemism, that Naga women do not have "any past or lost golden age". That the antithetical sphere of men's and women's validated the patriarchal culture and that preconceptions of Naga women enjoying equal status with men are deemed conclusions at face value.[40] Her argument is not without concrete evidences. She systematically underlines ancient structures, practices and customary values that advantages tribal men at the expense of their women. I must agree with Migliore that the "a Christian theology of the Holy Spirit will give attention to the work of the Holy Spirit in binding believers to Christ [and God] and creating new life and new community in him."[41] Sadly, the Christian identity of the tribals has not rectified the many deficiencies apparent in their dealing with women. Creating new life and new community in Christ through the Holy Spirit must necessarily imply change in the nature of erstwhile patriarchal communities into an egalitarian one. It must also imply a complete turnover in gender relations from a domineering to a mutual one.

The Bible testifies that the Holy Spirit is the Spirit of truth (Jn 14:17, 26) and the teacher of all that pertains to the will of God made known in the life, ministry and teachings of Christ (14: 16). In the "new covenant age" whereby the Holy Spirit is the "primary manifestation of the presence of the Trinity

---

[39] Panger Imchen, *Ancient Ao Naga Religion and Culture* (New Delhi: Ashok Gosain for Har-Anand Pub, 1993) 34. Cf., Eyingbeni Hümtsoe-Nienu, *God of the Tribes,* 218.

[40] See Lovely Awomi James, *Tribal Theology: Reviewing the Naga Traditional Worldview* (New Delhi: CWI, 2017).

[41] Migliore, *Faith Seeking Understanding*, 227.

among us" and "the one who is most prominently present with us now"[42] the Sophia, the feminine expression of the Holy Spirit, plays that role of a truth-teacher. The truth is essentially liberative. Migliore is right again to point out that "The Spirit frees us to take on the 'mind' of Christ (Phil 2:5), to live according to the 'law' of Christ (Gal 6:2)."[43] As the One who continues the work of Jesus Christ today, the Holy Spirit works in cohesion with the mind of the other two persons in the Trinity (Jn 16:13-15).

The church in particular must first of all fully manifest God's presence in the Spirit by promoting gender justice. The spirit-filled space of the ancient world was gender inclusive as discussed above. The church, the people of God, is to be filled with the Holy Spirit (Eph 5:18b) and consequently every space they occupy ought to reveal that inspiritedness. Sexist structures, practices or thought patterns that diminish the witness to the God of truth is a sign that the presence of the Spirit is absent. Fabricated lies that fuel misogyny encapsulated in proverbial sayings like "crabs and women do not have religion" or that "the wisdom of a woman does not cross the village gate"[44] are not only to be opposed but thrown to the pigs as though they were ominous (Cf., Mk 5: 1-13).

Sadly, there seems to be no perceptible change in the role and status of women beyond the charismata. In fact, the leaders of the prayer groups and homes mentioned above are all men, despite women being in majority. Questioning whether it's a case of God not speaking in favor of women's leadership would clearly contradict God's just mode of working. The obvious possibility, then, must be that the 'groups' have refused to listen to the voice of God deafened by the noise of masculine hegemony!

Keitzar's statement that "The traditional understanding of the Great Spirit, the spirit world, or the manifold works of the spirits all lead to a better understanding of the work of the Holy Spirit....Perhaps the Nagas can understand the doctrine of the Holy Spirit better because we have a background of the spirit worship (*sic*)"[45] will find validation when Christian/communities show reverential allegiance to the Holy Spirit by listening to the voice of truth symbolized in the just ways of God in Christ. It is not right that women's gifting is maximized only on occasions and circumstances that benefit individuals desperate for supernatural intervention. The freedom which women enjoy in relation to their charismatic gifts during special events should also become the

Wayne Grudem, *Systematic Theology: An Introduction to Biblical Doctrine* (Grand Rapids, MI: Zondervan, 1994), 634-35.

[43] Migliore, *Faith Seeking Understanding*, 228.

[44] Cf., Samuel Lalrinsanga, "Role and Status of Mizo Women," in *Women Then and Now: Sharing Untold Insights on Women of North East India*, ed Narola Imchen and Eyingbeni Hümtsoe (Jorhat, AS:WSC, 2011), 51.

[45] Renthy Keitzar, "The Indigenization of the Naga Christian Theology," in *In Search of Praxis Theology for the Nagas* (New Delhi: Regency Publication for CNBC, 2003), 41.

norm in everyday living and in all areas of life. Restoration of gender justice (Cf., Isa 42: 1-4; 61:1-4), then, will become a hallmark of communities living in the Spirit.

Conclusion

Keitzar is correct in observing that -

> The Naga Christians have not yet completely got rid of their subconscious belief in animism ['belief in spiritual beings(s)']. For example, the present day upsurge of the so-called charismatism among the Christians is, in fact, an explosion of the repressed animism. Most of the manifestations of charismatism are clearly external signs of primitive animatism and spiritualism....[46]

The crucial issue is the need for tribal churches to recognize that the spirit world of the ancestors is a space that affirms both genders. The charismatic phenomenon in Christianity cannot be fully detached from pre-Christian spirituality because of the ontological and epistemological continuity of the Triune God at all times and in all places. It is binding on Christian communities to accept that God has been pouring out his favor on women from time immemorial. Even today, God works in and through Holy Spirit to enable both women and men to experience God's righteousness but tribal communities continue to limit the scope of that divine gifting according to gendered socio-cultural boundaries. Thus, communities are poorer because women's presence in most areas is either customarily forbidden or deliberately restricted or habitually forgotten.

The essay reveals that irrespective of human distinctive factors like gender, age, class, and tribe, people who are faced with illness of different kinds – physical, psychological, mental or spiritual - seek out those who are endowed with charismatic powers and gifts. This is true in the ancient times as well as in the Christian era. Women have found a respectable place in the mystical realm. And they must now be accorded the same place in other dimensions of life. The Holy Spirit must guide Christians and their communities – *when the Spirit of truth comes, he will guide you into all the truth* (Jn 16: 13) – as those enabled by the Holy Spirit to practice truth and justice in its entirety.

---

[46] Renthy Keitzar, "The Indigenisation of Naga Christian Theology," *In Search of Praxis Theology for the Nagas* (New Delhi: Regency Publication for Council of Naga Baptist Churches, 2003), 41.

14

Tribal Understanding of Priesthood and Its Relevance for Today

S. Akatoli Chishi

Introduction

The term priest and the function of priesthood in the tribal society are much more fluid and less clearly defined when compared with the nature and function of priesthood of the highly organized hierarchies of the other societies. It is more complex again because of the many related role types that existed especially in the Indian tribal society. It is not easy to delineate in detail the tribal understanding of priesthood and to bring out its relevance in the context where there still exist gender inequalities in the churches or conflict in regard to initiation of women into priesthood. However, an attempt is made to uncover the understanding of priesthood where the main quality which qualifies them or sets them apart from others was their knowledge of the sacred and the profane. An attempt is also made in the last section to reconstruct some traditional values of the tribals.

1. Priest and Priesthood: An Overview

Priesthood is the office of a priest, a ritual expert learned in a special knowledge of the technique of worship and accepted as a religious and spiritual leader.

Throughout the long and varied history of religion, the priesthood has been the official institution that has mediated and maintained a state of equilibrium between the sacred and the profane aspects of human society and that has exercised a stabilizing influence on social structures and on cultic organizations. The term priest is derived etymologically from the Greek word *presbyteros* ("elder"), of which it is a contraction, and it is equated with the Latin word *sacerdos* (the Roman officiant at the sacrifices and sacred rites).[1]

In most common parlance, the priest is a religious functionary whose role is to administer an established religion - to celebrate the traditional rituals, practices, and beliefs. Weber explains that "it is more correct for our purpose in order to do justice to the diverse and mixed manifestations of this phenomenon, to set up as the crucial feature of the priesthood, the specialization of a particular group of persons in the continuous operation of a cultic enterprise, permanently associated with particular norms, places and times, and related to specific social groups."[2]

The main function or the essential characteristic of the priest is cultic. Worship, as the very expression of religious experience, however primitive or rudimentary its form may be, is the main concern of the priest. S/he guarantees the right performance of formalized acts of worship.[3] The priest mediates between God and humans; s/he not only interprets the divine will but also regulates and strengthens the relation between God and her/his fellow human beings. The basis of her/his existence and authority is a continuous and regular communion with the Divine. For the priesthood regular ritual (liturgical) observance and a fixed theology are essential.[4] Weber reiterated that there can be no priesthood without a cult, although there may well be a cult without a specialized priesthood because a rationalization of metaphysical views and a specifically religious ethic are missing in the case of a cult without priest.[5]

Another essential characteristic of the priest is her/his linkage with an organized religion, and legitimation by religious authorities. An extended, cross-cultural description of the priest is, "any religious specialist acting ritually for or on behalf of a community."[6] The priest inheres in a religious organization as a representative of that establishment, and her/his actions

---

[1] Edwin Oliver James, "Priesthood" in *Encyclopedia Britannica* https://www.britannica.com/topic/priesthood (2/10/2018).

[2] Max Weber, *The Sociology of Religion*, 4th rev. ed., trans. Ephraim Fischoff, intro. Talcott Parsons (Boston: Beacon Press, 1963), 30.

[3] Joachim Wach, *Sociology of Religion* (London: The University of Chicago Press, 1944), 365.

[4] Joachim Wach, *Sociology of Religion*..., 360-362.

[5] Max Weber, *The Sociology of Religion* ..., 30.

[6] Willard G. Oxtoby. "Priesthood: an Overview," *The Encyclopedia of Religion*, 1995 ed.

mediate between its traditions and the people.[7] Differing from other related roles, "the priest serves the altar, in the temple or shrine, as the representative of the community in her/his relations with the gods and the sacred order by virtue of the status and its functions that have been conferred upon her/him at her/his ordination, bestowing its sacredness and attendant taboos."[8] Bendix interprets Weber, and reiterated that the priest serves in a holy tradition, and "even when the priest possesses a personal charisma, her/his function is legitimate only by virtue of a regular organization of worship."[9] The traditional priest is also an important social figure because after her/his priestly training s/he becomes the custodian of societal or communal customs, knowledge and wisdom, taboos and the history of the society. In support of this view, Opoku affirms, "priests are repositories of communal knowledge and traditions."[10]

About the Levitical priests of Judaism, Brown points out that even "if a man was born into the priestly tribe, s/he still had to be installed in the priestly office."[11] Often the priest is the official representative of a religion. Greenwood, while affirming that the priest is called to be a witness, says, "The priest is required personally to be the representative of all the other members of the local church within, which she (the priest) presides to the wider community."[12]

Preparation and education play an important role in priesthood. The systematic training of priests is intended to help them to develop the faculties and abilities required for the performance of cults. It centres in the development and maintenance of the proper communion with the *numen*, from which the mana or 'sanctity' of the priests results. While ascetic practices are to bring body and will under the necessary control, meditation and prayer are destined to prepare the soul, and instruction and study to train the mind. History of the development of religions evidences that great systems of knowledge and schools of learning of various disciplines have emerged in association with centres of the training of priests.[13] The rational training and discipline of priests is distinguished from the combination of partly "awakening education" using

---

[7] Meredith B. McGuire, *Religion: The Social Context*, 5th ed. (California: Wadsworth Thornson Learning. 2002), 252.

[8] Edwin Oliver James, "Sacred Offices and Orders: Priesthood", *The New Encyclopedia Britannica: Macropaedia,* 15th ed. (1997).

[9] Reinhard Bendix, *Max Weber: An Intellectual Portrait* (New York: Doubleday. 1960), 109.

[10] K.A Opoku, *West African Traditional Religion* (Accra: FEP International Private Limited, 1978), 74.

[11] Raymond E Brow, *Priest and Bishop: Biblical Reflections* (London: Geoffrey Chapman, 1970), 9.

[12] Robin Greenwood, "What Priesthood now?" *Theology* 785 (September – October, 1995), 372.

[13] Joachim Wach, *Sociology of Religion…*, 362-3.

irrational means and aimed at rebirth, and partly training in purely empirical lores of magicians.[14]

2. The Office of the Priest

The office of priesthood in tribal society ranges from the medicine person, who magically manipulates the sacred power as a quasi-impersonal force, to the shaman, who, as an agent of divine or spiritual beings, may be at once a medicine man, a visionary, an occult diviner, and a genuine sacerdotal cult leader. Not infrequently, chiefs or headmen of a clan or village may become sacred person or ritual experts displaying supernatural insight and knowledge as the agents of spiritual beings. As such, they may eventually become prophets or sacral kings occupying a unique status in the community. This status may be acquired by accepted claims of descent from a mythical divine ancestor or god on whom the fertility of the crops and the welfare of the community in general are thought to depend. Occult power and insight may be derived from spirits with which the prophet or diviner is related in a trance or ecstasy, or else in dreams, visions, or auguries and oracles that make known the divine will. To occupy such a position, a strenuous course of training is frequently required, involving some knowledge of therapeutics (healing), herbs, poisons, and perhaps sleight of hand and similar techniques, together with the development of psychical and occult qualities. While charlatanry (pretensions to medical knowledge) is often practiced, the office also demands an understanding of the technical equipment calculated to bring about the results that are sought, and the proper type of temperament, conditions of mind, and state of emotion.[15]

The function of the priest as the mediator and maintainer of the equilibrium between the sacred and the profane in human society, and as the stabilizer of the social structures and the cultic organizations, determines the various criteria for holding the priestly office. In primal society the functions are accomplished by ritual experts who are trained in the special knowledge and techniques of magico-religious disciplines in which sacred power is believed to be inherent. They also are trained in disciplines that enable them to gain a supernormal psychic knowledge and in the techniques of mystical experience. As agents of the sacred power, they are believed to have the ability to control and manipulate through ritual natural processes and events and to engage in a sacramental relationship between humanity and the sacred order on which the community and its members depend for their sustenance, survival, and well-being.[16]

---

[14] Max Weber, *The Sociology of Religion…*, 30.

[15] E. O. James, *The Nature and Function of Priesthood* (London: Thames and Hudson, 1961), 277.

[16] Edwin Oliver James, "Priesthood" in *Encyclopedia Britannica* https://www.britannica.com/topic/priesthood (2/10/2018).

Because religious institutions and beliefs are intimately connected with other social institutions, those who are set apart to establish efficacious relations with the transcendental powers that are believed to control the universe, as well as human affairs and destinies, occupy a key position at the dynamic centre in the social structure. Thus, in certain types of societies the office and functions of the priest may be limited to those having a particular ancestry, those belonging to certain tribes, families and those initiated into certain professional orders.[17]

Besides such socio-cultural criteria, there are also certain personal requirements in various cultures for those who would become members of the priesthood. Celibacy, asceticism and religious experiences are among the personal requirements for those who aspire to or are chosen to assume the priestly office.[18]

The religious functions of priests are quite varied. In her/his specific role as the officiant of the rites that unite the sacred and the profane realms, the priest as a pontifex (from the Latin word that means maker of a bridge) celebrates or administers at the rituals of initiation into the cult or church, presides over ritual and offers sacrifices to the gods or to one God. S/He also functions as a perpetuator of the sacred traditions, practices, and beliefs and as a teacher, healer, counselor, and diviner.[19] The African traditional priest is a significant religious and social figure due to the essential roles he or she plays in the community. Mbiti posits that as an intermediary, the priest is also the religious symbol of God and the divinities among the people. S/he speaks and understands the language of the divine so s/he is expected to translate and interpret this language to the people whenever the need arises. The priest also performs ritual sacrifices and offerings on behalf of the community. For instance, when there are national disasters such as plagues, death, famine and drought, to mention a few, the priest offers the required sacrifice to God, the ancestors and the other divinities concerned.[20]

In all their respective offices, functions, and capacities, those who have exercised and manipulated sacred power have attained a uniquely prestigious position as the spiritual and social leaders par excellence. When perplexing and emotional situations that appear to be beyond human control, knowledge, skill, or techniques arise in a community, the people have a recourse in the priest,

---

[17] Edwin Oliver James, "Priesthood" in *Encyclopedia Britannica* https://www.britannica.com/topic/priesthood (2/10/2018).

[18] Edwin Oliver James, "Priesthood" in *Encyclopedia Britannica* https://www.britannica.com/topic/priesthood (2/10/2018).

[19] Edwin Oliver James, "Priesthood" in *Encyclopedia Britannica* https://www.britannica.com/topic/priesthood (2/10/2018).

[20] J. S. Mbiti, *African Religions and Philosophy* (Nairobi: East African Educational Publishers, 1969), 188.

who has the special knowledge of the relationship between the divine or sacred and the profane realms. The priest is often called upon at critical junctures in the lives of individuals (such as birth, puberty, marriage, and death) and in the life of a community (such as seasonal changes or at times of flood, drought, and famine).

Unlike the shaman and the medicine person, both of whom exercise their respective functions while relying largely on their own initiative and psychic and occult powers of divination, healing, and direct access to the spirit world at their command, the priest supplicates and conciliates supernatural forces superior to himself, guards the sacred tradition in his care, and acts as the master of sacrifice. The shaman or magician officiates in her/his own name and by her/his own methods and techniques; the priest serves the altar, in the temple or shrine, as the representative of the community in his relations with the gods and the sacred order by virtue of the status and its functions that have been conferred upon him at his ordination, bestowing its sacredness and attendant taboos.[21]

3. The Priest and its Relation and Differences with other Functionaries

The identity of the tribal priest may be better comprehended by differentiating and also by identifying its relations from other Religious functionaries. Some of which are discussed below:

a. Shaman

The priest is distinct from the Shaman.[22] The term shaman comes from Siberian Tungus noun *saman* which signifies "one who is excited, moved, raised". As a verb it means "to know in an ecstatic manner". Shaman is a person with "a high degree of nervous excitability". Like any other sacred person in the primal society, the shaman is a complex figure but the thing which is very clear about them is that they rely exclusively on psychic influences and experiences gained through dreams and visions, trance and ecstasy.[23] S/he is the charismatic[24] figure par excellence - one who actually displays the presence of the sacred

[21] J. S. Mbiti, *African Religions and Philosophy…*, 188.

[22] Verrier Elwin, "Saora Shamans and Shamanins" *The Religion of an Indian Tribe* (Bombay: Oxford University Press, 1955), 130-131; 469-483.

[23] E. O. James, *The Nature and Function of Priesthood* (London: Thames and Hudson, 1961), 27.

[24] Charisma denotes "a certain quality of an individual personality by virtue of which he is set apart from ordinary men and treated as endowed with supernatural, superhuman, or at least specifically exceptional powers or qualities. These are such as are not accessible to the ordinary person, but are regarded as of divine origin or as exemplary, and on the basis of them the individual concerned is treated as a leader". Cf. Max Weber, *The Theory of Social and Economic*

while in a state of ecstatic trance. Weston LaBarre writes, "the real difference between shaman and priest is who and where the god is, inside or out."[25] As far as the functions performed by a shaman are concerned, it is believed that s/he combines the functions of priest, prophet and magician, all in one. S/he is known to perform priestly functions and uses sacrifice as a central act in the process of healing and divination. He also performs rituals of sacrifice and appeasement to the gods or spirits once they have been forced to submit to the shaman's needs. Finally, because of fear of the shaman and her/his powers, s/he acquires a charismatic personality and qualities of leadership similar to a prophet.[26]

b. Magician

The Priest is not the magician. The Magician in present-day society is one who makes visible things disappear, or invisible things appear as a means of entertainment. But, that has not been the case always. The magician is usually self-employed though s/he may be the member of a hereditary caste or an organized guild. Rather than using a specialized doctrine of knowledge, the magician may derive his influence by virtue of personal gifts and knowledge of the supernatural world. The magician can have considerable power among her/his community and may be respected more out of fear than faith. s/he does not necessarily have a following as the priests do.[27]According to Wach, magic connotes forcing the *numen* to grant what is desired, while religion, with which priests are associated, means submission to and worship of the divine power upon which human feels dependent. Magician's authority is proportionate to the fulfilment of the expectations of the clients. The prestige is less firmly established and more dependent upon the professional successes than that of the prophet.[28] On the one hand Weber observes that in many religions, including Christianity, the concept of the priest includes a magical qualification. But, on the other hand, he concurs with Wach in asserting that the priest is a functionary of a regularly organized and permanent enterprise concerned with influencing the gods by means of worship, in contrast with the individual and occasional efforts of magicians who coerce gods by magical means. While the priest operates in the interests of her/his organization, the magician is self-employed. Moreover, the professional equipment of special knowledge, fixed doctrine, and vocational qualifications of the priest bring

---

Organization, trans. A.M. Henderson and Talcott Parsons (New York: Oxford University Press, 1947; Free Press Paperback Edition, 1964; 1966), 358-9.

[25] Cited by Charles Lindholm, *Charisma* (Oxford: Basil Blackwell, 1990), 158.

[26] http://egyankosh.ac.in/bitstream/123456789/21684/1/Unit-13.pdf.

[27] http://egyankosh.ac.in/bitstream/123456789/21684/1/Unit-13.pdf.

[28] Joachim Wach, *Sociology of Religion*..., 353-354.

her/him in contrast with sorcerers, prophets and other types of religious functionaries who exert influence by virtue of personal gifts (charisma) made manifest in miracle and revelation.[29]

c. Prophet

The priest is distinct from the prophet. The prophet is someone who confronts the powers and the established ways of doing things, claiming to be taken seriously on religious authority. Weber finds that "the personal call is the decisive element that distinguishes the prophet from the priest. The latter lays claim to authority by virtue of the service in a sacred tradition, while the prophet's claim is based on personal revelation and charisma. It is no accident that almost no prophets have emerged from the priestly class.[30] The priest, in clear contrast dispenses salvation by virtue of the office.[31] Emphasizing the distinctness of prophetic call, Wach opines, "The consciousness of being the organ, the instrument, or mouthpiece of the divine will is characteristic of the self-interpretation of the prophet."[32] Furthermore, Weber distinguishes between two types of prophets: exemplary prophets who point out the path to salvation by exemplary living, usually by a contemplative and apathetic-ecstatic life, and the emissary prophets who address their demands to the world in the name of a god. Naturally these demands are ethical, and often of an active ascetic character.[33] Vernon observes that prophets usually appear during periods of unrest, when the established value systems are being challenged. They find little welcome at peaceful times.[34]

According to Nisbet, the prophet and the magician have certain common features, namely, secret powers and assumption of importance in times of collective crisis or personal difficulty. But, they do differ.

[29] Max Weber, *The Sociology of Religion* ..., 28-30.

[30] Differing from Weber, Wach observes that, "It should be remembered that frequently spiritual and prophetic characters in the highest degree are found among priests. Several Hebrew prophets have emerged from their ranks e.g., Ezekiel and Zechariah". He adds that prophets usually come, not from the aristocracy, the learned, or the refined; but from the simpler folks, and are marked by frugaltty and simplicity. Cf. Joachim Wach, *Sociology of Religion*..., 361& 302.

[31] Max Weber, *The Sociology of Religion* ..., 46-47.

[32] Joachim Wach, *Sociology of Religion*..., 347. Max Weber, *Sociology of the World Religions: Introduction.*

[33] Max Weber, *Sociology of World Religions: An Introduction* in https://web.archive.org/web/20040404142710/http://www.ne.jp/asahi/moriyuki/abukuma/weber/world/intro/world_intro_frame.html (2/10/2018).

[34] Glenn M. Vernon, *Sociology of Religion* (New York: McGraw-Hill Book Company, 1962), 182.

> But, whereas the central function of the prophet is that of interpretation of the sacred tradition and of gaining access to the deity in ways denied the bulk of populace, the central function of the magician is that of effecting exceptions to the natural order ... The magician's role is that of the doer - but what he does is reserved for times of crisis and for activities which are affected by risk or uncertainty of outcome. His role is the outcome of special knowledge that he holds to himself and to his legitimate descendant.[35]

4. The Sacred Versus the Secular Powers[36]

According to the nature of the governance of a country, Weber identifies three types of relation between the secular and the sacred powers in the history of the world. While in the first type, a ruler is legitimated by the priests, in the second the high priest is also the king, and in the third, the secular ruler exercises supreme authority in sacred matters too.[37] For instance, Islam unlike most other religions, does not have a class of priests or clergy, in the strict sense of the term, we find that there was a time when the roles of Imam (the leader of the prayers in the worship rites in mosques) and ruler of the place were assigned to the same individual. When a governor was appointed to a province, he was also appointed as Imam to lead the prayers, and this practice continued for a long time. In fact, the honour of leading the prayers (imamat) in Islam was great as the honour of kingship, and the two offices, the office of the spiritual leader and that of the temporal leader were combined in one person for a long time. As the ruler himself was the Imam at the centre, so were his governors the Imams in the different provincial headquarters.[38]

According to Weber, in hierocratic domination, priestly power seeks ascendancy at the cost of the political power. At times it is projected even as a God-given tool for the subjection of anti-ecclesiastic forces. In practice, therefore, hierocracy seeks to turn the political ruler into a vassal and to deprive her/him of independent means of power. Meanwhile, hierocracy makes every attempt to protect itself: an autonomous administrative apparatus, a tax system (tithes), legal forms (endowments) for the protection of ecclesiastic

---

[35] Robert A. Nisbet, *The Social Bond: An Introduction to the Study of Society* (New York: Alfred A. Knopf, 1970), 169.

[36] Cf. T.N. Madan, "Secularism in its Place", in *Religion in India*, edited by T.N. Madan (New Delhi: Oxford University Press, 2000), 398ff.

[37] Max Weber, *Sociology of Rulership and Religion* in https://web.archive.org/web/20040605041128/http://www.ne.jp/asahi/moriyuki/abukuma/weber/society/ruler/ruler_relig/rul_rel_frame.html (5/10/2018).

[38] Maulana Muhammad Ali, *The Religion of Islam* (Delhi: Motilal Banarsidass Publishers, 1994), 291.

landholdings, bureaucratization of administration, and development of office charisma at the cost of personal charisma.[39]

In Weber's mind, the extreme opposite of any kind of hierocracy is Caesaro-papism - the complete subordination of the priestly to the secular powers. Herein religious affairs are but a branch of political administration. The political rulers fulfill these obligations either directly or with the assistance of the state-maintained priestly professionals. Caesaro-papism is nowhere found in its purest form. As a rule priestly charisma compromises with the secular power either tacitly or even through a concordat. On the whole, the general picture of the relationship between the two as portrayed by Weber is one of a cold war. Everywhere state and society have been greatly influenced by the struggle between military and temple nobility, between royal and priestly following. This struggle did not always lead to an open conflict, but it produced distinctive features and differences.[40]

According to Aberbach, even though there are important differences between the sacred and the secular, history of religion testifies to a close parallel between the two: while even in its secular forms, charisma has a religious dimension, traditional religious charisma is rarely devoid of political and other significance. Political charisma draws on the language, the spirit and even the ideological conviction of religion. Charismatic religious leadership is no less infused with politics. The devotees of religious charismatics are inspired not only by their message but also by their political skill and military success.[41]

Priests have often been throughout history regarded as the official go between the sacred and the profane. Throughout the long and varied history of religion, the priesthood has been the official institution that has mediated and maintained a state of equilibrium between the sacred and the profane aspects of human society and that has exercised a stabilizing influence on social structure and on cultic organization.[42] But, the various administrative duties derive from the cultic activities of priests. Therefore, the less the communion with the numen expressed in formalized cult, the closer s/he is to a magician.[43] As long as the mediation of the priest is desired to secure material or ideal

[39] Max Weber, *Sociology of Rulership and Religion* in https://web.archive.org/web/20040605041128/http://www.ne.jp/asahi/moriyuki/abukuma/weber/society/ruler/ruler_relig/rul_rel_frame.html (5/10/2018).

[40] Max Weber, *Sociology of Rulership and Religion* in https://web.archive.org/web/20040605041128/http://www.ne.jp/asahi/moriyuki/abukuma/weber/society/ruler/ruler_relig/rul_rel_frame.html (5/102018).

[41] David Aberbach, *Charisma in Politics, Religion and the Media: Private Trauma, Public Ideals* (London: Macmillan Press, 1996), 36.

[42] Edwin Oliver James, "Sacred Offices and Orders: Priesthood". The New Encyclopedia Britannica: Macropaedia, 15th ed. (1997).

[43] Joachim Wach, *Sociology of Religion*..., 365-366.

advantages, religion is still close to magic, but a higher stage is reached where it becomes the function of the priest to thank and to adore in his/her own and other's name.[44]

5. Priestly Requirements: An Approach from Tribal Perspective

The Tribal community/people in general possess good values and traits that are known since time immemorial. If Tribals are to have an integrative or holistic formation of priesthood in a tribal context, some of the following Tribal values can be taken into consideration.

(i) The Sense of the Sacred

In Tribal traditional conception, the sacred is not so much a category that is opposed to the profane, as Mircea Eliade maintained but a way of looking at reality in its wholeness. Traditional tribal regard the entire cosmos, when viewed in its totality (invisible and visible) as sacred.[45] The invisible penetrates the visible through a unique Being, God, known in various Tribal languages and named after both genders as: *Alhou* (Sumi), *Totatara-Rabuga* (Garo), *Pathian* (Mizo), *Amono Pfiipei* (Mao) and so on. All realities: invisible (divinities, ancestors, spirits) and visible (human, animals and inanimate objects) become sacred when viewed in their total relationship to the unique wholeness of God. The individual in a society is sacred from the perspective of his/her relationships with the totality of beings around him/her. The Tribal family is sacred because it reflects wholeness in unity of being. Certain persons, objects and places are sacred because they manifest this wholeness of being either symbolically or in actuality. A masked figure is sacred on account of its relationship to the invisible sacred reality it is representing. Certain trees are sacred either on account of their structure or their mode of existence which reflects life in its totality. Human speech becomes sacred when viewed in its relationship to the speaker and the totality of human beings. Places and things are sacred in so far as they reflect the unity of the beings which they symbolize.

For the Tribal, the sacred is not only associated with power, but it is also affiliated with the highest values in human life such as: honesty, justice, gentleness, patience, endurance, perseverance, sincerity in one's word, etc. A sacred person is expected to mirror these values. People's attitude towards the sacred is generally to keep a respectful distance without severing relationship

[44] Joachim Wach, *Sociology of Religion…*, 363.

[45] Mircea Eliade, *The Sacred and the Profane: The Nature of Religion* (New York: Harper & Row Publishers, 19961), 15.

completely. According to Rudolf Otto, "The sacred attracts and repels."[46] To maintain cordial relationship with the sacred implies the observance of a certain code of conduct on the part of humanity.

In Tribal culture, this respectful distance is best translated by the word 'taboo'. In every religious act taboo is observed by the tribals. Among the Naga tribes couple who commit incest is thrown out from the village for fear that their sin will be visited by the divine curse if they are allowed to stay in the village.[47] When a taboo is broken, it becomes abomination or pollution. If this taboo is directed against the land divinity, it becomes pollution against the land divinity. Ritual cleansing through confession of guilt with appropriate sacrifices is then made to restore the 'Sacred' of the culprit. Often the diviner gives the guidelines on how to remove the abomination.

The emphasis on the Tribal sense of the sacred can have far-reaching effects in the priestly formation today. It can create an attitude of deep respect for the things of God and anything associated with God. It will also foster a great appreciation for the value of the human person, the most sacred of all creatures. This explains why crimes like murder, abortion, calumny, disturbance of harmony, wanton destruction of neighbor's property, etc., are taboo. To be involved in any of these is to pollute the sacredness of the society. Humanity is sacred because of its vital link with transcendental realities of the world in its wholeness. Some of the ways through which Tribals internalize the sense of the sacred and the sacredness of a human being include: worship, covenants with divinities and others, oath taking, sacrifices, prayers and periodic festivals. Stimulating the sense of the sacred among the tribal society today will help all to respect the sacred of humanity and this I believe can be one of the criterions of priestly formation.

(ii) Corporate Existence

The sense of the sacred is concretely manifested through the Tribal concept of corporate existence in other words the concern for communitarian over against individuals. According to Thanzauva, communiterianism is a concept and life principle in which the homogenous people live together sharing their joys and sorrows in mutual love and care.[48] The same line of thought is also seen from the definition given by A. Wati Longchar when he stated that "the tribal religion is basically a community religion. To be truly human is to belong to the whole community, including the ancestors and creation, and to do so involve

[46] Rudolf Otto, *The Idea of the Holy* (London Oxford, New York: Oxford University Press, 1923), p. 25.

[47] Dr Samuel Longkumer & Mr Moanungsang, *A Reader in Primal Religious Traditions and their Select Movements in India* (Kolkata: Authors, 2012), 77-78.

[48] K Thanzauva, *Theology of Community: Tribal Theology in Making* (Aizawl: Mizo Theological Conference, 1997), 106.

the active participation in the beliefs, ceremonies, rituals and festivals of the community. A person cannot live in isolation from one's community."[49] These definitions from tribal theologians clearly explain the tribal understanding and importance of corporate existence. We also see the existence of communitarian spirit from the governance of the ethical principle known as *Sobaliba* in Ao Naga and *Tlawmngaihna* in Mizo. Both *Sobaliba* and *Tlawmngaihna* is to be self-sacrificing, unselfish, self-denying, preserving, co-operation, honesty, truthfulness, dedication, commitment, sociable, to endure patiently, to do whatever the occasion demands no matter how distasteful or inconvenient it may be to oneself or to one's own inclination etc.[50]

J.S. Mbiti seems to have exaggerated when subsuming the individual in the corporate existence of African society.[51] He/she remains an autonomous person who acts responsibly although his/her actions are governed by what may be regarded as "sensus commune" (communal sense). He/she takes into account the general aspirations, values and customs of the community to which he/she belongs before making a personal decision. These are ultimately rooted in transcendence or the sacred in its totality. Perhaps, it is in this sense that this affirmation of John V. Taylor becomes meaningful:

> The sense of the personal totality of all beings, and of a humanity which embraces the living, the dead and the divinities, fills the background of the primal worldview. This is the context in which an African learns to say, I am because I participate. To him the individual is always an abstraction; man is a family.[52]

Tribals need to emphasize the sense of community living and values to cut across ethnic and social boundaries and even gender boundaries. This has to be given a christological interpretation of the concept of neighbour as found in the Parable of the Good Samaritan (Lk 10:2937). The tribal society/church should be a society and church where the traditional tribal family and neighbourly spirit are nurtured and sustained. However, this sense of community cannot be fostered without a deep sense of justice.

---

[49] A. Wati Longchar, *The Traditional Tribal Worldview and Modernity* (Jorhat: The Author, 1994), 152.

[50] P. L. Lianzuala, "Towards a Theology of Mizo Tlawmngaiha," in *Good News for North East India: A Theological Reader*, edited by Renthy Keitzar (Guwahati: CLC, 1995), 119. A. Wati Longchar, "Sobaliba" in *Good News for North East India: A Theological Reader*, edited by Renthy Keitzar (Guwahati: CLC, 1995), 127.

[51] J. S. Mbiti, *African Religions and Philosophy* (London, Ibadan, Nairobi: Heinemann, 1969), 108.

[52] John V. Taylor, *The Primal Vision Christian Presence Amid African Religion* (London: SCM Press Ltd., 1963), 85.

(iii) A Sense of Justice

It is not an exaggeration to say that justice is at the hub of the human interactions in Tribal society. Indigenous justice systems are based on a holistic philosophy. Law is a way of life, and justice is a part of the life process.[53] For tribals, justice is more than the Aristotelian idea of giving each one his/her due.[54] For instance, in most of the tribal community the rich usually plays the dominant role in the society especially in their practice of Feast of merit. Feast of merit were given not for honour only but used as a means to share wealth with the poor.[55] Everyone especially the elders of the village are expected to say the truth without fear or favour, give to everyone what he/she is supposed to have, maintain fair relationships with neighbour, never tilt the balance in ontological relationships and so on. Religious leaders like priests, diviners, elders of all shades, etc. use their just fair judgements to prove their sincerity in discharging their duties. People will then respect them according to their truthfulness and sincerity. That is when they become real fathers of the society. Thus, even in the present context this sense of Justice need to instilled as well. The idea of 'leave all judgments to God' while an injustice is perpetrated equals to failure of fulfilling the assigned task to priesthood.

(iv) Sincerity in one's Commitment to a Cause

Traditional Tribal cultures attached great value to sincerity in one's words and pledge. It was an allied virtue to justice. They cherished someone who was always truthful and who stood by his/her word no matter the odds. Such an individual was entrusted with community responsibility and leadership. People needed him/her especially when the going was rough. He/she was often addressed as a truthful person, a just person, a person who perseveres in the face of difficulties.

Thus, in the present scenario of conflicts and confusion, everyone needs to be encouraged to express their views sincerely without fear of expulsion. This can be done by challenging them to be true to themselves because an atmosphere of insecurity and fear created through threats will suffocate sincerity. Thus, the greater tasks of the Priests have to be living examples of this virtue to counteract the rampant cult of hypocrisy and cheating that is taking root throughout the tribal society.

---

[53] Ada Pecos Melton, *Indigenous Justice Systems and Tribal Society* (2/10/2018).

[54] David L. Osborn, *Aristotle's Conception of Justice* https://scholarship.law.nd.edu/cgi/view content.cgi?article=3967&context=ndlr (5/10/2018).

[55] Takatmejen, *Studies on Theology and Naga Culture* (Delhi: ISPCK, 1998), 32.

Concluding Remark

The paper has elucidated the concept of the tribal priesthood and has shown how distinct the tribal priesthood was/is from the other priesthood tradition. The priesthood is a great blessing from God to all. All members of the Church should honor the priesthood and develop Christlike attributes in their relationships with each other in the home and the Church. Men and women have different but equally important responsibilities in the home and the Church. Priesthood power can help each person perform those responsibilities for the benefit of all. However, there is still a wrestle to the question "Can women become Priest"? To answer this we first need to ponder on the questions: what is the nature of the priesthood today? What form does the call to the priesthood take? What constitutes formation of candidates to the priesthood? Who determines a candidate's genuine vocation to the priesthood? What constitutes the ordination of the priest?

15

Tribal Ecclesiology

Esther Jish Rengma

1. Introduction

The twenty-first century has been called 'the century of the Church'. The characterization refers not to any expected or verified triumph of Christianity, but to the remarkable way in which ecclesiology has become a central subject of theological reflection. With this said, there is an identity catastrophe among the contemporary tribal Christian church and lack of authenticity and communitarian[1] value in the tribal church today. With exception to some of the indigenous churches having its own unique characteristics and distinctiveness, most Christian tribal Churches in North East India region do not have their distinguishable nature. This has created a need to explore and rediscover the community life of the Tribal Christian churches with a focus toward developing a contextual and relevant tribal Ecclesiology[2] as an ongoing g

[1] Communitarian is a philosophy that emphasizes the connection between the individual and the community. Its overriding philosophy is based on the belief that a person's social identity and personality are largely molded by community relationships, with a smaller degree of development being placed on individual. https://merriam-webster.com (accessed on 21/01/19).

[2] The word Ecclesiology comes from two Greek words meaning "assembly" and "word"- combined together to mean 'the study of the Church." Ecclesiology helps us to understand the role of the church and our role in the church. It teaches us about the ordinances of the church,

search for an authentic believing community. This paper attempts to explicate the etymological term of ecclesiology, meaning of the word *ekklesia* and Church, and the comprehensive tribal understanding of ecclesiology. In this article the term church, *ekklesia,* and ecclesiology are inter-changeably used as they all have similar connotation.

2. Etymology of the Word Ecclesiology

The roots of the word ecclesiology come from the Greek ἐκκλησίᾱ, *ekklēsiā* (Latin *ecclesia*) meaning "congregation, church"[3] and -λογία, *-logia*, meaning "words", "knowledge", or "logic", a combining term used in the names of sciences or bodies of knowledge. The similar word ecclesiology first appeared in the quarterly journal *The British Critic* in 1837, in an article written by an anonymous contributor who defined it thus: We mean, then, by Ecclesiology, a science which may treat of the proper construction and operations of the Church, or Communion, or Society of Christians; and which may regard men as they are members of that society, whether members of the Christian Church in the widest acceptation of the term, or members of some branch or communion of that Church, located in some separate kingdom, and governed according to its internal forms of constitution and discipline.[4]

The Ecclesiologist was first published in October 1841 and dealt with the study of the building and decoration of churches. It particularly encouraged the restoration of Anglican churches back to their supposed Gothic splendour and it was at the centre of the wave of Victorian restoration that spread across England and Wales in the second half of the 19th century. Its successor Ecclesiology today is still, as of 2017, being published by The Ecclesiological Society (successor to the CCS, now a registered charity).[5] The situation regarding the etymology has been summed up by Alister McGrath: "Ecclesiology is a term that has changed its meaning in recent theology.

how church leadership is to be chosen and structured, and what the church is to be doing in regards to believers (worship and discipleship) and unbelievers (ministry and evangelism). Above all, we must understand that the church is the Body of Christ and that each of us has a specific function and role within that body. Hence Ecclesiology is a vital subject to understand Gods' purpose for believers in the world today. It helps us to appreciate both, the Church at large as well as the Church as a local assembly.

[3] In the Greco-Roman world, *ecclesia* was used to refer to a lawful assembly, or a called legislative body. As early as Pythagoras, the word took on the additional meaning of a community with shared beliefs. This is the meaning taken in the Greek translation of the Hebrew Scriptures (the Septuagint), and later adopted by the Christian community to refer to the assembly of believers.

[4] James F White, *The Cambridge Movement: the ecclesiologists and the Gothic revival (revised ed.),* (London: Cambridge University Press, 1979), 48–49.

[5] Anon, "Ecclesiology", in *The British Critic Quarterly Theological Review and Ecclesiastical Record. London: J.G. and F. Rivington.* XXII (41) (1837): 218–248.

Formerly the science of the building and decoration of churches, promoted by the Cambridge Camden Society, the Ecclesiological Society and the journal The Ecclesiologist, ecclesiology now stands for the study of the nature of the Christian church."[6]

3. The Word *Ekklesia* and Church

Ekklesia and church are two sides of the same coin, however for deeper understanding; a brief explanation on both the terms has been presented.

3.1. Meaning of *Ekklesia*

The word *Ekklesia* is derived from the Greek verb *kaleo*, 'call', in its compound from *ekkaleo*, which means, "to summon" or "to call out". In classical Greek it is used for a company of people gathered together in response to a summons.[7] *Ekklesia* is used primarily to designate to a particular communal reality, not to describe its qualitative aspect. In The N.T. the word *Ekklesia* is an assembly of persons, which has been summoned for a particular purpose. The purpose may be secular or religious. The meaning may be regularly constituted (Acts19:39) or more spontaneous in origin (Vs. 32, 40). In the N.T *ekklesia* often refers to the occasion when a specific congregation gathers for prayer, instruction and deliberation (Acts11: 26, 12:5, 1Cor. 11:18).[8] It is also a community of believers, which has been gathered from the inhabitants of a specific area. Church thus means the community of believers or simply the followers of Jesus Christ who are in the service of the Lord or who are set apart for the service of the Kingdom of God.

In the O.T. the LXX uses *ekklesia* almost a hundred times as the translation for *qahal*. The basic meaning of both Lords is a meeting or gathering. People gather together or are summoned for any and every purpose. It is the people and the purpose, which give significance to the *qahal*. *Qahal* may be a gathering of men called up for military (Gen 49:6, Num 22:4, Ezek 16:40) or for civic action. Those who assemble may be prophets (Psalm 19:20) or princess (Num 16:3, 1Chron 28:8). Probably the most significant of *qahal* in the O.T. is the assembling of Israel before God on Horeb. (Deut 4:10, 9:10) When God sealed His covenant with them. This served to define the significance of the

---

[6] McGrath, Alister E. "Ecclesiology", *The Blackwell Encyclopedia of Modern Christian Thought* (Oxford: Blackwell, 1999), 127.

[7] Edmund Hill, "Church", in *The Dictionary of Theology*, edited by Joseph A. Komonchak, May Collins and Demrmont A. Lan (Wilmington: Michael Glazier, 1987), 185.

[8] William Stewart, *The Nature and Calling of the Church* (Bangalore: The Christian Students Library, 1958), 5.

ekklesia of Israel, but it did not give to the term *qahal* or *ekklesia* a fixed, technical meaning.[9]

3.2. Meaning of the Word "Church"

The English word "Church," like equivalent in the other Germanic languages, derives from the Greek adjective *Kuriakos,* meaning "belonging to the Lord." In other word the original term was *kuriakon doma* or *kuriakos domos* "the Lord's house." Perhaps the first situation would be the building in which the Christians met for worship and that is still the first dominant reference in ordinary English.[10] Church comes from a Greek word which means "belonging to the Lord or master."[11] "The Church is the whole body or Congregation of persons who are called by God the Father to acknowledge the Lordship of Jesus the Son, in word, in sacrament, in witness and in service, and through the power of the Holy Spirit to collaborate with Jesus' historic mission for the sake of the kingdom of God."[12] The word Church is used in variety of meanings of which the following are the most important:

(a) It is used for a building in which people meet for worship. In most Indian languages a distinctive word is used for such a building.
(b) In the Creeds and in other places the word "Church" refers to the whole company of Christ's people. This is the Universal Church of the Creeds.
(c) Sometimes the word "Church" is used to refer to this universal company on earth. In this sense, though generations rise and pass away, we think of the Church as living on from generation to generation. We refer to this Church on earth when we speak of "Church History".
(d) The term Church uses for single organizations or "denominations" or even "communions" which are often referred to as Church etc.[13]

The Church is one of the most fundamental realities of the Christian faith.[14] Therefore, the Church is the community of all true believers for all times.

---

[9] P. S. Minear, "Idea of Church," in *The Interpreter's Dictionary of the Bible*, edited by A. D. George Arthur Buttrick et al., (New York: Abington Press, 1962), 609.

[10] Edmund Hill, "Church," in *The Dictionary of Theology,* 185.

[11] *The World Book of Encyclopedia*, 1959 ed., vol. 13, s.v. "Church," 1433.

[12] *The Encyclopedia of Religion*, 1995 ed., vol. 3, s.v. "Church," 473.

[13] William Stewart, *The Nature and Calling of the Church* (Bangalore: The Christian Students Library, 1958), 5.

[14] R. S. Greenway, "Church," in *New Dictionary of Theology*, edited by Sinclair B. Ferguson and David F. Wright (Leicester: Intervarsity Press, 1988), 140.

4. The Tribal Understanding of Ecclesiology

The present understanding of the Church is self-centred ecclesiology, deviated with the biblical understanding of *ekklesia* i.e., the community of called out people or the people of God. The Churches are institutionalized and have a tendency to be self-centred in their way of doing ministry and mission, busy to maintain and enlarge them. The activities of the church tend to be ritualistic. Primary attention is given to maintaining the institutionalised church, which is bureaucratic rather than a living community. Its ministry is rigid and hierarchical to the extent that women and lay participation in the decision making is still minimal. There is a need to go beyond the traditional bilateral dialogues to embrace the local spiritual needs. The Churches are challenged to pay more attention to and develop capacities to assist articulating the relationship of self-understanding (ecclesiastical) and self-representation (ecclesiology) among different tribal churches and communities.

The present structure of the Church is male oriented and so it is difficult to include women's concerns and marginalized people's needs. This might be due to our patriarchal culture, inherited patriarchal theology and ministry from the West. To a greater extend, women are denied a significant and active role in the life of the Church. The agenda of women is commonly not one of the mainstream concerns of the church.[15] In such a scenario we need to envision a new paradigm of church for the tribal communities where the church as the body of Christ is fully accomplished. Church should become a common place where people irrespective of gender, economic status, educational background or social standing, feels comfortable and able to freely mingle with people from all the section of the comunity.

The *Ekklesia*, in its true sense in the primitive church, has wonderful natures. The new insights that we got from the Ecclesiology of the Tribal Church and the resourceful findings for tribal ecclesiology may be summed up as follows:

4.1. The Church as Community

The Christian Community is regarded as the anticipation of God's ultimate plan with humanity and the whole of creation in union and communion with the Triune God.[16] As the people of the early Christian Church need the institution of the Church as the main base for their religious authenticity and existence, the tribal are required to have community home as Thanzauva pointed out for

---

[15] Limatula Longkumer, "Wider Ecumenism and Ecclesiology", in *Ecumenism in India Today: A Search for a Relevant Ecclesiology and Churches and Theological Education in India*, edited by James Massey (Bangalore: BTESSC/SATHARI, 2008), 45-46.

[16] John Fuellenback, *Church Community for the Kingdom* (Orbis Book: New York, 2002), 147.

teaching and learning the ethic of living. Building the house for bachelors and ladies was a common practice for the tribal community. The community home, so called house for the bachelors and ladies or community hall plays a vital role to mould the life of the young people in the past days. This institution is very similar to a hostel but different from the hostels in functioning.

The hostel is mainly set up for the study, but the dormitory for bachelors and ladies community home was multi-purpose. The community home or so called dormitory was taken care of by the parents and the senior bachelors and ladies. They are just teachers who always correct them and guide them in their fellowship. There was no institution apart from this, thus parents and the senior leaders were the teachers in their teaching and learning.[17] A similar idea is found in the concept of *Qahal* and *Synagogue* where people come to listen to the reading of *Torah* and basic teaching of their religious life. *Qahal* and *Synagogue* also have multi-dimensions for teaching and learning. In this, the Church as Community does not seek an alternative, nor search to create a new concept of the Church. Rather, it is an attempt to focus on building up the understanding of the Church as well their participation and meaningful fellowship of community. On the one hand the concept of Church could be seen as transforming the community bound in love and unity in Christ. The concept of the Church is seen as the force to unite and treat all the community members' equality without any barriers. Participation and fellowship in one through Christ is considered as equal with the communitarian moral values of life in common. This does not mean to say limiting Christ to the communitarian arena alone but comparatively the binding force in Christian Church and communitarian life is valued.

Another concept of the church is ***Kiononia*** that is as Sharing Community. Here the Church is perceived primarily as *Koinonia* or Community. The word *Koinonia* plays a dominant role in the ideas of New Testament. From the verb meaning "to chance a share in," "to come into community," or "to come into fellowship," to "have something in common" or "to act together," it was a meaning of participation and partnership.[18] *Koinonia* is first Greek word for community (intimate sharing) on the level of the purely human.[19] In cases of Christian community, *koinonia* means an offer to all human beings involved in moral struggles and need aspect of it.[20] It aims personal growth through

[17] K.Thanzauva, *Theology of Community: Tribal Theology in the Making* (Aizwal: Mizo Theological Conference, 1997). 134.

[18] Choan-Seng Song, *Theology from the Womb of Asia* (London: SCM Press, 1988), 173.

[19] Robert Duncan Culver, *Systematic Theology: Biblical and Historical* (Great Britain: Christian Focus Publication, 2005: reprinted ed., 2006), 821.

[20] Thomas F. Best and Martin Robra, eds., *Ecclesiology and Ethics-Ecumenical Ethical Engagement, Moral Formation and the Nature of the Church* (Geneva: WCC, 1997), 9.

interpersonal relationships in the community.[21] Paul speaks of *koinonia* beyond ethnic group and family to a community which exists on the basis of the gospel. *Koinonia* can be best applied to the Church or the Christian communities.[22] *Koinonia* is also the word used to apply that Jesus Christ shared human physicality. Similarly Paul used *koinonia* as participator in Christ and the Church.[23] *Koinonia* is generated and nurtured as Churches and Christian reflect together on issues of ethical concern, and seek a response to the challenges facing humanity and the creation today. The Church as *Koinonia* has provided a necessary entry point for moving away from the institutional and structural understanding of the Church to a more relational character of the life of the Church in its vertical and horizontal dimension of fellowship.

Therefore, the concept of *koinonia* is the core of the communitarian life which is the binding force. And without a sense of the holy, there can be no appreciation of the human and no formation of human community.[24] Therefore the idea of *koinonia* is closer to the concept of community life found in the tribal practices in North East India. The Church as community of people can be seen only when we critically explore in the depth of the concept of *koinonia* which is basically known as fellowship where loving, sharing, and caring prevails.

4.2. The Church as the Center of Selfless-ness Service to the Community and Society

It is the teaching of selfless-ness which makes the tribal people reserved, slow to express themselves even to the extent of telling a lie. It is based on the principle of self sacrifice to the community or society when there arise some problem. Helping others is the means by which one should become self reliance.[25] Today, the Church is not limited to spiritual growth alone but it represents economics prosperity, social upliftment, justice and the church also speak about over all development of individual's life. In this regard, the Church can be a model to work for the welfare of community as a whole, and moulding and shaping the life of its members into good citizens and fruitful life. The Church as a voluntary organization can lead their members to extend help to the needy people and helpless people. Therefore, the Church can be

[21] John Fuellenback, *Church Community for the Kingdom*, 147.

[22] Thomas F. Best and Martin Robra, eds., *Ecclesiology and Ethics-Ecumenical Ethical Engagement, Moral Formation and the Nature of the Church*, 35.

[23] Michael Kinnamon, *Truth and Community: Diversity and its Limits in the Ecumenical Movement* (Michigan: William B. Eerdmans Publishing Company, 1988), 12.

[24] Charles G.Adam, "Christian Social Ethics in the Formation of Community," in *Faith and Witness: Baptist World Alliance-1988-1990*, edited by William H. Brackney with Ruby J. Burke (Alabama: Sanford University Press, 1990), 64.

[25] K.Thanzauva, *Theology of Community: Tribal Theology in the Making*, 158 – 159.

a center of the selfless-ness to the community and society. In the recent past tribals were known for their selfless service toward community. Today's church can emulate and revive those rich experience.

4.3. The Church as Praxis Gathering

The two Hebrew words for *ekklesia* are *qahal* and *eda*, '*eda* mostly means the people of God (Israelites) whether assembled or not while *qahal* denotes the actual assembly/meeting. Those *qahal* assembles were always for some specific purposes, as assembly in action. Those assemblies were assemblies for actions, sometimes for war, sometimes for worship etc. In fact, they were praxis assemblies. Such nature was found also in the early Christian Community. Apostles did many wonders and signs, tirelessly and earnestly taught, preached, healed others and supervised the community.[26]

The sense of community is also so strong among the tribals that they give priority to their community in their thinking and actions, rather than to their individual personal needs. The people were recognized by their community. They do not usually ask their name first, but they were identified by their village community. As Thanzauva said that the village community becomes their own identity. They tell the name of their village rather than telling their name because the village community is their own identity.[27] These practices are still visible in the tribal community in North East India. This is so because a person is insecure without the protection of the community. If a person is affected the whole community suffered.[28]

The tribal understandings of the community also come as a result of knowing the individual human person and concept of life with the community. For them the communitarian life is not just a response to the necessity of life, but also a concept and principle of the tribal community.[29] Everybody is committed faithfully to the community as a sign of love and participation. Without which the community life would have no meaning. Thus the tribal understanding of community is not far from the early Christian Churches and their practices as witnessed in the earlier times.

---

[26] H. Joseph Lalfakmawia, "General Background of the Term Ekklesia', *in (Ekklesia) Indian Conversations: A Study of the Church*, Edited by Samuel George, H. Joseph Lalfakmawai and Ajungla Jamir (Visakhapatnam: Christian World Imprints, 2015), 12.

[27] K. Thanzauva, *Theology of Community: Tribal Theology in the Making*, 115.

[28] A.Wati Longchar, *The Traditional Tribal World View and Modernity* (Jorhat: ETC, 1995), 8.

[29] R. L. Hnuni, "Women in the Context of the Bible and Mizoram," in *Towards A Tribal Theology: The Mizo Perspective*, edited. K. Thanzauva (Aizawl: Mizo Theological Conference, 1989), 88.

4. 4. The Church as Strengthening Community

Acts 9:31 tells us that the church (*ekklesia*) throughout Judea, Galilee, and Samaria had peace and was built up. The word for build up here is *oikodomeo*. This word can be translated as strengthen or build up or make more able. It means to help improve ability to function in living responsibly and effectively. The early *ekklesia* communities built up itself and strengthen the members to live responsibly and effectively. It is a member-oriented community. The same verse too says that the number of the community was multiplied. But, this is not the main emphasis here. Rather, the *ekklesia* community gave emphasis on the so-called lay people, the members. It strengthened and made them more able. Thus, the community as a whole could live responsibly and effectively.[30] Community life is the most integral and important part of the tribal System. Community interest comes first. The strength of the tribal is based upon the life of the community. The tribal people considered every member as equally important, there is no life without community, which means community life, was their culture and heritage. Communitarianism is a concept and life of tribal community in which homogeneous people live together sharing their joys and sorrows in mutual love and care. The fundamental idea of communitarianism is that human beings are, by nature, social beings. They are not simply isolated because it is necessary to do so to protect their individual rights and freedom, and to fulfill their economic interest.[31]

5. The Church as Faithful Community

For community to exist there must be a common unity, a common centre, focus, and direction. Community can centre on anything imaginable. The whole Church members should testify as the believing community.[32] Community is a gift that it is from God's grace and it is through faith that the Church lives.[33] It is not based on mutual admiration, emotional attraction, or common personalities, but is a result of being drawn together by God. As for the Christian, we find our centre in Jesus. He is the basis, the cohesive force, the guide, and the goal of Christian community. Not only is the Christian community based on Jesus Christ, but Christians also affirm that there can be no authentic, nor lasting community apart from Jesus Christ. Community can be opened and free only as we see it as a gift rather than a human creation. Christian community is a

---

[30] H. Joseph Lalfakmawia, "General Background of the Term *Ekklesia*', 13.

[31] K. Thanzauva, *Theology of Community: Tribal Theology in the Making*, 106.

[32] Hans Küng, *The Church maintained in Truth: A Theological Meditation* (London: SCM Press Ltd., 1980), 13.

[33] Hans Küng, *The Church maintained in Truth: A Theological Meditation*, 57.

living testimony to the reality and power of the resurrection.[34] In the years being faithful is a

5.1. The Church as Sharing Community

The basic principle of the sharing community was more of commitment and dedication, self denial, willingness to surrender their belonging. Probably the most visible and amazing aspect of true Christianity is how Christians love and share together. The Christian fellowship communicates being with God through the sharing of the sacrament made for each other.[35] Given the love that defines our existence, we can do no other. Sharing is not a law, but an inevitable result of being bound together in love and unity. Some people would define community as the people with whom we deeply share our lives. No one claimed private ownership of any possessions, but everything they owned was held in common (Acts 2:44;4:2). They sold their possessions and goods and distributed the proceeds to all, as any had need (Acts 2:45). There was no accumulation of wealth or goods for one's own benefits. The rich shared their possessions with the poor.[36]

Community life does not involve a continual process of sharing and mutual support among all the members. The basis of our love for each other must be spiritual rather than a human relationship, for in human relationships we selfishly reach out to other persons and seek to bind to them. Our faith is the basis of our sharing together. We see each other as bearers of the good news of the gospel.[37] Our brothers and sisters are signs of God's grace and love to us. The more we love and share, the more we learn of the coming of the kingdom of God. Our sharing together is a concrete and visible anticipation of the kingdom which is coming and is already present among us.

5.2. The Church as *Diakonia* Community

The word *diakonia* is derived from the Greek word which means "servant" or "minister."[38] In the broad sense the meaning of *diakonia* refers to the service towards the humanity. This service was a mutual service Jesus' followers were committed themselves to undertake *diakonia* for the sake of Christ. They were to serve the Lord in the persons of the needy (Mat. 25:31-46) and to use gift for the benefits of others. Their service to the community was to imitate

[34] C. Norman Kraus, *The Community of the Spirit* (Grand Rapids: Eerdmans, 1974), 23.

[35] Walter Kasper, *Theology and Church* (London: SCM Press Ltd., 1989), 156.

[36] H. Joseph Lalfakmawia, "General Background of the Term Ekklesia', 14.

[37] Art Gish, *Living in Christian Community* (Sutherland: Albatross Books, 1979), 58-64.

[38] Peter A. Angels, "Diakonia," in *Dictionary of Christian Theology* (New York: Harper and Row Publishers, 1985), 69.

Jesus' model of the good shepherd.[39] The life in the community is known by the individual participation for the benefit of the community. Traditionally, common life is used to signify things in common, no one person has more of the community's goods than any other; community recreation centers on the common room. Certainly these can be external expressions of the will to community; they can be also positive hindrances to the full development of the individual and the consequent death of community.[40] The Christian Church should bear feeling of oneness to witness the communitarian life as an example to the people around us. As the members of Christ should participate equally to be the witness and develop full potential of community life. In the age of individualism and materialism the concept of service to the community which is one of the important cardinals of the church must be cultivated.

5.3. The Church as the Kingdom of God

The Kingdom of God is one of the most important themes in Biblical Theology. God has extended His mercy and grace to the human race by allowing us to glance at the role of the Kingdom of God in His plan for the redemption of the entire world. Most importantly, God took the initiative by revealing to humankind a fuller part His kingdom of program through the ministry of Jesus of Nazareth.[41] In the Old Testament the term "kingdom of God" indicates that God intends to show himself by enabling and demanding a certain arrangement of the sociopolitical life of His people and ultimately in the universal salvational dimension of His kingly rule.[42] George Ladd said, "The Kingdom is primarily the dynamic reign or kingly rule of God, and derivatively, the sphere in which the rule is experienced. In Biblical idiom, the kingdom is not identified with its subjects. They are the people of God's rule who enter it, live under it, and are governed by it. The Church is the community of the Kingdom but never the Kingdom itself. Jesus' disciples belong to the kingdom as the Kingdom belongs to them; but they are not Kingdom. The Kingdom is the rule of God; the church is a society of men."[43] Therefore, the church becomes a sign of the kingdom of God when relationships within the Christian community are characterized by the recognition of the personal value and worth of each human

---

[39] Sinclair, Ferguson, B., "Ministry," in *Dictionary of Theology* (Illinois: Inter-Varsity Press, 1988), 430.

[40] Sister Helen Marie Beha, *Living Community* (Milwaukee: The Bruce Publishing company, 1967), 23.

[41]. Eric Chabot, "The Kingdom of God," The *Messianic Outreach*, edited by Elliot Klayman Columbus: Messianic Literature Outreach, 2008), 3.

[42] Hans Schwarz, *Christology* (Grand Rapid: William B. Eerdmans Publishing Company, 1998), 312.

[43] Wayne Grudem, *Systematic Theology: An Introduction to Biblical Doctrine* (Secunderabad: OM Books, 2003: reprinted ed., 2005), 863.

being. It is the community of those who are experiencing the presence of the kingdom and actively awaiting its final fulfillment.[44] Therefore, the Church is called to live as that force within humanity through which God's will for the renewal, justice, community and salvation of all people is witnessed to. A Christian Community lives in anticipation of the Kingdom of God.

5.4. Ecclesiology for Eradication of Poverty

Poverty is deceptive. It has four guises i.e, moral, material, mental, cultural and the fruits of poverty are ignorance, homelessness, hungry, diseases. So the tribal church must strive to eradicate poverty in all categories by doing evangelism for justice, stressing on education, sharing equally human as well as material resources and must strive towards human dignity.[45] Acts 4:34, 35 tell us that there was not a needy person among the members of the *ekklesia* (Koinonia community) because the haves sold their lands or houses and those proceeds were brought to the leaders (Apostles) and were distributed according to their own need. It is the wonder of the wonders that there was not a needy person' within that community because the haves became the benefactors, at their own expense, for the have-nots, which actually is contradictory to the worldly standard of the present day Church.[46] The Church is nothing else than the community or gathering of the saints and of the godly, believing men on earth which the Holy Spirit gathers, preserves and rules.

5.5. Ecclesiology for Striving Towards Equality

In that *ekklesia* (assembly) every citizen had the right to speak and to propose matters for discussion. A decision was only valid if it won a certain number of votes.'[47] *The ekklesia* has democratic nature in which equality was maintained. It was not monopolized by a certain wealthy leader/citizen, but the majority in number determined decision of any proposal. In the *ekklesia,* every individual has real significance. Keeping that characteristic, the leaders of the *Koinonia* community of the early believers listed to the congregation and examined themselves (Acts 6:1ff). No one claimed for private ownership of any possessions, but everything they owned was held in common (Acts 2:44; 4:32).[48] Though there are many characteristics of tribal communities that

---

[44] *Church and World: The Unity of the Church and the Renewal of Human Community* (Geneva: WCC Publication, 1992), 23.

[45] Joseph Vadakkam, *A Priests Encounter with Revolution an Autobiography*, Bangalore: C.L.S. 1974, 118-137.

[46] H. Joseph Lalfakmawia, "General Background of the Term *Ekklesia*', 14.

[47] Lothar Coenen, 'Church," in *The New International Dictionary of the New Testament Theology*, vol.1, ed. Colin Brown (Grand Rapids: Zondervan Publishing House, 1975), 291.

[48] H. Joseph Lalfakmawia, "General Background of the Term Ekklesia', 12.

are discriminative and patriarchal in nature, there have been collective efforts among the tribal scholars and theologians striving towards equality in and through the life and ministry of the church.

6. Conclusion

If an *ekklesia* model of the Church is to be envisaged we must continue to exercise our responsibility as the people of God by calling the 'malestream' church to conversion. Like the early Christians, we must continue to model and build *ekklesia* communities that are not governed by control, subordination and obedience but realize the freedom of the children of God. We must celebrate and appreciate all the gifts of the Spirit that are given to us for the building up of the community. If our diverse struggles for equality, dignity, and well-being in society and church continue, this radical democratic tradition can become an ever expanding reality.

The Church is called to rebuild the kind of community that shares, give hope and substance to the claims of faith. Called to community by His creation in the image and likeness of God and Humankind can realize themselves only by union with others because the community is called to express Christian unity and fellowship with God in order to build a sense of communitarian life into a significant Christian unity in Christ. The Church and Community cannot be separated since both are grounded in communion with the people. Both the Church and the community cannot be active without participation and fellowship. In this sense where in a community even a single person cannot be mistreated, the same idea is found in the Christian community that all the members are equally treated. As suggested in this article, the true meaning of the church as *the people of God or the Lord's house*, where it emphasizes the community life as the true essence of tribal people have to be fully realized, also ecclesia as the assembly where people assemble and come together for common good is to be encourage and advocated.

In this era of individualism and materialistic competition even among the tribal, people have completely lost the community life. Therefore, this paper has attempted to relive and revive the concept of tribal ecclesiology through community consciousness. The Images and the metaphors of the ecclesia as the true people of God, fellowship of the believers, and as the new creation should be encouraged. Moreover, the nature of the tribal ecclesiology as community, praxis gathering, strengthening community, sharing community, serving community, faithful community, as ecclesiology for striving towards equality and eradication of poverty is the need of the hour. To this end it is the responsibility of every theologically trained people and all the servants of God to labour hard so that we may experience real community life.

16

Reading Rizpah's Lament (2 Sam 21:1-14) *vis-à-vis* Tribal Women

Akani Kinimi

Introduction

I would like to begin with a couple of questions. Why do we interpret texts, particularly the Bible? What is at stake for us as individuals and as members of communities in the ways we prepare ourselves to hear and choose to interpret biblical texts? A closer look at the biblical world and the present context reveals that issues and concerns of contemporary communities are appropriate conversation partners in reading and interpreting the Bible. Hence, the intent of this article is to explore some of the ways in which feminist biblical scholars, in particular tribal women, can meet the challenge of adequately and sensitively interpreting biblical texts and the biblical tradition in the light of their experience and situate tribal women and their contribution within a broader context.

1. Theoretical Framework

The lament of Rizpah and her remarkable vigil in 2 Samuel 21:1-14 has long struck me as one of the intriguing and moving stories in the Bible. Yet it is rarely written about and, I suppose, even more rarely preached about. This lament has received considerably less attention from biblical scholars; more focus is on dealing with events in the life of King David. Furthermore, most of the interpretation of this passage is about Saul and bloodguilt against his house that has resulted in a three-year famine, and about David's efforts to alleviate the crisis. Rizpah is not considered as the main character in the story. This is an apt example of excluding women's experiences from biblical interpretation and, how women's experiences and their contributions toward the broader community are eventually forgotten. The problem is that women's voices, both biblical and contemporary, have been sidelined. For long, the only experiences that have been used to interpret on the Bible have been men's. Thus, the vantage point of this writing would be the concept of rediscovering traditions that have been ignored or covered up which is a key part of feminist biblical interpretation.

1.1. Feminist Hermeneutics

Over the years many significant developments took place in the field of general hermeneutics as well as Biblical hermeneutics. A feminist interpretation of the Bible is one of the interested approaches. Along with the development of feminism in general, this approach began in theological circles due to women's growing desire to be liberated from the limitations that the ideology of patriarchy placed on them. Women realised that altering the dominant perspective from which the Bible is read, can bring about new interpretation possibilities. This resulted in what is known as *feminist Biblical interpretation*.[1]

Feminist biblical interpretation is on part in the larger struggle for women's liberation. It helps women combine this struggle with belief in scripture. Feminist hermeneutics also challenges patriarchal interpretations of the Bible and finds ways for the Bible to be empowering to women. It does this by looking at the Bible in two ways: how the Bible worked in Israelite culture and how it is applied to contemporary culture. Feminist biblical exegesis works to create an egalitarian reading of the Bible, where men and women have different roles, but those roles are of equal importance. Gender, as well as how gender is viewed by the surrounding society, can also impact how a person interprets the Bible.[2]

Societal ideologies of sexism, racism, and heterosexism constrain our notions of reality and condition our awareness and responses to differences among humans. Feminist hermeneutics, as it theorises from the perspectives of victims and those on the margins, unmasks the socially constructed nature

[1] C. Nunes & H.J.M. van Deventer, "Feminist interpretation in the context of reformational theology: a consideration," *In die Skriflig* 43/4 (2009), 740.

[2] Samantha Gerstein, *Feminist Biblical Interpretation* (Capstone Project, 2012), https://www.artsci.uc.edu/content/dam/artsci/departments/judaic%20studies/Docs/Capstone_Final.pdf.

of 'reality' and its core concepts, such as woman, man, sex, gender, and difference.[3] In the end, women learn that the Bible can be beneficial to women, and women do have an important role within religion and society.

1.2. Tribal Women's Biblical Hermeneutics

The tribal women's biblical hermeneutics is sensitive to the male dominated interpretation that distorts women's godly image and, ignores the stories and experiences of the women in the Bible. As Asangla Lemtur asserts, "our reading and interpretation of the Bible is 'piestic' and 'other worldly' that fail to address the existential problems of the people. Our reading is also based on the socio-religious and cultural context, which is of men's domination."[4] Thereby, tribal women's biblical hermeneutics strives to challenge the male favoured interpretation of the Scripture and brings the text meaningful and liberative for women as well as all oppressed groups. The concern is how to re-read and re-interpret the Bible from tribal women's perspective in order to discover fully the hidden roles and status of women and the liberating and transforming dimensions of women's quest for justice.

Limatula Longkumer rightly affirms, "Bible reading should be a tool to empower and transform people's lives and should not be a tool to perpetuate oppressions and discriminations."[5] Thus here, Tribal women's reading engages in its conversation with biblical text having a view that women's struggle for justice is worth discovering. And it asserts the importance of tribal women's experience as being the crucial base for their approach as it not only invokes insight but also consciousness of the need for empowerment and transformation of the oppressed and downtrodden.

2. The Story of Rizpah

2 Samuel 21:11 identifies Rizpah her as a wife/concubine of Saul. The Hebrew term *pilegesh*, refers to a legal wife of secondary rank. Rizpah, then, was a widow of the former king Saul. She was the mother of two sons, Armoni and Mephibosheth, whose deaths were called for to settle a claim against the house of Saul. As a member of the deposed house of Saul, a woman, and a widow, Rizpah had no official power to oppose their execution, yet the dramatic deed she performed afterwards was of such magnitude that it influenced a king

[3] Beverly J. Stratton, *Out of Eden: Reading, Rhetoric, and Ideology in Genesis 2-3* (Sheffield: Sheffield Academic Press, 1995), 196.

[4] Asangla Lemtur, "Reading the Bible from Naga Women's context," *Side by Side: Naga Women Doing Theology in Search of Justice and Partnership*, edited by Limatula Longkumer and Talijungla Longkumer (Kolkata: CCA-EGY & NWTF, 2004, reprint 2013), 104.

[5] Limatula Longkumer, "Tribal Feminist Reading of the Bible," in *Tribal Theology and the Bible: A Search for Contextual Relevance*, edited by Yangkhao Vashum (Jorhat: Tribal Study Centre, 2011), 141.

to give them a proper burial. Her action is described in one verse, but it is absolutely pivotal, for it changes the entire course of events.[6] Rizpah's long and solitary vigil outwardly demonstrated her private loss in a public action that commanded King David's attention.

The emphasis on the passing of time and the cycles of day and night bears testimony to Rizpah's determination and tenacity. Even though Rizpah's deed receives only a small amount of narrative space, it is the focal point of the story. Her isolation from the other characters in the tale, demonstrated by her silence and her solitary vigil, symbolises her "otherness," her alliance with the dead. Whereas the Gibeonites and David are shown actively discussing and deciding the fate of Saul's house, Rizpah's vigil ultimately determines it. David and the Gibeonites offer a sacrifice of atonement, aimed at cleansing the land of evil. By protecting the exposed corpses from desecration and by prompting David to have the remains buried, Rizpah prevents a horrible profanity.[7] Rizpah's action ushers in the divine receptivity to human supplication that brings the story to closure: "God heeded supplications for the land after that" (v. 14).

3. Rizpah's Lament *vis-à-vis* Tribal Women's Lament

Most of the victims of injustice do not always have the liberty to voice out loud against the perpetrators of injustice and oppressors. However, many have found nonverbal ways of expressing their resistance to their oppressors' actions that have sought to deny their humanity and assault their dignity. These acts of protest serve as a testimony to the resilience of the human spirit that desperately seeks to survive even amid the most terrible of circumstances. Moreover, the very act of resisting dehumanisation underscores the incontrovertible and indestructible nature of human dignity.[8] As Beverly Mitchell argues, "The dignity of being a human made in the image of God was manifested precisely in the bearing witness to the violation and in the protest against those violations, whether the assaults were physical, emotional or spiritual."[9] The acts of resistance of these women are often quite subtle in nature. These acts of resistance are, however, by no means insignificant or trivial. Indeed, this ability to act in spite of the best attempts of individuals and/or circumstances that seek to crush them attests to the fact that even in the most precarious situations, women will fight for and claim their dignity in the face of dehumanisation.

---

[6] J. Cheryl Exum, "Rizpah," *Word & World* XVII/3 (Summer 1997), 261.

[7] J. Cheryl Exum, "Rizpah,"267.

[8] L. Juliana M. Claassens, *Claiming Her Dignity: Female Resistance in the Old Testament* (Collegeville, Minnesota: Liturgical Press, 2016), xiii.

[9] Beverly Eileen Mitchell, *Plantations and Death Camps: Religion, Ideology, and Human Dignity* (Minneapolis, MN: Fortress Press, 2009), 4.

3.1. Lament as Counter Violence

There is a lot that this text does not say. For instance, Rizpah's voice is never heard, her action of mourning the death of these victims of violence is accompanied by silence. It does not take much to imagine this bereaved mother weeping silently as well as wailing at the top of her voice. So, Rizpah's lament is to be understood in the context of women who, through the ages, have mourned the death of their loved ones.[10] Luis Riviera-Pagan writes how "in the wake of war," women's lament has served as a means of "resistance against the perennial proclivity to make force the arbiter of human conflicts."[11] Rizpah's lament in the wake of the terrible violence that has destroyed the lives of her sons and the sons of Merab may on all accounts seem futile. Her lament most certainly cannot bring her sons back to life. And yet as Judith Butler points out, "To grieve, and to make grief itself into a resource for politics, is not to be resigned to inaction, but it may be understood as the slow process by which [an individual] develop[s] a point of identification with suffering itself."[12] Rizpah's lament thus offers us some important perspectives regarding the nature of resistance in the face of violence. By lamenting, Rizpah transcends the dignity-destroying effects of violence, so attesting to the universal truth that to be human means to resist those forces that seek to assault, violate, or obscure one's human dignity. The very act of resisting as exemplified in Rizpah's lament is hence a sign that this person is maintaining some basic sense of what it means to be human. In very difficult circumstances, Rizpah shows tremendous courage in the face of violence.

3.2. Lament as Non-violent Resistance

Rizpah's lament serves as an act of silent public protest regarding the injustice committed and as a testimony to the futility of violence that affects the community as a whole. Gerald West, reading Rizpah's lament in terms of non-violent resistance argues that Rizpah's lament constitutes a hidden transcript over against the dominant ideologies and theologies of those in power. According to West, Rizpah's lament constitutes a prime example of female resistance in that she was "caring for the dead while and because men in power did not care for the living." Rizpah did not speak out. But, her act of solidarity with the victims and her lament demanded a response, from David and from

---

[10] L. Juliana M. Claassens, *Claiming Her Dignity: Female Resistance in the Old Testament*, 9.

[11] Luis N. Riviera-Pagan, "Woes of Captive Women: From Lament to Defiance in Times of War," in *Lament: Reclaiming Practices in Pulpit, Pew, and Public Square*, edited by Sally A. Brown and Patrick D. Miller (Louisville, KY: Westminster John Knox, 2001), 121–134.

[12] Judith Butler, *Precarious Life: The Powers of Mourning and Violence* (London: Verso, 2004), 30.

God. God responds first, and the rain falls on Rizpah and the dead (10a). David then also responds, recognising his accountability and responsibility.[13]

We thus see how Rizpah continued day after day in her self-imposed duty of mourning the violent death of her sons, so becoming an enduring example of embodied lament that moves the community to face the tragic death of the sons of Saul and to adequately mourn their deaths. Rizpah's lament constitutes a powerful means of resisting the derealisation experienced by Saul's sons. Her lament serves as a type of obituary for these victims of violence. By means of Rizpah's public grief over these seven victims of violence, the lives of her sons and her stepsons are recognized and prevented from falling into oblivion.

3.3. Lament and Transformation

Rizpah's six-month vigil lamenting the brutal death of her children has a transformative effect on all who witnessed her resolve to effectively mourn the violence that had destroyed the lives of Saul's sons and grandson. So, we see how God hears her cries and sees her lament when it finally starts to rain.[14] Reading of the text notes that the rain is not connected with the blood sacrifice demanded by the Gibeonites but closely linked with Rizpah's lament. According to verse 10, Rizpah conducted her solitary vigil until it started to rain again. The divine response of giving rain again (v. 14) is associated with the community satisfactorily mourning the victims of violence, a process initiated by Rizpah's lament. Moreover, Rizpah's lament also has a profoundly transformative effect on King David. It is significant that in response to Rizpah's vigil for her sons as well as the sons of Merab, King David finally is obliged to respect the dignity of the dead by giving these victims of violence a decent burial. With this act, something of the humanity of Saul's sons is recovered. It is moreover significant that David also, after all this time, decides to bury the bones of King Saul and his son Jonathan when he heard what Rizpah had done (vv. 11-12). Rizpah's display of grief thus helps David to deal as well with the community's failure to adequately mourn the tragedies of the past.[15]

Judith Butler writes that at the heart of mourning's ability to effect transformation on an individual, as well as on a political, level is the recognition of a common human vulnerability. It is, on the one hand, the realisation that as humans we are all profoundly vulnerable to violence that may eradicate our being; on the other hand, as vulnerable human beings, we are also dependent on

[13] Gerald West, *Doing Contextual Bible Study: A Resource Manual* (KwaZulu-Natal, SA: Ujamaa Centre for Biblical and Theological Community Development and Research, 2007), 38-39.

[14] L. Juliana M. Claassens, *Claiming Her Dignity: Female Resistance in the Old Testament*, 14.

[15] L. Juliana M. Claassens, *Claiming Her Dignity: Female Resistance in the Old Testament*, 15.

the other for the physical support of our lives. So it is significant that Rizpah's lament extends beyond her own sons to another woman's sons as well. By weeping also for Merab's children, Rizpah embodies an important principle voiced by Butler, i.e., being able to recognise the suffering of another.[16]

Finally, Rizpah's lament is significant in that it offers an important way out of violence. Her lament over the tragedy that had befallen her people breaks the cycle of violence that for a very long time existed between the Israelites and the Gibeonites.[17] It is thus by reading one's own suffering through the lens of someone else that we may derive a principle by which we vow to protect others from the kinds of violence we have suffered.

Concluding Remarks

In a most brutal display of narrative violence, the bodies of Saul's seven sons and grandsons, who have been murdered and dismembered, are seen strewn all over the field in 2 Samuel 21:1-14. These members of Saul's household have been the victims of a malicious cycle of violence caused by petty politics between the Gibeonites' and David. The seven sons of Saul were executed because Saul did not honour an old treaty that existed between them and Israel. We learn that violence begets violence and old feuds can return with a vengeance. And not just bloodshed, the dead were not even given the decency of a burial. Here in this story, one finds a heart-wrenching image of a mother weeping for her sons, an image that reminds us of the hundreds and thousands of mothers who on a daily basis are faced with the calamity of losing a child. In 2 Samuel 21:10, one encounters Rizpah, the widow of King Saul, lamenting the merciless killing of her two sons as well as the sons of her stepdaughter Merab. She is said to have kept a six-month vigil "from the beginning of the harvest until the rains poured down on them from the heavens" (v. 10) for these victims of violence. Rizpah does not have much of a part in this narrative, at least not a speaking part, and her presence in the text constitutes little more than one sentence. Yet Rizpah emerges as one of the prime examples of female resistance in the face of violence in the biblical text. In the contemporary context, tribal women have been lamenting and some voicing out the poor condition of the women and the corrupted society. Most of the time, their voice goes unheard, yet we can see their persistence. In their resistance against oppression, suppression, violence, corruption, injustice, etc., the story of Rizpah can be an encouraging influence for the tribal women today.

---

[16] Judith Butler, *Precarious Life*, 31.

[17] L. Juliana M. Claassens, *Claiming Her Dignity: Female Resistance in the Old Testament*, 16.

17

Hearing the Voices of Female Commercial Sex Workers (FCSWs)[1] in Nagaland: Tribal Women's Perspective

Zuchobeni Ezung

Introduction

The church is not just an institution characterized by religious rituals and dogmas alone, but 'a called out community' to engage in the affairs of the society. There are myriad issues that confront the church in modern society. But, how do religious beliefs contribute to shaping the present society, and what is the role of the church in modern society? The church is expected to show a preferential option for the vulnerable through its ministry of solidarity. The church cannot claim to be borderless when some sections are excluded because of their lifestyle. It is imperative for the church to show solidarity to the vulnerable such as the commercial sex workers by bringing them back into the mainstream of Christian way of life. Commercial sex workers include men, women and transgender people who consider sex work as a viable choice of job; however it entails high risks of abuse from customers and law enforcement authorities, susceptible to murder, HIV and AIDs and STDs, and

[1] The abbreviation "FCSWs" shall be used henceforth for Female Commercial Sex Workers throughout the paper.

exclusion from the church and society, and health care and social services, thus increasing their vulnerability to exploitation and stigmatization.

Taking into consideration the life situations of FCSWs, it is pertinent to hear and listen to their voices that raise important theological questions: Are we not created in God's image? Why are we excluded from the church and society? Why do people consider us as untouchables and sinners? In what ways can the church address our various needs and concerns? Christian theology needs to address all these pertinent issues and concerns, without which it will remain incomplete. Christian theology needs to build an inclusive community to enable FCSWs experience the fullness of life within the salvific plan of God. Against this backdrop, the paper attempts to concentrate the life situations of FCSWs in Nagaland with special reference to Dimapur Town to enable them to experience a sense of belongingness in the church and society, today. The rationale behind focusing Dimapur Town is basically due to the high percentage of FCSWs among the locals who do not only pose danger to their lives alone but also to others with their irresponsible lifestyle. Thus, the paper is an attempt to hear the voices of FCSWs with 'Solidarity' as the methodological framework apart from constructing an inclusive tribal ecclesiology through the lens of tribal women to draw its significance for the ministry of the churches in Nagaland.

I. Methodology

The paper will employ Mercy Amba Oduyoye's[2] "solidarity" as a theological method to articulate the reality of FCSWs in Nagaland with the task of fostering inclusive ecclesia that is accommodating and liberating. In addition K.C. Abraham and Jürgen Moltmann concepts of solidarity will be highlighted to supplement Oduyoye idea of solidarity. For Oduyoye solidarity is not only verbal and ideological but to be expressed in concrete liberative acts.[3] Liberative solidarity calls for inclusiveness of the whole community. The church cannot afford to segregate among themselves over issues and differences for "a house divided against itself does not stand."[4] Solidarity as a harbinger of life in oneness could be a possible paradigm to address issues and realities like that of FCSWs so that wholeness of life is restored in the church. The church needs to be informed of these new insights to move towards inclusion for all members of the community. To complement the paper, the presenter will also employ the Naga cultural practices towards the full inclusion of FCSWs in the church and society.

---

[2] Mercy Amba Oduyoye is Africa's first and foremost woman theologian.

[3] Mercy Amba Oduyoye, "The Meaning of Solidarity" in *A Reader in Feminist Theology*, ed., Prasana Kumari (Madras: Gurukul Publication, 1993), 120.

[4] Oduyoye, "The Meaning of Solidarity" in *A Reader in Feminist Theology...*, 115-116.

II. Social Location of FCSWs in Nagaland with Reference to Dimapur Town

Globally, commercial sex is legal in one form or another in over 100 nations around the world. 49% of the world offers legal sex works, 39% makes illegal and 12% offer limited legality.[5] As far as laws are concerned, prostitution in India is not illegal per se. However, certain activities related to prostitution are regarded as contraventions of law (e.g. pimping, soliciting such services at public places, carrying out such activities in hotels).[6] Worldwide 80% of the world population of sex workers are female and range in age between 13-25 years. 90% are dependent on a pimp, 70-95 % experienced physical assault during sex work; 60-75 % is raped while working as a sex worker.[7] There are an estimated 3 million sex workers in India, according to the country's Ministry of Women and Child Development, and many of them are children who have been forced into it.[8] Northeast India has around 63,000 people infected with HIV, and 80% are affected by sex routes. Dimapur is a state where the numbers of commercial sex workers are rising every year, as per 2016 record the total sex workers comprise of 50% local girls and 50% immigrant girls.[9] There are estimated 1800- 3500 sex-workers in Dimapur,[10] with the said district registering the highest prevalence of HIV in the state,[11] and recently it was reported that the state has 20000 HIV positive cases in Nagaland.[12] Such figures are strong indications of loopholes in the system. Statistically speaking, commercial sex is a dangerous job where many workers face death, beating, and rape every day. It is different from one country to the other, but the risk remains the same,

---

[5] http://www.nswp.org/resource/who-implementingcomprehensive-hivsti-programmes-sexworkers-practicalapproaches- collaboration (Accessed on 7/10/2018).

[6] "Prostitution In India: Understanding The Conditions Of Prostitutes," *Youth Ki Awaaz in Society*, https://www.youthkiawaaz.com/2011/03/prostitution-in-india/ (Accessed on 1/10/18).

[7] https://septemper 2016 nobullying.com/prostitution-statistics/ (Accessed on 9/10/18)

[8] www.refinery29.com › Entertainment News › Queer Voices › World News (Accessed on 1/10/18).

[9] www.nagalandpost.com/ChannelNews/State/StateNews.aspx?news (Accessed on 2/10/2018).

[10] Alexandra Devine, K Bowen, B Dzuvichu, R Rungsung R and M Kermode, *Pathways to sex-work in Nagaland, India: Implications for HIV Prevention and Community Mobilisation.* https://www.ncbi.nlm.nih.gov/pubmed/20390501 (Accessed on 3/10/18).

[11] "HIV Prevalence in Nagaland Expected to Decrease," *The Morung Express*, October 4 2018. 5.

[12] The Principal Secretary for Health and Family Welfare, Govt. Of Nagaland, Himato Zhimomi while addressing the state consultation programme on HIV & AIDS (Prevention and Control) Act, 2017 in Kohima on October 16 also pointed out the number. "Treatment Accessibility a Challenge to HIV & AIDS Control in Nagaland," *The Morung Express*, October 17 2018. 1.

even among the FCSWs in Dimapur Town. Many FCSWs have few rights and are not treated as employees. There is no health care, retirement, and for many sex workers, there is no hope.[13] Romila Chawla laments that the experience of FCSWs is pitiable as they lose the devotion and care of good men throughout their lives. They lose their reputation, status among respectable women in the church and society.[14] A survey was undertaken by the Prodigal's Home, a non-governmental organization (NGO) in Dimapur Town also found that FCSWs were considered as the most vulnerable community. A majority of them were between 15 to 24 years of age with no savings, and they were habitually abused and assaulted by thugs, customers, Naga Political Groups (NPGs), and security personnel, mainly for money. They are often beaten up for being a sex-worker and often get assaulted from the customers if they decline to conform to their sexual fantasies. The study concludes that sex workers of Dimapur were among the high-risk groups, and the study calls for further research on women's vulnerability and gender insensitivity in society.[15]

FCSWs from the Naga tribe prefer non-Naga clients, presumably for fear of being recognized. Naga men also avoid Naga girls but prefer those from the other sister states. Most of the girls comprised of school drop-outs, college-going and hostlers from Dimapur. Many girls do not bother casual sex in return for big money.[16] State Government officials deny their existence, but social marginalization and stigmatization are aspects of their lives.[17] Adding to their woes, the Naga church and society has been antagonistic towards FCSWs. Noyingbeni Ezung, a social worker opines that FCSWs have no

---

[13] https://septemper 2016 nobullying.com/prostitution-statistics (Accessed on 9/10/18).

[14] Romila Chawla, *Globalization and Sex Tourism* (New Delhi: Arise Publishers and Distributors, 2006), 30.

[15] Paula Banerjee, *Borders, Histories, Existences: Gender and Beyond* (New Delhi: Sage Publications India, Pvt. Ltd., 2010), 179-180.

[16] Telephonic interview with Mhabemo, Social Worker, Dimapur Town, 10/10/18. See also, Nagaland Post also reported that in Dimapur city, most of the local girls refused to reveal their identities. Some were highly educated, some were school drop-outs and few uneducated. The reasons for being in the "business" ranged from-unemployment, high economic demands on their living standards or wanting to earn extra money. Some girls from the rich family background were in the business purely "for enjoyment. *Rising number of sex workers in Dimapur*, Nagaland Post, Staff Reporter Dimapur, July 28, 2013. http://www.nagalandpost.com/ChannelNews/State/StateNews.aspx?news=TkVXUzEwMDA0MjE1Nw (Accessed on 10/09/18).

[17] Santosh Kumar Sharma, Shri Kant Singh and Bedanga Talukdar, "Understanding the Factors Associated with Alcohol Use among Female Sex Workers in a High HIV Prevalence Northeast State of India," in *Journal of Infectious Diseases and Treatment*, 2/1:12 (June 30, 2016): 1. https://infectious-diseases-andtreatment.imedpub.com/understanding-the-factors-associated-with-alcohol-use-among-female-sex-workers-in-ahigh-hiv-prevalence-northeast-state-of-india.pdf (Accessed on 1/10/18).

ecclesial and social standing. The sociocultural belief of the people towards sex-work is taboo and thus FCSWs deserved condemnation and isolation.[18] FCSWs go through common health struggles i.e., HIV and this stigma are carried on throughout their lifetime. FCSWs are called with derogatory names such as *Rendi* (Nagamese), *Lonsülonphyoe* (Lotha), *Nüktapangda Tsür* (Ao), and *Tughalimi* (Sema).[19] Such intolerant attitude has not only caused them deep psychological guilt, shame, and distress but also detach them from the mainstreams, the church, and society. This calls forth for the churches in Nagaland to address this pertinent issue while making efforts to make the church borderless for all community.

III. Pathways to Sex-work among FCSWs

Economic compulsions constitute the major factor in the causation of FCSWs. It is not the cause that every FCSWs accepts money for her services, there are many FCSWs who hail from well to do families. In India, there are many FCSWs who are compelled to adopt sex work to feed themselves and their dependents. Some voluntarily get into sex work in order to live a well to do lifestyle.[20] There are also some social causes which comprised of marital factors, bad neighborhood, and Illegitimate Motherhood.[21] In India, there has been a religious sanction to prostitution. In some parts of India, every family was supposed to offer one daughter to the temple where apparently she was supposed to serve gods with total dedication. They were known as devadasis–god slaves. But, in actual practice, they lived a life of prostitution as pleasure girls of courtiers and kings. In many cultures, a guest is honored by the offer of wife or daughter by the host.[22] Coming closer home to Nagaland, some years back, a study was carried out by Alexandra Devine et al., and who had identified four main routes to commercial sex in Dimapur, Nagaland (1) To obtain money to meet basic needs for self and family; (2) To obtain money to purchase drugs or alcohol; (3) Being coerced, tricked or forced into sex-work; and (4) For pleasure.[23] Against this backdrop, the church needs to transcend the pulpit ministry to the public space.

---

[18] Telephonic interview with Noyingbeni Ezung, Social Worker, Dimapur Town, 4/10/18.

[19] Telephonic interview with Mhonchumi Yanthan, Social Worker, Dimapur Town, 5/10/18.

[20] Haveripeth Prakash, "Prostitution and its Impact on Society-A Criminological Perspective," in *International Research Journal of Social Sciences* Vol. 2(3), 31-39, March (2013): 34.

[21] Prakash, "Prostitution and its Impact on Society-A Criminological Perspective"..., 35.

[22] Prakash, "Prostitution and its Impact on Society-A Criminological Perspective"..., 36.

[23] Alexandra Devine et al., (Accessed on 03/10/18).

IV. A Case Study: Hearing the Voices of Stakeholders and FCSWs

Ms. Susie[24] comes from a lower class family from Kohima, Nagaland. At a very young age, her mother passed away and she lives with her father and step-mother where she was not allowed to go to school. She has two stepbrothers but due to less family income, they are both school dropouts. Looking at her family's condition and the tortures from her stepmother, she decided to settle down in Dimapur to earn money, so she ran away from home. At first, she was working as a helper in one family in Dimapur. But, the work was huge and payment was not satisfied, so she met a lady from that locality who was involved in a sex racket. When she was 19 years, she started to work as a sex worker in the supermarket area. In the beginning, she was happy with her earning but it did not give her any peace and happiness as she was compelled to choose this profession. She sacrificed her youth and sold herself to the sex trade. Sometimes in the sex trade, she faces harassment and unwanted comments where she suffered physically, emotionally and mentally. She feels guilty, depressed and rejected since no one to depend wholly.[25]

The following interviews are the factual presentation of the voices emerging from various stakeholders of the church and society. The interviews are confidential with their names changed. The interviews were done for the purpose of hearing the voices of the FCSWs from the church ministers' in the context of the LBC in Dimapur Town by keeping Mercy Amba Oduyuoye's "Solidarity" approach to understand the life situations of the FCSWs. In Dimapur, there are 14 LBC (sector churches not included) and through the interview, it had come to the light that out of 14 Churches only 3 at most are doing ministry towards the FCSWs. And thus in this case study church leaders, NGOs, church congregation, and FCSWs were interviewed and thus some of the interviews shall be discussed below:

Many interviews were conducted, and only a few responses were positive while the majority of the Church leaders (LBC) responded negatively that their churches do not do any ministry or charity work towards the FCSWs. The questions were mainly based on their acceptance, membership, and participation in the liturgy. Very few agreed but upon some conditions, only if the FCSWs change their lives. Many of the churches never talk about sex education in the church as it is considered a taboo. The churches also consider this kind of social issue needs to be addressed by the Women department or by NGOs.[26] Such wrong understanding of the church leaders has aggravated the conditions of FCSWs. Both senior citizens and youths of the congregation

[24] A fictitious name for the client.

[25] A Case study conducted in the month of September 20, 2018.

[26] The writer conducted a telephonic interview on some Lotha Baptist church leaders in Dimapur on 8/10/2018.

were also interviewed, they are aware of the social issues and their responses were more positive towards FCSWs. They should be encouraged to reclaim the space by removing the destructive ecclesial and social barriers that isolate them with moral laws and creeds. Several NGOs who are engaged in charity work of the FCSWs express that if the churches are involved in this area it would help in reducing the rising percentage of FCSWs in Dimapur (and even across the state of Nagaland) and also check the high alarming rate of HIV infected and affected people. Some of the Care Homes such as the *Miqlat*[27] ministry run by NBCC provide vocational training and it does not only deal with the physical, social, and emotional wellbeing but also with the spiritual wellbeing of a woman.[28] In the Care Homes, FCSWs are taught in tailoring and handicraft works for their livelihood. The Care Homes also expect the churches to take a way forward in reaching out to the FCSWs[29] through intensive counselling, home visitations, fellowships, and engagement to enable them to live a responsible lifestyle. Thus, it is only through hearing the voices of the voiceless, the essence of ecclesia can be realized.

V. Fostering a Theology of Solidarity vis-à-vis FCSWs: From Exclusion to Inclusion

The case study has clearly shown that the girl went through socio-economic and religious circumstances. She experienced loneliness, guilt, shame, and rejection by her own family, society, and exclusion from the church and society. Having described the case study, we shall discuss the relevance of constructing a theology of solidarity that may lead to the inclusion of FCSWs in the church and society:

a) Experience as the Genesis of Emancipation

Tribal culture, customs, and traditions maintain the dignity of every citizen in a community. Yet, the understanding of rights is not altogether liberative for all. It also consists of oppressive elements of social practices that de-humanize women. At times our culture does not give a woman the due right of her identity. When women experience an indiscriminate violation of rights, there is little or no reaction on the part of the religious leaders and the church.[30] The church must stop asking why FCSWs are into sex-work, and instead try

---

[27] Miqlat is a Hebrew word which means "shelter, refuge."

[28] *One New Humanity, Nagaland Baptist Church Council*, Platinum Jubilee 1937-2012, 156.

[29] Interview conducted on some NGOs and the congregation of the church on 29/9/2018.

[30] Asangla Lemtur, "Towards a New Horizon of Developing Tribal Feminist Faith Articulation," in *Building Theologies of* Solidarity, eds., Hrangthan Chhungi, Raj Bharath Patta and P. Mohan Larbeer (Bangalore: BTESSC, 2012), 68.

to know what might have compelled them to choose this profession. God's incarnation into this world through Christ is to save sinners who believe and accept Him (Jn. 3:16). Matthew also recorded the term prostitute (sex workers) twice in his writing. Matthew mentions the words of Jesus who created a welcoming space for the most hated sections of the society: 'Truly, I tell you, the tax collectors and the prostitutes are going into the kingdom of God ahead of you' (Matt. 21:31-32). This statement of Jesus did not only turn upside down the value system of His time, but He completely revolutionized the inclusion of the vulnerable under the scheme of God's Kingdom.[31] John 7:53-8:11 narrate unnamed woman caught, paraded, publicized and exposed before the world, and as far as the Mosaic Law is concerned, she deserves to be punished, and stoned to death. But, the religious system and structure have forgotten that adultery is a crime committed by two persons. The central questions are-Is she really caught in adultery or a victim in the story in order to test the power of Jesus? Whatever the reason, the existing system condemned her and her actions, but Jesus never condemned her instead saved her from the clutches of victimization.[32] This shows that Jesus accepts everyone and affirms belongingness without any distinction and discrimination.[33]

b) Extending Solidarity to the Vulnerable

Solidarity affirms acceptance of common humanity and origins as children of the One God. Church acting in solidarity with the marginalized will be living out the Christian theology of creation that sees humanity-male and female as bearers of the image of God.[34] For Oduyoye, solidarity is not only verbal and ideological but to be expressed in concrete liberative acts.[35] K.C. Abraham holds solidarity as a process of seeing reality as the poor see it and in togetherness build new community by struggling for their justice (the subalterns).[36] Abraham further asserts that only in solidarity with the people (such as the FCSWs) can we witness the liberating power of God in Christ. The cross of Christ symbolizes the sign of solidarity. Solidarity is not even about

---

[31] Hisako Kinukawa, *Women and Jesus in Mark: A Japanese Feminist Perspective* (New York: Maryknoll, 1994), 130-131.

[32] Laila, L. Vijayan, "Building Theologies of Solidarity with the Victims of Sexual Violence," in *Building Theologies of Solidarity*, eds., Hrangthan Chhungi, Raj Bharath Patta and P. Mohan Larbeer (Bangalore: BTESSC, 2012), 90.

[33] Rongsenmarla, "A Study on the Prostitutes in and around Dimapur" (B.D unpublished Thesis, Senate of Serampore, 2008), 17.

[34] Oduyoye, "The Meaning of Solidarity," in *A Reader in Feminist Theology*…, 117-118.

[35] Oduyoye, "The Meaning of Solidarity," in *A Reader in Feminist Theology*..., 120.

[36] K. C. Abraham, *Liberative Solidarity: Contemporary Perspective on Mission* (Thiruvalla: Christava Sahitya Samithy, 1996), 69.

absolute equality, it is about just relationships.[37] Jurgen Moltmann understood solidarity as standing shoulder to shoulder, struggling together, suffering for one another and living with one another in a single community. It is a concept that expresses a Christian way of life and the prime motives behind Christian action.[38] This will be possible only when there is a subjective readiness on the part of the people victimized by the society at large to engage in a struggle for the removal of exploitation. Their consciousness has to be awakened to the necessity and legitimacy of such a struggle.[39]

The church as a body of Christ needs to co-suffer and co-travel with the vulnerable. Such action has been exemplified through the suffering and death of Christ on the cross for the sake of the other, which in this case is the entire human race. Not only reforming and transforming their lives with the values of Christ but also dismantling the destructive nexus among some of the stakeholders that trap and chain them for their vested interests. The church displays solidarity when it demonstrates a willingness to seek an understanding of power and begin to change the tradition that decrees that only men can exercise power over the whole community and even over associations of women.[40] The church needs to re-affirm human dignity which comes with moral responsibility and accountability. It is the responsibility of all human beings to relate with one another and be accountable to God for one's relationships with others. Failure to act responsibly involves an abuse of power that brings infliction in the lives of others.[41] In this regard, the patriarchal society has not only looked down at the women folks but also those at the margins such as FCSWs.

c) Re-orienting the Patriarchal Structures

Naga daughters give paramount importance to the value of her family yet they are not eligible co-owners in the family inheritance with the sons making them dependent in the society. Due to this patriarchal nature of the society, male members dominate the socio-economic, political, and religious affairs and women play only the subordinate role.[42] Aphuno opines that "Nagas are patriarchal and the mores of the society kept women subordinate."[43] Tribal

[37] K. C. Abraham, *Transforming Vision: Theological-Methodological Paradigm Shift* (Tiruvalla: Christava Sahatya Samithi, 2006), 282.

[38] Jürgen Moltmann, *The Power of the Powerless* (London: SCM Press Ltd., 1983), 107.

[39] Moltmann, *The Power of the Powerless*..., 52.

[40] Oduyoye, "The Meaning of Solidarity," in *A Reader in Feminist Theology*..., 124-126.

[41] Lemtur, "Towards a New Horizon of Developing Tribal Feminist Faith Articulation," in *Building Theologies of* Solidarity..., 70.

[42] Limatula Longkumer, *Naga Women in Theological Education: Problems and Prospects* (Jorhat: CCA-EGY Unit & Naga Women Theological Women Theological forum, 2004), 16.

[43] Aphuno Chase-Roy, 'Can Naga Women Birth Fire?' in *In God's Image*, Vol. 19 no. 4 (Dec. 2000), 27-29.

theology begins with the experience of the marginalized and moves to solidarity with the oppressed toward transformation and justice. Such theology becomes imperative for the church to know the experience of the FCSWs. Theological articulations should induce justice to the deprived such as the FCSWs and strongly move towards correcting the hierarchal structures of the society, or else theology becomes inadequate to liberate the victims.[44] In such a context, churches need an action-reflection attitude to help FCSWs to come out of human-induced segregation and victimization. Interfacing of feminist and tribal theology should lead to action-oriented or action-reflection theology to addresses the structural issues in the society and moves towards bringing about structural changes and transformation.

d) Voicing for the Justice of the Vulnerable: A Transformative Solidarity

The partnership is recognition of one's responsibility to be in active partnership, empowering others to become active partners in determining the quality of the life of the church as a community and of its presence in the world.[45] The goodness of God's creation permeates to the entire cosmos, including FCSWs who are equally created in God's image.[46] Hostility towards women, which includes FCSWs, is to be replaced with solidarity for the vulnerable. Churches need Jesus' model of acceptance towards fellow human beings without being judgemental. Solidarity is realized when churches see itself more and more engaged in doing justice to humanity and the vulnerable in the community.[47] FCSWs have for so long been isolated and discriminated by the church and society, this erroneous action has violated their dignity and identity as humans created in God's image. Any theology that denies the humanness of the other is, in fact, a denial of one's own humanness. Exclusive theologies should be replaced with inclusive articulations of faith through dialogue and interfacing.[48] The present realities challenge us to ponder our response to this so-called social evil? Isn't it our duty to do something for those people who are into commercial sex? Can commercial sex in any form be justified? It still remains a 'taboo' subject for most moral champions and moral experts. In a world where celebrities change

[44] Lemtur, "Towards a New Horizon of Developing Tribal Feminist Faith Articulation," in *Building Theologies of Solidarity* ..., 72.

[45] Oduyoye, "The Meaning of Solidarity," in *A Reader in Feminist Theology*..., 124-126.

[46] Stephen Harold Riggins, "The Rhetoric of Othering in the language and Politics of Exclusion," in *Others in Discourse*, ed., Stephen Harold Riggins (Thousand Oaks: Sage Publications, 1997), 3.

[47] Oduyoye, "The Meaning of Solidarity," in *A Reader in Feminist Theology*..., 126-130.

[48] Lemtur, "Towards a New Horizon of Developing Tribal Feminist Faith Articulation," in *Building Theologies of Solidarity* ..., 74.

partners like changing dresses, where divorces are as often as marriages, where trading in everything from a human egg to sperm is considered to be fair, where displaying one's body and sex appeal is the most fashionable business, why FCSWs still remain as a taboo? We need to show solidarity towards these FCSWs and include them into our community, where they can enjoy a dignified life, experiencing the true meaning of life.[49] There is a need to replace the attitude of xenophobia into *philoxenia*, the fear of the other into a love of the other such as FCSWs.

e) De-constructing the Concept of 'Perfectness' in God's Creation

The anthropological explanation of God's creation as good is articulated by St. Augustine[50] while the human tendency is to classify FCSWs as "other" while God sees people without any discrimination. The wrong interpretation of scripture based on the holiness and purity law by the church leaders has secluded the FCSWs from God's kingdom. Such wrong interpretation has denied inclusion of the other. It needs to permeate the message of hope and full inclusion of the other.[51] Exclusion only epitomizes otherness.[52] FCSWs come under the category of the "other" due to ecclesial and social rejection. Our understanding of church is limited only to the so-called "perfect people." But, perfection is a human construct, since, in creation, God said 'good,' and not 'perfect.' The goodness of God's creation permeates to the entire cosmos, including FCSWs who are equally created in God's image. The ministry of the church towards FCSWs must develop a positive attitude of love and acceptance to them as individuals created in God's image. According to Russell, being a misfit allows the individual to understand the meaning of hospitability and honor difference from the side of the stranger. For her, God's welcoming of the stranger or misfits and our partnership in this welcoming action[53] would provide a way of understanding their (FCSWs) experience. Before FCSWs are misfits, they are Humans. The issue is not their actions but their very being as human.

---

[49] Phanenmo Kath, "Globalization and Commercialization of Sex: Jesus' Model in Restoring a Dignified Life to the Commercial Sex Workers," in *Tribal Women and Globalization,* ed., Narola Imchen (Jorhat: Women Studies Centre, 2008), 53.

[50] Mark Ellingsen, *The Richness of Augustine: His Contextual and Pastoral Theology* (Louisville: Westminster John Knox Press, 2005), 56.

[51] Telephonic interview with Renbemo Ovung, Senior Citizen, Dimapur Town, 10/10/18.

[52] Stephen Harold Riggins, "The Rhetoric of Othering in the language and Politics of Exclusion," in *Others in Discourse*, ed., Stephen Harold Riggins (Thousand Oaks: Sage Publications, 1997), 3.

[53] Letty M. Russell, *Just Hospitality: God's welcome in a world of Differences* (Westminster: John Knox Press, 2009), 13.

VI. Constructing an Inclusive Tribal Ecclesiology from the Lens of Tribal Women

a) Re-reading the Bible through the Eyes of Tribal Women

Male and female images of the divine are equivalent rather than complementary. Ruether does, however, find other strands in biblical theology which contradict and point beyond this patriarchal view of God. Patriarchy is not only the subordination of females to males but the whole structure of Father-ruled society.[54] While Yahweh echoes many traits of the warrior king, this God transcends patriarchy. God is identified with liberation from slavery and oppression. Salvation is envisioned as deliverance from systems of social oppression and restoration of an egalitarian society of equals.[55] This is true with women who are voicing out for equality in the church and society. Limatula Longkumer observes that the Naga patriarchal society has allowed males to dominate the socio-economic, political, and religious affairs whereas women and children take the subordinate role.[56] If God is identified with upholding justice and equality, then, there is a need to articulate a theology that moves towards equal participation of women in all spheres of life. The church must induce justice to women who are deprived of their biblical and constitutional rights and move towards correcting the hierarchal structures of the society, or else theology becomes inadequate to liberate the vulnerable.[57] The New Testament also expressed its prophetic consciousness to all marginalized groups in every society, and singles out class, ethnicity, and gender as the divisions to be overcome by redemption in Christ. Therefore, if the God of the Bible is beyond patriarchy, why should the church and society look down FCSWs? Such a liberative solidarity act would enable them of the transformation of their lives.

b) Re-narrating the Tribal Folklores with Alternative Narrative

A story is told among the Lotha Naga tribe that many years ago, there lived a young widow with her daughter who was the most beautiful girl in the village, that every young man liked her.

> There was a man who wanted to marry her. So one day the young man asked her to accompany him in the forest to collect some bamboo shoots. She agreed to accompany him to the forest for that purpose. Legend

---

[54] Rosemary Radford Ruether, *Sexism and God-talk: Toward a Feminist Theology* (Massachusetts: Beacon Press, 1993), 48.

[55] Radford Ruether, *Sexism and God-talk: Toward a Feminist Theology*..., 62.

[56] Longkumer, *Naga Women in Theological Education: Problems and Prospects*..., 16.

[57] Lemtur, "Towards a New Horizon of Developing Tribal Feminist Faith Articulation," in *Building Theologies of Solidarity* ..., 72.

> says that he took her to an isolated place and murdered her for reasons unknown. Nobody could understand what might have provoked the young man to kill the beautiful young woman. The poor widow anxiously waited for her daughter for so many days, weeks and months, but there was no sign of her. As life moved on, one night, she saw her daughter in a dream who narrated the whole sequence of the event which led to her death at the hand of the young man. The following day, the widow went to the place where her daughter was murdered, and there she found the bones of her daughter and some fungus plants were growing from the bones of her daughter. She then plucked the fungus and went home, and kept those carefully. After some days, the young widow asked a favor to the young man for some domestic work. The young man extended his help to the poor widow. She wisely welcomed him to do the work. After completing the works, the poor widow offered him a rice beer and food made with the fungus. As soon as the young man ate and drank, he felt down on the ground and died instantly.[58]

From the above folklore, we can find that the oppression of women is nothing new; it is in existence since time immemorial. Some of the folklores contain the underlying realities of society. If we have to critically analyze the story, it is possible that the woman might have been abused, raped and murdered by the young man. It is also possible that the victim might have resisted with all force against the advances of the man, and eventually lost her life. The poor widow, lowly regarded by the society was left with no options as nobody came to give her hope and justice. It is in all probability that her voice was not heard by the society because the story unfolds that there was not even a single person who came to comfort/support her. Similarly, even in the present society, there are many who are at the edge of the society crying for help and support. Some of the myths and legends are full of violence inflicted to women, and it is essential to re-read and re-narrate those with new eyes. Just as the Bible was written from the perspective of men, so also many of the folklore. There will be certainly many liberative elements contained in the tribal folklores where women have also played a vital role in the society, but their stories are neither mentioned nor narrated. Rather, their subservient roles are mentioned in galore. The church and society seem to be ignorant or blind to their plights. Many women are crying in silence like the poor widow in the story. The ministry of Jesus was with the sinners, and His ministry was often in the public space. Should not the church also emulate Jesus' ministry to reach out to the margins that are at the periphery of society? The church without the margins is incomplete. Thus, it is imperative for the church to create a space where everyone will feel included and not excluded owing to ecclesiastical and doctrinal dogmas.

---

[58] Lilanthung Lotha, *Our Lotha* (Wokha: by the author, 1996), 147-148.

c) Re-visiting the Communitarian Spirituality (Khümtsüng Model)[59]

The cultural tradition of tribal society is blessed with rich customs, religious beliefs, and practices. Such cultural traditions have been instrumental in developing various contextual theologies. In particular, the communitarian model of the Lotha Naga fore-parents which I have christened as *Khümtsüng* like in any other tribes can be a model for developing an inclusive tribal ecclesiology to extend solidarity to FCSWs. This model is grounded in the teachings of the Bible. Under the *Khümtsüng* model, all the people within the village are inter-dependent and inter-related to each other. The tribal society was controlled by strict laws in all aspects of their life. The social codes prohibited people from violating tribal laws with regard to political, religious, moral and social life. For instance, a person is prohibited to anger the malevolent spirits, or a person who commits murder is banished from the community, or whenever, a man impregnates a woman; the male is asked to pay a fine in the form of "Vokho Echa"[60] to the family of the girl, this is done to compensate the loss incurred upon the woman's family. There are also cases where thieves were put inside a cage and kept them in the public square to reform their habits. It was an important tool to reform someone who is at conflict with the tribal norms. The punishments were not to destroy the person but to reform him/her with a view to bringing him/her back into the mainstream. The tribal laws also prohibit anyone from making fun of the poor, destitute and helpless as it would invoke the wrath of the spirits, and brings a curse upon the instigator. The people were also dependent on the malevolent spirit for their various blessings, and the nature for survival and wellbeing. Therefore, it becomes imperative for them to appease the spirits with various rites and rituals, while paying reverence to nature by being a good steward of resources, rather than being exploitative.[61] This model underscores compassionate love in action, towards the entire cosmos, thereby reflecting the boundless love of Christ.

Therefore, it is significant for the churches to re-visit such models to create a space for the vulnerable community whom God gives the preferential option for them. Such an approach would change from hostility to solidarity towards the FCSWs while re-affirming the inclusive nature of the triune God. The Bible is replete with examples of God's selfless love and cares for the vulnerable such as His protection of the poor, the alien, the widow, and the

---

[59] "Khümtsüng," a communitarian model denotes a unified community under the of the Lotha Naga fore-parents where everyone is concerned for each other's wellbeing. Basically, everyone remains inter-related and interconnected to one another in everything.

[60] "Vokho Echa" i.e., a pig is imposed as a fine upon the male by the female family.

[61] Telephonic interview with Rhanthungo Kikon, an octogenarian citizen, Dimapur Town, 1/10/18.

orphan (Deut.10:18; Prov.22:22-23; 23:10-11). Although prostitution is sinful, prostitutes are not beyond God's scope of redemption and forgiveness. They can be reformed through the involvement of the church. The Bible records God used a prostitute named Rahab to further the fulfillment of His plan. As a result of her obedience, she and her family were rewarded and blessed (Jos. 2:1; 6:17-25). The implication here is that God did not completely forsake Rahab, even though she was a harlot, yet, God intervened and changed her life. If God would reach out and use Rahab to fulfill His plan, why should the church remain hostile towards FCSWs? Should not the church also show solidarity to the FCSWs so as to transform and transform their sinful lives? Thus, the church as a community of faith should shed of its hostility towards FCSWs with the spirit of solidarity in order to redeem them from a life of sinfulness to a life of fullness in Christ.

d) Empowering FCSWs through Rehabilitation Programmes

It is encouraging that some NGOs (Prodigal Home, Bethesda Welfare Society, Good Samaritans, and Sisterhood Network) and related organizations in Nagaland have started rehabilitation programmes and creating self-reliance projects for the sex worker. Still, there are thousands who need to be rescued and need a hand from the churches towards charity work but churches have been so far insignificant on its role towards FCSWs. There should be more employment opportunities for the FCSWs who are forced to this profession under economic compulsion. Alternative opportunities should be provided in order that they will not turn back to the same profession, for instance, skill training programmes like tailoring, weaving, knitting etc, should be set up and financial grant should be sanctioned in order to help them, to stand on their own feet. Besides, the rehabilitation center should be linked with job placement agencies to provide them job according to their ability. The church also needs to articulate comprehensive policies to empower FCSWs through a variety of instruments focusing on their capacity building, promoting social awareness through Bible study and seminars on gender issues, removal of all references derogatory to the dignity of women, and promoting an inclusive theology from the eyes of women. There is a need to rework the status of FCSWs and Naga women in general in the church and society through rewriting history, as written records and oral traditions often shape people's sensitivity, belief, and worldviews. Thus, empowering women requires a collective response from all the stakeholders of the church and society.

e) Fostering Inclusion through Festivals

Festivals such as *Tokhu Emong, Moatsu, Ahuna/Tuluni* festivals can foster equality and unity in society. During the festival, both the young and old, rich and the poor, men and women sing songs and perform dances to express their appreciation and veneration to the Supreme Being for helping the crop to grow well, while they also give the best offerings to the deity for the abundant blessings.[62] Shimray opines that during festivals "Individual differences sink and the whole population participates in the festivals with a sense of unity and equality."[63] In all probability, festivals are not only centered on rituals and joyous celebrations but to reaffirm the inclusion of the whole community without any discrimination and distinction on the basis of gender, status, etc. Just as the celebration of festivals strengthen the community in terms of relationship building and cooperation, the church needs to exercise its ecclesial responsibility of welcoming and including everyone to experience the love and mercy of God through its compassionate ministry. The spirituality of the yesteryears may enlighten the present generation to foster inclusion of the vulnerable such as FCSWs who are often called with various derogatory names and which have often isolated, dehumanized, and stigmatized them. The context of FCSWs needs to be addressed in our theological assertions and formulations. The basis for Christian affirmation of human dignity stems from our faith conviction that all human beings are made in the image of God. Each person, no matter how badly damaged whether, by their own doing, the abuse of others, or some combination of both carry the image of God, that capacity for loving relationships in God's service. The church as an agent of God needs to show great enthusiasm to search for viable alternative occupations for FCSWs. The church may utilize some of the values and virtues of the festivals in its pastoral ministry to foster inclusion, equality, and justice among the various sections of the community. Imbibing and practicing such values can create a great impact in hearing the voices of the silenced FCSWs in the church and society. Thus, the church may critically revisit the cultural values and virtues to the quest towards the full inclusion of FCSWs as well as inculcate them some of the life skills to enable them to live a more dependent and responsible lifestyle.

Conclusion

The rising number of commercial sex workers is alarming in the state of Nagaland. In light of this, should prostitution be legalized in Nagaland? There have been questions on the mandate of legalizing prostitution in India. This may not be a great solution for the given problems which require more of a paradigm shift in the mindset of people, but given the clandestine nature and no regulation of industry, it would certainly be a step towards damage control.

---

[62] *Information about Tsungremmong Festival, www.indovacations.net/english/Tsungremmong-Festival.htm* (Accessed on 5/10/18).

[63] Quoted by Takatemjen, *Studies on Theology and Naga Culture* (Delhi: ISPCK, 1998), 22.

Legalizing would pave way for licenses and registration, whereby sex workers would have their own identity, access to public facilities, and other services. A serious check on the spread of HIV & AIDS will help in controlling the other related activities which have associated with prostitution, etc.[64] Legalizing prostitution in no way condones sexual promiscuity but such approaches may be explored to check the rising prevalence of HIV infection in the country/ state. The alarming rise of prostitution in the state should stimulate churches to bring out alternative narratives of street ministry, visiting Red-light areas, distribution of pamphlets on health issues, induction of reformed FCSWs to reach out to the sex-workers, and collaborating with various stakeholders. Such proactive approaches can help reduce HIV prevalence while reforming sex workers to live a more dignified life. The basis for Christian affirmation of human dignity stems from our faith conviction that all human beings are made in God's image. Oduyuoye approach of "Solidarity" can stimulate the church to relate to the FCSWs through acts of selfless love and compassion while moving towards building an inclusive community that embraces the entire cosmos.

[64] "Prostitution In India: Understanding The Conditions Of Prostitutes," *Youth Ki Awaaz in Society*, https://www.youthkiawaaz.com/2011/03/prostitution-in-india/ (Accessed on 1/10/18).

18

Barrenness in Women: A Retrospect

Elivi Chishi

Introduction

The joy of finding out that one is conceiving followed by the seven or nine months of responsibility to be taken care of and loved; The first cry of the baby, the first hold of the baby, the long nights of sleeplessness, the feeding to the intense giggles and small burps . . . the journey of motherhood begins. *Motherhood completes a woman* is a cliché that is familiar to our ears. Well if that is so how do we address the issue of barrenness in women? There is no such thing as an incomplete woman: for each woman is wholly created by God in His image (Genesis 1:27).

Psalm 113:9 - "He settles the childless woman in her home as a happy mother of children. Praise the Lord."

1. A Look into the Tribal views on Barrenness

Generally speaking, the Naga tribal society that we proudly acclaim ourselves to be a part of, is patriarchal in nature. It is a society where men get the first, the most important and the last say in any issue. A society where the birth of a male child is held in high jubilant for the heir, the lineage to the bloodline rights belongs to the male population. A society where women are proudly acknowledged in words, lauded for their progress and at the same time held back because of being a woman. A society where one of the foremost duties of a woman is to procreate and in some cases procreate till one gets the male heir to the family. In such a scenario barrenness has no place for discussion: a woman who cannot bear a child is seen as not fulfilling her duties. Even in the educated and so-called *broad minded* crowds barren women are sometimes looked at with eyes of pity and sympathetic thoughts. Such women are stigmatized by the society that they rightfully and proudly belong to. We boast at the fact that we are a Christian dominated society where God and His Word take the foremost importance. The Biblical teachings and sayings are where the faith of the tribal Christians rest. Being a tribal society, the issue of blessings and curse also takes a strong foot in any issue. Children are considered a great blessing in the lives of families.

Psalm 127:3 - "Children are a heritage from the Lord, offspring a reward from Him."

So, now the question that arises is - Does not having children mean one is cursed or that the blessings of God did not befall on them? The issue of barrenness and fertility is no doubt a sensitive one to be discussed. A society where culture, traditions and customs are rightfully embraced the issue of barrenness is discussed as being unblessed by God from hush tones, behind the doors of homes or sometimes even the heated talk of neighborhood gossips. Well, let us delve into the biblical world and try to catch a glimpse of how the Bible portrays barrenness.

2. Being Barren and Being Fertile

Bearing a child is one of the core responsibilities given by God in the Book of Genesis ("to go forth and multiply" Gen 9.7). Apparently the Bible also records women who were barren. Being barren also means infertility which is the inability of a person, animal or plant to reproduce by natural means.[1] In the following we shall retrospect some aspects of barrenness through the eyes of the Biblical records.

On the forefront, it appears that the Bible gives "fertility" a very important place in the Hebrew thought. However, this thought has a higher frequency towards the women. It must be noted that infertility is not solely a female phenomenon because even a male can be sterile. Nonetheless woman in the ancient times were seen with much contempt than their counterpart in this regard. In addition, one of the very important duties, if not the most important in the Hebrew world was to bear children. Needless to say, this

[1] Cf., "Barrenness," *https://www.merriam-webster.com/dictionary/barren*, 3rd February, 2018.

put immense pressure on a woman/wife to bear children. F. E. Deist is of the opinion that this may explain the prevalence of concubines and the polygamy practices of the ancient times.[2] Further, fertility also gave woman good status in the society as it was considered as a divine blessing from God.[3] However, in contrast, a family's childlessness is also blamed upon the woman/wife of the family.[4] Such a woman is construed to be "desolate," "in misery." "a womb that is never satisfied," "disgraced," "she joins the poor" which was a symbol of her vulnerability in the society.[5] J. S. Baden dwells upon "barrenness" as a disability. "Fertility must be considered the default and infertility the abnormality, just as health is the default and sickness the abnormality."[6] This adds further insecurity on the concept of barrenness of a woman from not just having an empty womb but a freak of nature.

On the other hand woman with offsprings were considered as blessed. "Blessing" therefore envelops childbearing. An example we often see is the blessing of a wife/woman (Psalms 128.3) where upon a woman is blessed to be "like a fruitful vine within your house; your children will be like olive shoots around your table."

3. Biblical View on Children

The Bible also has a very clear understanding about children. There are numerous stories and metaphors that depict the importance given to a child. However we shall focus our attention only to certain select texts to prove our point and come up with an assessment of Biblical thinking. Blood kinship is a very vocal idea in the Bible where children stand at the forefront. A child is identified by which family he/she belongs to, and accordingly, identified and also distributed power in the village of early Israel.[7]

In the Biblical thought, the provision of a child or a "seed" in the Pentateuch is one of the major themes running in the Pentateuch. We see in the book of Genesis (chapter 12 ff) how God promises Abram, that his offspring to multiply the land and also bring fame and honor. Further down the chapters

---

[2] Ferdinand E. Deist, *The Material Culture of the Bible: An Introduction* (London: Sheffield Academic Press, 200), 234.

[3] J. S. Baden, "The Nature of Barrenness in the Hebrew Bible," edited by Candida R. Moss and Jeremy Schipper in *Disability Studies and Biblical Studies* (New York: St. Martin's Press, 2011), 15.

[4] Deist, *The Material Culture of the Bible*, 234.

[5] Dorothy Jean Weaver, "1 & 2 Samuel," in *The IVP Woman's Bible Commentary,* edited by Catherine Clark Kroeger and Mary J. Evans (Illonis: Intervarsity Press, 2002), 157.

[6] Baden, "The Nature of Barrenness in the Hebrew Bible," 14.

[7] V. H. Matthews, "Family Relationships," in *Dictionary of the Old Testament Pentateuch* edited by T. Desmond Alexander and David W. Baker (Secunderabad: OM Authentic Books, 2003), 291-292.

of Genesis we see how God gives Abraham this "blessing" as a reward for his obedience to Yahweh. The Blessing came in the form of his son Isaac. In a nutshell, despite the promise of land that is also attached to the asset promised to Abram, the blessing of the child by far supercedes the blessing of the land. The child was going to act as the reassurance of God's promise to Abram long after his life on earth.[8] We also come across certain passages in the Bible (Elijah and the Shunnamite woman) where the prophet Elijah blessed the Shunnamite woman with a child (the story says that the woman had everything material wise) who was always helping Elijah during his stay in the town. On the economic front, children were considered as an extra help in their agrarian context then. Children were also an assurance in their context as they would ensure the parental properties remained in the family line.[9]

4. God's Hand in Fertility

In the ancient times, the reality of the spiritual and the material world were seen as one. This adheres also to childbearing where God is seen as the hand behind fertility. Genesis 49:25 reveals that God creates fertility by the blessing of the breasts and of the womb. The Bible acknowledges Yahweh/God as the one in control of a woman's barrenness or her fertility. God alone has the power to "lock" or "open" the womb (cf. I Sam. 1.5, Gen. 29.31, Ps. 113.9).[10] With the Hebrew as was also the case in the ancient Mesopotamian, "deities were seen to play a crucial role throughout the process of childbirth, from conception till childbirth."[11]

4.1. The Causality of Barrenness

The concept of barrenness may not be very apparently presented in the Bible, however as we collect bits and pieces it becomes more evident. It appears that barrenness had different causality. Though the concept refers to a woman unable to bear children and not having the chance of a life to begin, on the other hand it is also a "result of God depriving a person of the ability to reproduce. In some cases it acts as a distinct sign of His disfavour" (Lev. 220.20-21).[12] In other instances the Lord uses barrenness to help people recognize His sovereignty

---

[8] Carroll R., "Orphan," in *Dictionary of the Old Testament Pentateuch* edited by T. Desmond Alexander and David W. Baker (Secunderabad: OM Authentic Books, 2003), 620.

[9] Carroll R., "Orphan," in *Dictionary of the Old Testament Pentateuch,* 620.

[10] Deist, *The Material Culture of the Bible*, 234.

[11] Baden, "The Nature of Barrenness in the Hebrew Bible," 15

[12] George Burgess, *Barriers and Bridges: A Biblical Guide to Understanding Impairments, Afflictions, and Sufferings Within Today's World* (Hartford: Asdeon Publishing Company, 2005), 57.

over particular situations and all things in general.[13] "Michal was King Saul's daughter, and the first wife of David (1 Samuel 19). Michal remained barren until her dying day (2 Samuel 6:23). But, even her infertility had a purpose. God saw the bigger picture, because He is the one who wrote and illustrated the whole story. And because Michal had no children, no descendant of Saul ever regained the throne of Israel."[14] God was at work writing the history of humankind. Here, in all these examples of women we see the handiwork of God in the unfolding of his great purpose.

Further, in the narration of the patriarchs, the concept of barrenness finds their fulfilment with the divine opening of the womb by God in order to fulfil His promise and to bring unspeakable joy to the woman. Some of such women were Sarah, Rebekah and Rachel to name a few. The biblical writers record the power of God in bringing fertility as a symbolic act that "corresponds to concerns for the poor and the weak in the society."[15] Hence, the concept of barrenness also engulfs a metaphorical meaning in some sense. The opening of Leah's womb may be considered a "transformation from the ordinary to the extraordinary," and as in Deuteronomy 7.14-15 may be rightly considered a divine blessing.[16] In the story of Leah the divine hand of God transformed Leah from a sobbing wife with no child to a happy, proud and joyous mother. In the same way, being barren and fertile was God's way to metaphorically convey his pleasure and displeasure to his people.

Now this further leads us to new question of quest on the issue of barrenness. It must also be brought to perspective that being barren also begs the question; has sin done this? Is God's punishment at work? No. The Bible contradicts itself here. In some instances we find God passes a divine judgment and one is barren. But, in this instance the answer is otherwise. There in the stories of the great women of the Bible who were barren initially and later on went on to conceive (we have the examples of Sarah, Rebekah, Rachel, Manoah's wife, Hannah and Elizabeth). In all of these stories there is no indication that such barrenness was the result of God's disfavour. However, in contrast, it appears that God wanted to establish His presence/power in "their lives and the lives of their children."[17] God has gone on to work and establish his greatness through the lives of these women. All the source of blessings in their lives begins with barrenness. What was once considered empty and

---

[13] Burgess, *Barriers and Bridges*, 57.

[14] Logan, *Women in the Bible who Struggled with Infertility. http://withgreatexpectation.com/infertility/women-in-the-bible-who-struggled-with-infertility/*, 3rd February, 2018.

[15] Dorothy Jean Weaver, "1 & 2 Samuel," in *The IVP Woman's Bible Commentary,* edited by Catherine Clark Kroeger and Mary J. Evans (Illonis: Intervarsity Press, 2002), 157.

[16] Baden, "The Nature of Barrenness in the Hebrew Bible," 15.

[17] Burgess, *Barriers and Bridges*, 58.

fruitless now seemed to be fulfilled and bearing fruits through the work of God in their lives.

The picture of God's divine plan through these women would appear as:

- Sarah and Rebekah – Eventually gave birth to Isaac and Jacob – the two of the patriarchs.
- Rachael – Eventually gave birth to Joseph who went on to become the second most powerful man in Egypt
- Manoah's wife – Eventually gave birth to the mighty Samson
- Hannah – Eventually gave birth to the great prophet Samuel.
- Elizabeth – Eventually gave birth to John the Baptist.[18]

The above evidences clearly suggest that the barrenness these women had before becoming fertile was not a case of God's punishment on them. This was a case of God's divine plan to state His presence and redemptive purpose.[19] Therefore, we can establish that, though there are cases where being barren were considered punishment/curse from God, at most instances this was not the case. Barrenness actually opened up ways to let God display his works and fulfil his divine plans for the welfare of humankind.

5. Redoing our Tribal Views on Barrenness

Now with a better idea on the biblical views on barrenness, it is time that we readjust our glasses, get a better lenses to see through the work of God in the barrenness of a woman. Lukewarm Christianity is what describes the bulk of our Christian population. No one wants to be addressed as such but our action pronounces otherwise. We proudly acclaim and celebrate our relationship with God and being Christian is what has separated us from our savage ways. However, if we still adhere to the same old thinking of considering barrenness as a curse and treat such women with shame and continue to stigmatize them . . . where is the picture of being the Christians that we call ourselves to be?

The Bible clearly indicates that it is God at work even in the midst of barrenness that He has His divine fulfilment at progress. It can begin when the tribal mindset of demeaning women consciously or unconsciously is put to a stop. When we learn to respect and accept women simply because of who they are, instead of making them feel inferior or threatened by their existence, then we can proudly call ourselves real Christians. Motherhood no doubt makes a woman feel complete but that does not necessarily make a barren less complete.

---

[18] Burgess, *Barriers and Bridge*, 58.

[19] Burgess, *Barriers and Bridges*, 58.

Conclusion

The world in general is described as an advanced and technology prompted one. Despite all the progress humankind has made, it is the ways of our thoughts that still tie us down to the ungodly and unchristian character. Let us work on making our place a safe society that protects our women not only from physical harms but also a society that provides emotional and mental support - a society that works together to fully recognise the creation of God and wait for God's plan to unfold in the barrenness of a woman.

Contributors

Zhodi Angami – Associate Professor in the department of New Testatment, teaching at Eastern Theological College (ETC), Jorhat, Assam. He is also the present Dean of Post Graduate Studies.

Lovely Awomi James – Associate Professor in the department of Christian Theology, teaching at Eastern Theological College, Jorhat, Assam. She is also the present HOD of the department.

Razouselie Lasetso – Professor in New Testament and Greek, teaching at Eastern Theological College, Jorhat, Assam. He also serves as the Dean of Doctoral Studies Center of the College.

Akani Kinimi – Assistant Professor in the department of Old Testament, teaching at Eastern Theological College, Jorhat, Assam. She is also the Dean of Women Study Center of the College.

Manini Chuseote – She served as Assistant Professor in the department of New Testament at Eastern Theological College. At present, she is doing her doctoral studies at United Theological College, Bangalore, Karnataka.

Narola Imchen – Professor in the department of History of Chrisianity. At present, she is the Principal of Eastern Theological College, Jorhat, Assam.

Mekronyi-ü Thele – She served as Assistant Professor in the department of Missiology at Eastern Theological College. Presently, she is doing her doctoral studies at Aizawl Theological College, Mizoram.

Esther Jish Rengma – Assistant Professor in the department of Christian Theology, teaching at Eastern Theological College, Jorhat, Assam.

S. Akatoli Chishi – Associate Professor in the department of Religions, teaching at Trinity Theological College, Dimapur, Nagaland.

Vimeno Lasetso – Assistant Professor in the department of History of Christianity, a faculty at Eastern Theological College. At present, she is on study leave for her doctoral studies.

Marlene Ch. Marak – Associate Professor in the department of Communications, teaching at Eastern Theological College, Jorhat, Assam.

Eyingbeni Hümtsoe-Nienu – Associate Professor in the department of Christain Theology. At present, she is serving as the Principal of Baptist Theological College (BTC), Pfutsero, Nagaland.

Zuchobeni Ezung – Assistant Professor in the department of Christian Theology, teaching at Witter Theological College (WTC), Vankhosung, Wokha.

Elivi Kibami – Principal of Children Education and Training Center (CETC), Chekiye Village, Dimapur.